Study Guide

T0369639

Chemistry
for CSEC®

OXFORD
UNIVERSITY PRESS

Great Clarendon Street, Oxford, OX2 6DP, United Kingdom

Oxford University Press is a department of the University of Oxford.
It furthers the University's objective of excellence in research, scholarship,
and education by publishing worldwide. Oxford is a registered trade mark of
Oxford University Press in the UK and in certain other countries

First published by Nelson Thornes Ltd in 2013
This edition published by Oxford University Press in 2015

British Library Cataloguing in Publication Data
Data available

978-1-4085-2248-6

12

Printed by CPI Group (UK) Ltd, Croydon CR0 4YY

Acknowledgements

Cover photograph: Mark Lyndersay, Lyndersay Digital, Trinidad
www.lyndersaydigital.com
Illustrations: Include artwork drawn by GreenGate Publishing Services
Page make-up: GreenGate Publishing Services

Thanks are due to Juanita Hunte-King, Paul Maragh and Farishazad
Nagir for their contributions in the development of this book.

Contents

Contents

Introduction

This Study Guide has been developed exclusively with the Caribbean Examinations Council (CXC®) to be used as an additional resource by candidates, both in and out of school, following the Caribbean Secondary Education Certificate (CSEC®) programme.

It has been prepared by a team with expertise in the CSEC® syllabus, teaching and examination. The contents are designed to support learning by providing tools to help you achieve your best in CSEC® Chemistry and the features included make it easier for you to master the key concepts and requirements of the syllabus. *Do remember to refer to your syllabus for full guidance on the course requirements and examination format!*

Inside this Study Guide is an interactive CD which includes electronic activities to assist you in developing good examination techniques:

- **On Your Marks** activities provide sample examination-style short answer questions, with example candidate answers and feedback from an examiner to show where answers could be improved. These activities will build your understanding, skill level and confidence in answering examination questions.
- **Test Yourself** activities are specifically designed to provide experience of multiple-choice examination questions and helpful feedback will refer you to sections inside the Study Guide so that you can revise problem areas.

This unique combination of focused syllabus content and interactive examination practice will provide you with invaluable support to help you reach your full potential in CSEC® Chemistry.

1 States of matter

1.1

The three states of matter

LEARNING OUTCOMES

At the end of this topic you should be able to:

- describe the three states of matter in terms of arrangement, motion and proximity of particles
- explain the nature of solids, liquids and gases in terms of the particulate theory of matter.

DID YOU KNOW?

Atoms are so small that there are millions and millions of them in a pinhead. To line up hydrogen atoms the width of a large pinhead, you would need 10 000 000 000 000 000 atoms.

EXAM TIP

Many of the particles in a liquid are touching one another. Make sure that you don't draw them well separated from each other.

| Figure 1.1.1 | Particles in a solid |

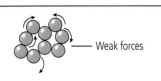

| Figure 1.1.2 | Particles in a liquid |

Solids, liquids and gases

The three states of matter are solids, liquids and gases. Most substances can exist in all three states depending on the temperature. For example, water is

- solid (ice) below 0 °C
- liquid (water) between 0 °C and 100 °C
- gas (steam) above 100 °C.

The particulate theory of matter

- All matter is made up of particles.
- The particles either vibrate (as in solids) or move from place to place (as in liquids and gases).
- There are forces of attraction and repulsion between the particles.

The particles that make up matter can be atoms, molecules or ions.

- An **atom** is the smallest particle that cannot be broken down by chemical means.
- A **molecule** is a particle containing two or more atoms. The atoms can be the same or different.
- An **ion** is an atom or group of atoms with either a positive or negative charge.

We can explain the nature of solids, liquids and gases by looking at:

- how the particles are arranged
- how close the particles are to each other
- the motion of the particles
- the strength of the attractive forces between the particles.

(See Figures 1.1.1–3.)

Solids

Arrangement of particles: regular pattern

Closeness of particles: very close or touching each other

Motion of particles: vibrate around a fixed point but do not move from place to place

Attractive forces between the particles are strong.

Liquids

Arrangement of particles: irregular – no particular pattern

Closeness of particles: very close or touching each other

Motion of particles: move (slide) over each other slowly

Attractive forces between the particles are weaker than in solids but stronger than in gases.

Gases

Arrangement of particles: irregular pattern

Closeness of particles: far apart

Motion of particles: move everywhere rapidly

There are almost no attractive forces between the particles.

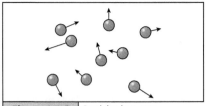

Figure 1.1.3 | Particles in a gas

Explaining the nature of solids, liquids and gases

Solids

Solids have a definite shape and volume and cannot be compressed (squashed together). They do not flow like liquids (see Figure 1.1.4). This is because the strong attractive forces between the particles keep the particles close or touching each other.

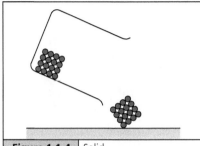

Figure 1.1.4 | Solid

Liquids

Liquids have a definite volume but they do not have a definite shape and they can flow (see Figure 1.1.5). For this reason, they can take the shape of the container in which they are placed. The forces of attraction between the particles are not very strong, so the particles have enough energy to slide over each other. Liquids cannot be compressed (squashed) very easily. This is because the particles are close together.

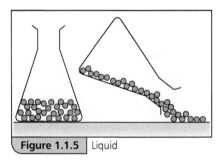

Figure 1.1.5 | Liquid

Gases

Gases do not have a definite shape or volume. They can spread everywhere (Figure 1.1.6). This is because there are hardly any forces of attraction between the particles. Their density is very low compared with that of solids or liquids. They can be compressed because the particles are far apart.

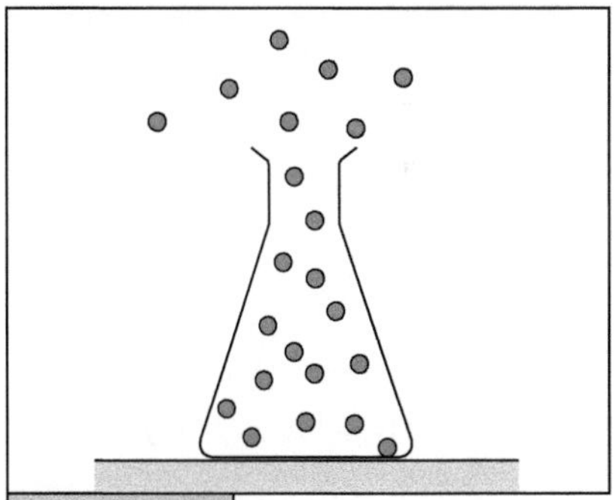

Figure 1.1.6 | Gas

KEY POINTS

1. The three states of matter are solids, liquids and gases.

2. In solids the particles are regularly arranged and close together, and only vibrate on the spot.

3. In liquids the particles are irregularly arranged and close together, and slide over each other.

4. In gases the particles are irregularly arranged and far apart, and move rapidly everywhere.

5. Solids have a definite shape, liquids take the shape of their container and gases spread everywhere.

6. Solids and liquids cannot be compressed easily, but gases can be.

1.2

Diffusion

EXAM TIP

If you are asked to define diffusion, it is better to give an answer about the spreading or random movement of particles rather than the movement of particles from high to low concentration. Although the overall direction of movement of particles is from where their concentration is high to where it is low, some particles are moving in the opposite direction because the movement is random.

Diffusion

In liquids and gases, the particles are in constant random movement. Random movement means that the particles go in any direction. The particles in liquids and gases are constantly changing direction and colliding with others. The idea that particles are in constant motion is called the **kinetic particle theory**.

Diffusion is the spreading movement of one substance through another due to the random movement of the particles.

- In diffusion the overall direction of movement is from where the particles are more concentrated to where they are less concentrated.
- Diffusion in gases is faster than in liquids. This is because the particles in gases move faster than those in liquids.

Examples of diffusion

Diffusion of potassium manganate(VII) in water

A crystal of potassium manganate(VII) (also called potassium permanganate) is placed in water. The colour of the manganate(VII) gradually spreads out through the water until there is the same depth of colour throughout (Figure 1.2.1). This is because both the manganate(VII) particles and the water particles in solution are in constant motion, bumping into and bouncing off each other.

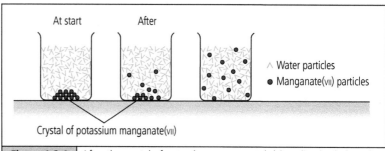

Figure 1.2.1	After the crystal of potassium manganate(VII) has dissolved, the colour of the manganate(VII) gradually spreads throughout the water.

Diffusion of gases

Hydrogen chloride and ammonia are gases. A long glass tube is set up as shown in Figure 1.2.2.

- The hydrochloric acid gives off hydrogen chloride gas and the aqueous ammonia gives off ammonia gas.
- After a few minutes a white ring is seen nearer one end of the tube.
- The ring is nearer the hydrochloric acid end.

We can explain this using the particle model.

- The hydrogen chloride and ammonia particles (molecules) are in constant motion.
- They bump into and bounce off air molecules and so move along the tube.
- The white ring is formed where the hydrogen chloride and ammonia have met and reacted to form a white solid.
- The white ring is nearer the hydrochloric acid end because hydrogen chloride is a heavier molecule than an ammonia molecule. Heavier molecules move more slowly than lighter ones.

Osmosis

Osmosis is a special case of diffusion. **Osmosis** is the overall movement of water molecules through a selectively permeable membrane from where the water is at a higher concentration to where it is at a lower concentration.

Osmosis can be demonstrated using thin strips of pawpaw fruit placed in distilled water or sugar solution (Figure 1.2.3). The contents of the cells of the fruit can be thought of as being a solution of different substances in water. The cell membrane is selectively permeable.

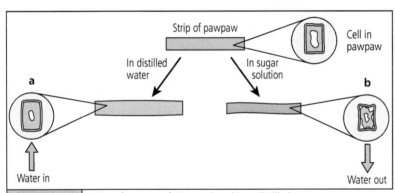

Figure 1.2.3 Strips of pawpaw fruit are placed in **a** distilled water, **b** sugar solution.

In distilled water the strips become longer and more rigid. This is because:

- the water outside the cells is more concentrated than inside the cells
- water passes into the cells by osmosis.

In sugar solution the strips become shorter and softer (flaccid).

- The water outside the cells is less concentrated than the water inside the cells. This is because there is sugar as well as water in the solution.
- Water passes out of the cells by osmosis.

Some uses of sugar and salt

Sugar or salt are used to preserve food. They stop bacteria and fungi from growing. The cells of all organisms depend on water for survival. Foods with a high concentration of sugar or salt remove water from bacteria or fungi by osmosis, so they die.

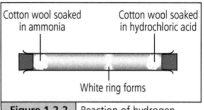

Figure 1.2.2 Reaction of hydrogen chloride and ammonia

DID YOU KNOW?

Salts such as Epsom salts (magnesium sulfate) can be used to control garden pests such as slugs and beetles. The salt is sprayed on the earth around the plants or on the leaves. Slugs avoid the plants because of the water-withdrawing properties of the salt. Some gardeners use sodium chloride for this purpose but this may cause 'leaf burn'.

KEY POINTS

1 Diffusion is the spreading movement of one substance through another due to the random movement of the particles.

2 Osmosis is the movement of water molecules through a selectively permeable membrane from where the water is at a higher concentration to where it is at a lower concentration.

3 Results from experiments on diffusion and osmosis provide evidence for the particle theory.

Changing states

At the end of this topic you should be able to:

• explain the terms freezing, melting, boiling, evaporation, condensing and sublimation

• interpret heating and cooling curves in terms of forces between the particles.

EXAM TIPS

• The terms 'evaporation' and 'boiling' have slightly different meanings. Evaporation of a liquid can happen below its boiling point. Boiling occurs when the whole liquid bubbles and both gas and liquid are present in balance with one another.

• We usually use the term 'vapour' for the gaseous form of a substance that is normally liquid or solid at room temperature.

• We sometimes use the term 'vaporisation' for the change liquid ⟶ gas.

Changes of state

When we heat a solid it turns into a liquid. Further heating turns the liquid into a gas. On cooling, the gas turns into a liquid. Further cooling turns the liquid into a solid. These changes of state are given special names.

• **Melting**: solid ⟶ liquid
• **Boiling/evaporation**: liquid ⟶ gas
• **Condensing**: gas ⟶ liquid
• **Freezing**: liquid ⟶ solid

Energy and changes of state

• In melting and boiling/evaporation, energy is absorbed (taken in).
• In condensing and freezing, energy is released (given out).

(See Figure 1.3.1.)

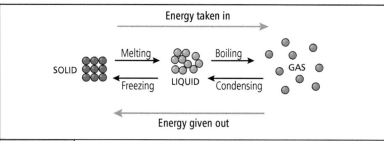

| **Figure 1.3.1** | Energy is required to melt and boil a substance. Energy is released when a substance condenses or freezes. |

Heating and cooling curves

Figure 1.3.2 shows how the temperature of a solid changes when it is heated slowly to form a liquid and then a gas.

We can explain the shape of the curve using ideas of energy (heat) transfer to the particles.

1 AB: Increasing heat energy increases the vibrations of the particles in the solid. So the temperature of the solid increases.

2 BC: The forces of attraction between the particles are weakened enough so that the particles slide over each other. The temperature is constant because the energy is going in to overcome the forces between the particles instead of raising the temperature. The substance melts.

3 CD: Increasing the energy increases the movement of the particles in the liquid. So the temperature of the liquid increases.

4 DE: The forces of attraction between the particles are weakened enough so that the particles move well away from each other. The temperature is constant because the energy is going in to overcome the forces between the particles instead of raising the temperature. The substance boils.

5 EF: Increasing the energy increases the speed of the gas particles. So, the temperature increases.

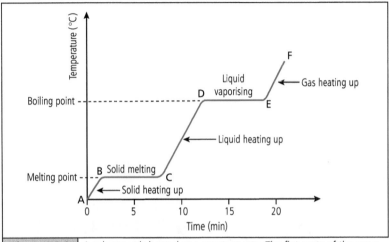

Figure 1.3.2 A substance is heated at a constant rate. The flat parts of the curve show where the substance is melting (B to C) and boiling (D to E).

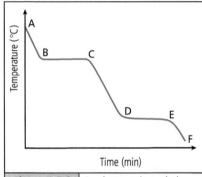

Figure 1.3.3 A substance is cooled at a constant rate. The flat parts of the curve show where the substance is condensing (B to C) and freezing (D to E).

Figure 1.3.3 shows how the temperature of a gas changes when it is cooled to form a liquid and then a solid.

1 When the gas is cooled, the particles lose kinetic energy (movement energy). The temperature falls (AB).

2 The particles become attracted to each other.

3 Energy is released and the gas turns to a liquid (BC).

4 When the liquid is cooled, the particles lose more energy. The temperature falls (CD).

5 Energy is released and the liquid turns to a solid (DE).

Sublimation

Sublimation is the direct change of a solid to a gas on heating without any liquid state being formed. It also refers to the direct change of a gas to a solid on cooling without the liquid state being formed.

$$\text{Solid} \underset{cool}{\overset{heat}{\rightleftarrows}} \text{Gas}$$

For example, solid carbon dioxide changes directly to carbon dioxide gas when heated.

2 Mixtures and separations

2.1

Elements and compounds

Elements

An **element** is a substance made up of only one type of atom. Elements cannot be broken down into anything simpler by chemical reactions.

Some examples of elements are shown in Figure 2.1.1. The structures look different but each one of them only has one type of atom. Chlorine has only chlorine atoms, carbon has only carbon atoms and so on.

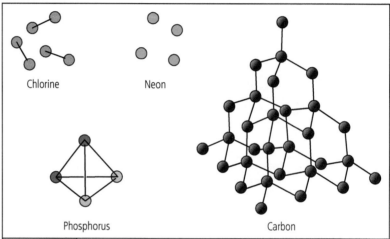

Chlorine   Neon

Phosphorus   Carbon

Figure 2.1.1 Each of these four elements is only made up of one type of atom.

Chemical bonds

In Figure 2.1.1, the atoms of chlorine, phosphorus and carbon are joined by chemical bonds.

- A chemical bond is shown by a line joining the atoms.
- A chemical bond shows that there are strong forces holding the atoms together.
- The bonds shown here are called covalent bonds (see 5.2).

Compounds

A **compound** is a substance made up of two or more different atoms (or ions) joined together by bonds.

Compounds always have a fixed amount of each element in them. For example, a water molecule always has two hydrogen atoms and one oxygen atom. In sodium chloride (salt) the ratio of sodium ions to chloride ions is always 1 : 1 (see Figure 2.1.2).

There are two main groups of compounds:

- molecular (or giant molecular), where atoms are bonded together (see 5.2)
- ionic, where positive and negative ions form 'ionic bonds' (see 5.1).

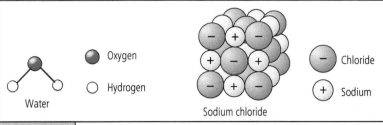

| **Figure 2.1.2** | Water is a molecular compound of hydrogen and oxygen. Sodium chloride is an ionic compound of sodium and chloride ions. |

Physical and chemical properties

Physical properties are ones that do not generally depend on the amount of substance present. Examples are:

- melting and boiling points
- density (mass of substance divided by volume of substance)
- strength
- hardness
- electrical and thermal conductivity.

Chemical properties describe how elements and compounds react with other substances. For example:

- Sodium reacts with chlorine to form sodium chloride.
- Sodium reacts with water to form sodium hydroxide and hydrogen.

Reacting elements

Compounds often have very different properties from the elements they are made from. We can see this by comparing the properties of sodium, chlorine and sodium chloride. Sodium chloride is the compound formed by the chemical reaction when sodium burns in chlorine gas.

Table 2.1.1   Some physical properties of sodium, chlorine and sodium chloride

	Sodium	Chlorine	Sodium chloride
State	Solid	Gas	Solid
Colour	Silvery	Green	White
Boiling point (°C)	883	−35	801
Density (g cm⁻³) at room temperature	0.97	0.00296	2.17

Table 2.1.2   Some chemical properties of sodium, chlorine and sodium chloride

	Sodium	Chlorine	Sodium chloride
Reaction with oxygen	Burns to form a white powder	Does not react	Does not react
Reaction with water	Reacts to form an alkaline solution	Reacts to form an acidic solution	Does not react – just dissolves

Pure substances and mixtures

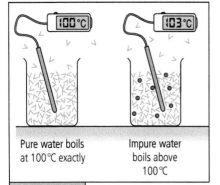

Pure water boils at 100°C exactly

Impure water boils above 100°C

Figure 2.2.2

Pure substance or mixture?

Elements and compounds are examples of pure substances. If a substance is pure, we cannot separate it into any other parts (components) by physical means. Pure water has only one component in it – water molecules. Pure sulfur has only one component in it – sulfur molecules. The composition of a compound is fixed (see 2.1).

A **mixture** is an impure substance that contains two or more different components. It consists of two or more elements or compounds which are not chemically bonded together (see Figure 2.2.1). A solution of sodium chloride (salt) in water, for example, is a mixture because it contains two components: salt and water.

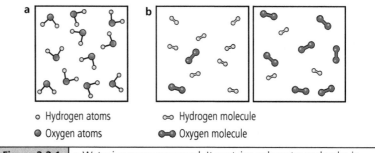

| o | Hydrogen atoms | ∞ | Hydrogen molecule |
| ● | Oxygen atoms | ●● | Oxygen molecule |

Figure 2.2.1   **a** Water is a pure compound. It contains only water molecules in which there are two hydrogen atoms for every oxygen atom. **b** A mixture of hydrogen and oxygen can have varying amounts of hydrogen and oxygen in it.

Pure or impure: comparing boiling points

Pure substances have sharp melting points and boiling points. The melting point of water is exactly 0°C and the boiling point is exactly 100°C at atmospheric pressure.

If a substance is impure, the impurities will affect its melting point and boiling point.

• The boiling point of a liquid is increased by adding other substances. Making water impure by dissolving a lot of sodium chloride in it raises the boiling point from 100°C to about 103°C (Figure 2.2.2). The more salt that is dissolved, the greater the rise in the boiling point.

• The melting point of a substance is decreased by adding impurities. Adding salt to water makes it freeze at temperatures below 0°C.

Mixtures can be separated by physical means

The components of a mixture can be separated by physical means such as filtration or distillation. For example, a mixture of sand and salt can be separated by:

1 dissolving the salt in water – the sand does not dissolve

2 filtering the mixture – the sand remains on the filter paper and the salt solution goes through

3 the water is evaporated from the salt solution to leave salt (Figure 2.2.3).

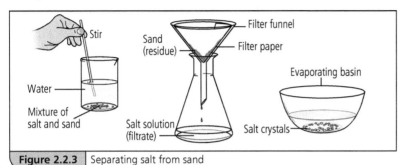

| Figure 2.2.3 | Separating salt from sand |

Comparing compounds and mixtures

Table 2.2.1   Differences between a compound and a mixture

Compound (pure substance)	Mixture
Composition is fixed	Composition is variable
Cannot be separated by physical means	Can be separated by physical means
Physical properties are different from the elements from which they are made.	Physical properties, e.g. colour and density, are the average of the substances in the mixture.

Comparing a mixture of iron and sulfur with the compound iron sulfide

Iron is a silvery metal and sulfur is a yellow non-metal. Iron sulfide is a compound of iron and sulfur. It is made when iron and sulfur are heated together. It contains sulfur atoms bonded to iron atoms. Some of the differences between the mixture (impure substance) and the compound (pure substance) are shown in Table 2.2.2.

Table 2.2.2   Differences between iron sulfide and a mixture of iron and sulfur

Iron and sulfur (mixture)	Iron sulfide (compound)
The colour is a mixture of tiny yellow and silver spots.	The colour is brown-black.
The iron can be separated from the sulfur using a magnet.	The iron cannot be separated from the sulfur using a magnet.
The sulfur can be dissolved in an organic solvent leaving the iron as a solid.	Iron sulfide does not dissolve in organic solvents.
When the mixture is formed, no heat is given off.	When the compound is formed, heat is given off.
Hydrogen gas is formed (by reaction with iron) when an acid is added. The gas does not smell.	Hydrogen sulfide gas is formed when an acid is added. The gas smells of bad eggs.

| Figure 2.2.4 | This waste pond is a mixture of water and chemical waste from the extraction of aluminium. |

2.3 Solutions, suspensions and colloids

Solutes, solvents and solutions

When you shake sugar in water, the sugar disappears to form a **solution**. The sugar dissolves in the water. All parts of the solution formed are exactly the same. This is an example of a homogeneous mixture. 'Homogeneous' means the same throughout. The main component of the solution is called the **solvent** and the minor component is called the **solute**.

A solution is a uniform mixture (homogeneous mixture) of two or more substances.

A solute is a substance that is dissolved in a solvent. The solute can be a solid, a liquid or a gas.

A solvent is a substance that dissolves a solute. The solvent can also be a solid, liquid or gas.

Solutions

In solutions:

- The particles are so small that they cannot be seen. They are less than 1 nanometre in diameter. (1 nanometre = 1 millionth of a millimetre.)
- They are generally transparent. Light can be transmitted through them. The exception is a solution of a solid in another solid.
- The particles cannot be separated by filtration, and do not separate out by letting the mixture stand for a while.

Table 2.3.1   Types of solution

Solute	Solvent	Example
Solid	Liquid	Seawater (salt dissolved in water)
Solid	Solid	Bronze (tin dissolved in copper)
Gas	Liquid	Carbonated water (carbon dioxide dissolved in water)
Liquid	Liquid	Rum (ethanol dissolved in a mixture of liquids)
Gas	Gas	Air (mixture of nitrogen, oxygen and other gases)

Suspensions

When you shake powdered clay with water, the mixture appears milky. The clay particles can just about be seen. We call this a **suspension** of clay in water. When you leave the mixture of clay in water for a little while, the clay particles settle to the bottom of the container. The settling of the solid is called **sedimentation**.

A suspension is a mixture of small particles dispersed in another substance, and in which the small particles settle on standing.

In suspensions:

- The particles are large enough to be just visible. They are more than 1000 nanometres in diameter.
- They are opaque (not transparent) to light. Light is scattered by them (see Figure 2.3.1).
- The particles can be separated by filtration. The particles undergo sedimentation – they eventually settle to the bottom of the container in which they are placed.

Colloids

Colloids have some of the properties of solutions but are more like suspensions in many ways. They consist of one type of particle (solid, liquid or gas) dispersed throughout another. An example is mayonnaise, where particles of vinegar are dispersed in vegetable oil (see Figure 2.3.2).

In colloids:

- The particles are not large enough to be visible. They are larger than those in a solution but smaller than those in a suspension, so are between 1 and 1000 nanometres in diameter.
- They are opaque (not transparent) to light. Light is scattered by them (see Figure 2.3.1).
- The particles are too small to be separated by filtration.
- The particles do not undergo sedimentation. They do not settle on standing.

Table 2.3.2   Examples of colloids

Nature of colloid	Type of colloid	Example
Solid dispersed in gas	Aerosol	Smoke particles in air
Gas dispersed in liquid	Foam	Whipped cream
Liquid dispersed in liquid	Emulsion	Milk (fat in water)
Solid dispersed in liquid	Sol	Paint
Liquid trapped in solid	Gel	Jelly

KEY POINTS

1 A solute dissolves in a solvent to form a solution.

2 A solution has particles that cannot be seen. They are generally transparent and the components cannot be separated by sedimentation.

3 A suspension has particles that can be seen. Suspensions scatter light and the components can be separated by sedimentation.

4 A colloid has particles intermediate in size between those in a solution and those forming the dispersed part of a suspension. Colloids scatter light and the components cannot be separated by sedimentation.

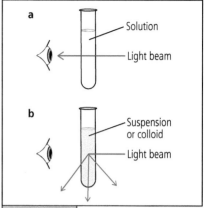

Figure 2.3.1   **a** Light is transmitted through a solution. **b** Light is scattered by the small particles present in a suspension or a colloid. The light is not transmitted directly to the observer.

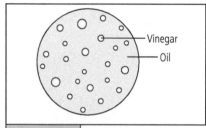

Figure 2.3.2   Mayonnaise is a type of colloid called an emulsion (see Table 2.3.2). Droplets of vinegar are spread throughout the vegetable oil.

Figure 2.3.3   Vinegar is a solution, so is transparent to light. Milk is a colloid, so scatters light and appears opaque.

How solubility changes with temperature

Solubility

If a solvent dissolves a particular substance, we say that the substance is very soluble in that solvent. If the solute does not appear to dissolve in the solvent, we say that the substance is insoluble. Solubility depends on both the solute and the solvent. Some substances may be insoluble in water but soluble in other solvents. For example, sulfur is insoluble in water but dissolves in some organic solvents.

If, at constant temperature, a solution can dissolve more solute, we say that the solution is unsaturated. If the solution cannot dissolve any more solid and excess solid is present, we say that the solution is saturated.

The **solubility** of a solute in a solvent is the number of grams of solute needed to form a saturated solution per 100 grams of solvent used. The temperature must always be quoted. This is because solubility varies with temperature.

DID YOU KNOW?

Some solutions can hold more solute than in a saturated solution. We call these solutions *supersaturated*. Hydrated sodium thiosulfate contains water of crystallisation in its structure. When this compound is heated gently, it dissolves in its own water of crystallisation. This solution contains more sodium thiosulfate than a saturated solution of sodium thiosulfate in water. Adding a speck of dust or tiny crystal to the supersaturated solution results in the whole solution crystallising.

The effect of temperature on solubility

When we warm saturated solutions of most substances, the solutions become unsaturated. For most solutes in water, solubility increases as temperature increases.

A **solubility curve** shows the mass of solute dissolved to form a saturated solution per 100 grams of solvent at different temperatures. The solubility curves for a number of different solutes in water are shown in Figure 2.4.1.

From these graphs we can see that:

• At 0 °C, potassium carbonate is the most soluble in water and potassium nitrate is the least soluble.

• At 80 °C, potassium nitrate is the most soluble and sodium chloride is the least soluble.

• The increase in solubility with temperature is greatest for potassium nitrate.

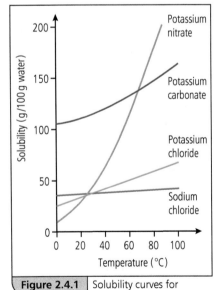

Figure 2.4.1 Solubility curves for potassium nitrate, potassium carbonate, potassium chloride and sodium chloride

- Sodium chloride shows only a very small increase in solubility as the temperature is increased.
- The increase in solubility with temperature is usually a smooth curve or an almost straight line.

Calculations using solubility curves

The solubility curve for potassium nitrate is shown in Figure 2.4.2. We can use information from this curve to deduce:

- the temperature at which crystals start to form when a saturated solution is cooled
- the mass of solid deposited when a saturated solution is cooled.

1 At what temperature does a saturated solution containing 140 g potassium nitrate first form crystals as it is cooled from 80 °C?

- Draw a line XY from 140 g on the vertical axis to join the curve.
- The line YZ gives the temperature at which potassium nitrate is just soluble. So 70 °C is the maximum temperature at which crystals will start to form.

2 Calculate the mass of potassium nitrate that would come out of solution when a saturated solution of potassium nitrate is cooled from 80 °C to 40 °C.

- At 80 °C a mass of 170 g of potassium nitrate dissolves (lines ABC).
- At 40 °C a mass of 65 g of potassium nitrate dissolves (lines DEF).
- On cooling from 80 °C to 40 °C the mass of potassium nitrate that comes out of solution is (170 g – 65 g) = 105 g.

Fractional crystallisation

Fractional crystallisation can be used to separate two dissolved substances which have different solubilities at different temperatures. A warm concentrated solution containing the two solutes is cooled. A larger proportion of the solute with the lower solubility crystallises out. The solute with the higher solubility remains in solution. The crystals still contain a small amount of the solute with higher solubility. So the procedure is repeated several times to improve the purity. Filtration is used to separate the crystals from the solution.

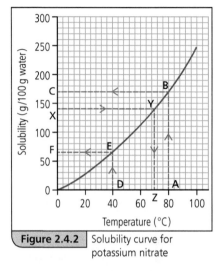

Figure 2.4.2 | Solubility curve for potassium nitrate

EXAM TIP

If you are asked to draw a solubility curve or similar curves from data provided, make sure that you draw the curve of best fit and do not draw straight lines from one point to another.

KEY POINTS

1 The solubility of a solute in a solvent is the number of grams of solute needed to form a saturated solution per 100 grams of solvent used.

2 The solubility of most substances increases with temperature

3 The information from solubility curves can be used to calculate the mass of solid deposited when a saturated solution is cooled.

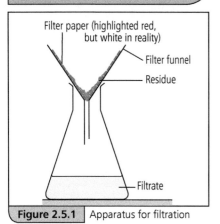

Figure 2.5.1 Apparatus for filtration

Filter paper (highlighted red, but white in reality)
Filter funnel
Residue
Filtrate

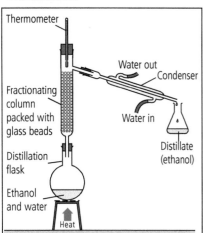

Figure 2.5.3 In fractional distillation the components move up the column at different rates, which depend on their boiling point and the temperature of the column.

Thermometer
Water out
Condenser
Fractionating column packed with glass beads
Water in
Distillate (ethanol)
Distillation flask
Ethanol and water
Heat

Filtration

Filtration separates undissolved solids from a solution or liquid (see Figure 2.5.1). The spaces in the filter paper are very small, so the tiny particles in solution can flow through but the particles in the solid are too large to flow through. They get trapped on the filter paper.

- The solution passing through the filter paper is called the **filtrate**.
- The solid remaining on the filter paper is called the **residue**.
- The solid is washed with a suitable solvent to remove traces of solution.

Crystallisation

We obtain crystals from a solution by the following method (see also Figure 2.5.2):

1 Gently heat the solution in an evaporating basin to concentrate it.

2 Evaporate the solvent until a saturated solution (crystallisation point) is reached. This is reached when a drop of the solution forms crystals when placed on a cold tile.

3 Leave the saturated solution to cool and form crystals.

4 Filter off the crystals and dry them between filter papers.

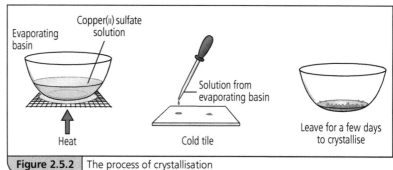

Figure 2.5.2 The process of crystallisation

Copper(II) sulfate solution
Evaporating basin
Heat
Solution from evaporating basin
Cold tile
Leave for a few days to crystallise

Simple distillation

Simple distillation is used to separate a liquid from a solid, e.g. to separate salt and water from a solution of sodium chloride. Distillation involves the processes of boiling and condensation. It works because the components to be separated have very different boiling points.

The procedure for separating water from salt by simple distillation is as follows (see also Figure 2.5.3):

1 Heat the solution of salt in water in a distillation flask.

2 The water boils first because it has a much lower boiling point than salt.

3 The steam goes into the condenser.

4 The condenser is at a lower temperature than the boiling point of water, so the water condenses here, and is collected in a flask.

5 The salt remains in the distillation flask because it has a much higher boiling point than water.

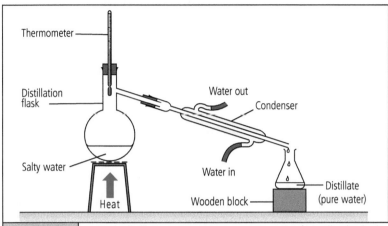

| **Figure 2.5.4** | A simple distillation apparatus to separate water from dissolved salt |

Fractional distillation

Fractional distillation is used to separate two or more liquids with different boiling points from each other (Figure 2.5.5). This method is used to separate petroleum fractions (see 12.4) and to purify alcohol from a mixture of water and alcohol.

- The more volatile components in the liquid mixture (the ones with the lower boiling points), boil first, so as they move up the column, the vapour contains more of the more volatile component.

- There is a gradient of temperature in the column, which is hotter at the bottom than at the top.

- More of the less volatile components (the ones with higher boiling points) condense lower down because they have higher boiling points, so the more volatile components move further up the column.

- As the mixture is heated more and more, the vapours move up the column. The ones with lower boiling points move ahead of those with higher boiling points.

- The components of the mixture reach the condenser in turn. They change from vapour to liquid in the condenser and the fractions containing particular components of the mixture are collected one at a time.

The boiling point and therefore the distance moved up the column depends on:

- the size of the molecules – smaller molecules of similar types tend to have lower boiling points than larger molecules and so move further up the column than larger ones

- the mass of the molecules – lighter molecules of similar types tend to have lower boiling points and so move further up the column than heavier ones.

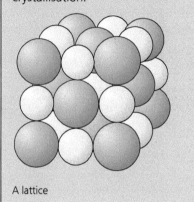
KEY POINTS

1 In filtration, the filtrate passes through the filter paper and the residue remains on the filter paper.

2 Crystallisation is carried out by heating a saturated solution and then leaving the solvent to evaporate.

3 Distillation is a process involving boiling and condensing.

4 The separation of substances by distillation depends on the differences in boiling points of the components in the mixture.

Extracting sucrose

At the end of this topic you should be able to:

- describe the extraction of sucrose from sugar cane
- explain the importance of crushing, filtration, precipitation, treatment under vacuum crystallisation and centrifugation in the extraction of sucrose.

Figure 2.6.1 Sugar cane plants

DID YOU KNOW?

Sugar cane originally came from south-east Asia. It was first brought to the Caribbean by Christopher Columbus in the 1490s, but it did not become important in the Caribbean economy until the Dutch introduced it from Brazil in about 1625. In the following century, sugar cane rapidly replaced cotton and tobacco as the major crop produced in the Caribbean.

Laboratory versus industrial extraction

The apparatus used in the laboratory for extracting compounds or making new compounds is often different from that used when the compound is extracted or made on an industrial scale. The principles, however, are the same. It is difficult to extract sugar from sugar cane in the laboratory by grinding, filtration and evaporation for the following reasons:

- Considerable force is needed to extract the juice from the fibrous sugar cane.
- Ordinary laboratory filters get blocked and it would take too long to filter the sticky filtrate.
- Simple evaporation leaves a treacle-like substance with few crystals and this easily chars on overheating.

Sugar from sugar cane

Extraction of sugar cane juice

1 Cane sugar stalks are harvested and sent to the factory.

2 The stalks are cleaned by jets of water to remove soil, and the leaves are stripped off.

3 A shredding machine cuts up the stalks into small chips.

4 The chips are crushed and rolled flat under a spray of hot water.

5 The sugar cane juice extracted from the crushing and rolling is a slightly acidic green suspension. The fibrous material (bagasse) is removed.

6 Calcium hydroxide is added to neutralise the acidity and remove some of the impurities. The impurities form a sediment. This process is called clarification.

Filtration

Non-sugar impurities are removed by a continuous filtration process in special industrial filters. This leaves a syrup containing about 85% water.

Evaporation (boiling)

The syrupy sugar extract is passed successively into three or four boilers (evaporators) in order to concentrate it. In each successive boiler the pressure is decreased. This is to prevent the sugar from getting charred. The concentrated juice then contains about 35% water.

Crystallisation

1 This takes place under vacuum in a crystallisation pan, where the syrup is evaporated until it is saturated with sugar.

2 A few crystals of sugar are added to help more sugar crystals to form.

3 The mixture then contains a thick syrup called molasses together with sugar crystals.

Centrifugation and drying

A centrifuge is a machine that spins round and round at very high speeds. The force of the spinning pulls heavier particles downwards and separates them from lighter particles. This process is called **centrifugation**.

1 A basket centrifuge (Figure 2.6.2) is used to separate the molasses from the sugar crystals. The mixture is placed in the perforated basket (a basket with tiny holes in it). This is spun round at a high speed.

2 The sugar remains in the basket. The molasses are forced out through the holes in the basket.

3 The sugar crystals are dried in air using a type of tumble-drier.

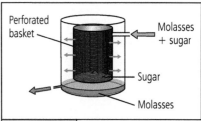

Figure 2.6.2 Simplified diagram to show the idea behind a basket centrifuge

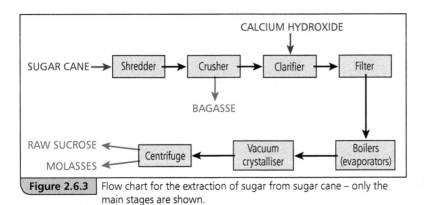

Figure 2.6.3 Flow chart for the extraction of sugar from sugar cane – only the main stages are shown.

EXAM TIP

When revising sugar extraction concentrate on the most important points which are relevant to separation techniques: filtration, precipitation, treatment under vacuum, crystallisation and centrifugation.

KEY POINTS

1 The main stages in sucrose extraction are filtration, precipitation, treatment under vacuum, crystallisation and centrifugation.

2 Calcium hydroxide is used to neutralise the juice extracted from the sugar cane and to precipitate impurities.

3 The sugar solution is concentrated by evaporation under reduced pressure.

4 Crystallisation is done under vacuum.

5 Sugar crystals are separated from molasses by centrifugation.

Chromatography and use of a separating funnel

At the end of this topic you should be able to:

- describe chromatography
- describe the use of a separating funnel
- explain how chromatography and the use of a separating funnel depend on the differences in solubility of the components in the solvents used.

Paper chromatography

Paper chromatography is used to separate a mixture of different dissolved substances. The method is often used to separate the different pigments (coloured compounds) present in food colourings and inks. Figure 2.7.1 shows how to carry out paper chromatography of a mixture of coloured dyes.

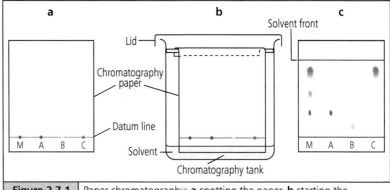

| **Figure 2.7.1** | Paper chromatography: **a** spotting the paper, **b** starting the chromatography, **c** the finished chromatogram |

EXAM TIPS

- You must draw the datum line in pencil because the graphite in the lead does not dissolve in the solvent. If you use ink, the different colours in the ink would move up the paper!
- You must make sure that the solvent level is below the datum line. Otherwise the components would wash off into the solvent and would not separate.

1 Draw a pencil line (the datum line) on a piece of chromatography paper (a type of fine-grained filter paper).

2 Put a spot of concentrated dye mixture, M, on the datum line using a very fine glass tube (capillary tube).

3 Small spots of pure substances, e.g. A, B and C, that you think are in the dye mixture, can also be placed on the datum line for comparison.

4 A chromatography tank is set up with the solvent level below the datum line.

5 As the solvent moves up the paper, the dyes separate.

6 The paper is removed when the solvent front is near the top.

The spots on the chromatogram can be compared with those of known dyes. For example, in Figure 2.7.1(c), the mixture, M, contains dyes A and C as well as a third dye.

We can identify the components in the mixture because, for a particular solvent, they travel a certain distance compared with the solvent front.

How chromatography works

The separation of the components in the mixture depends on the solvent or mixture of solvents used.

- With a single solvent, the separation of the components in a mixture depends on the solubility of the component in the solvent and the attraction of the component to the paper. Components that are attracted more to the paper move more slowly up the paper.

- In a mixture of two solvents, one solvent is attracted to the paper more strongly than the other. If a component in the dye is more soluble in the solvent that is more strongly attracted to the paper, it will not move as fast during chromatography. If a component in the dye is more soluble in the solvent that is less strongly attracted to the paper, it will move faster during chromatography.

Using a separating funnel

A **separating funnel** is used to separate immiscible liquids that have different densities. Immiscible liquids are liquids that do not mix. Figure 2.7.2 shows how we use a separating funnel.

We can use a separating funnel to separate two solutes dissolved in a solvent. An example is a solution of iodine and potassium iodide in water (see Figure 2.7.3). Iodine is more soluble in hexane than in water, but potassium iodide is more soluble in water than in hexane. We can separate the iodine from the potassium iodide in the following way:

1 Put the solution of iodine and potassium iodide in a separating funnel.

2 Add hexane to the separating funnel (hexane is immiscible with water).

3 Shake the contents of the funnel to mix the solutions.

4 Most of the iodine moves to the hexane layer and the potassium iodide remains in the water.

5 The layer of potassium iodide in water is run off, leaving the iodine in the hexane layer.

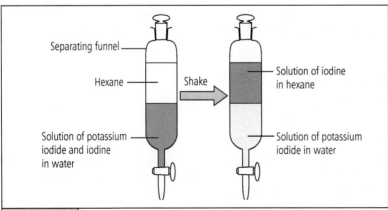

Figure 2.7.3 When a solution of iodine and potassium iodide in water is shaken with hexane, the iodine moves to the layer of hexane.

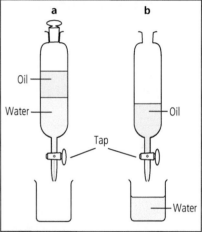

Figure 2.7.2 **a** A mixture of oil and water is allowed to settle into two layers. **b** The lower, denser layer is run off into the beaker.

KEY POINTS

1 Paper chromatography is used to separate a mixture of two or more different solutes in a solution.

2 In paper chromatography, a solvent carries the components of the mixture up the paper at different rates.

3 Paper chromatography can be used to identify the components in a mixture.

4 A separating funnel is used to separate two immiscible liquids.

3 Atomic structure

3.1 The structure of atoms

Subatomic particles

An atom is the smallest uncharged particle that can take part in a chemical change. Atoms are made up of even smaller particles. We call these particles subatomic particles.

• At the centre of each atom is a tiny **nucleus**.

• The nucleus contains two types of subatomic particle: **protons** and **neutrons**.

• Around the outside of the atoms are subatomic particles called **electrons**.

• The electrons are arranged in **electron shells** (also called energy levels).

• In a neutral atom, the number of electrons is equal to the number of protons.

Scientists have developed different models of the atom over the past 100 years. We can draw different models of the atom. In each of these models, it is difficult to show the exact position of the electrons because sometimes they are nearer the nucleus and sometimes further away. Figure 3.1.1 shows two useful models of an atom.

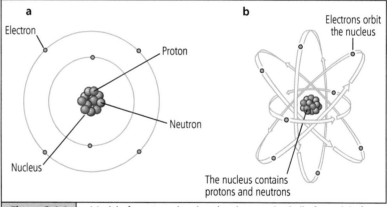

Figure 3.1.1 | **a** Model of an atom showing the electrons in shells, **b** model of an atom showing electrons moving around the nucleus

Putting elements in order

• The number of protons in the nucleus of an atom is called the **atomic number**.

• Each atom of the same element has the same number of protons.

• The atoms of the elements can be arranged in order of their atomic number (proton number). Hydrogen has one proton, helium has two, lithium three and so on.

• The periodic table is an arrangement of all the elements known, in order of their atomic number. See 4.1 for more information.

Electron shells

In one model of the atom, the electrons move at high speed at certain distances from the nucleus in vague regions of space that have the shape of a sphere. In a simplified model we show the electrons in circular orbits around the nucleus. These orbits are the electron shells (see Figure 3.1.2).

- The first shell is nearest the nucleus. It holds a maximum of two electrons.
- The second shell is further away from the nucleus. It holds a maximum of eight electrons.
- The third shell is even further away. It starts filling up when the second shell has eight electrons.

The electron arrangement of elements 1 to 20

The **electron arrangement** in an atom (also called the electron configuration or electronic structure) is deduced by adding electrons, one at a time to the shells, starting with the inner shell. (Remember that the number of electrons in an atom equals the number of protons.) We write the number of electrons in each shell as a number separated by commas. For example:

- Hydrogen atom: 1 proton, so 1 electron. The electron goes into the first shell, so the electron arrangement is 1.
- Helium atom: 2 protons, so 2 electrons. Both electrons go into the first shell, so the electron arrangement is 2.
- Lithium: 3 protons, so 3 electrons. Two electrons go into the first shell, but this shell is then full, so the third electron goes into the second shell. Therefore the electron arrangement is 2,1.
- Sodium: 11 protons, so 11 electrons. Two electrons go into the first shell and eight electrons into the second shell. Then the second shell is full, so the eleventh electron goes into the third shell. Therefore the electron arrangement is 2,8,1.

The electron arrangements of the atoms of the first 20 elements are shown in Figure 3.1.3.

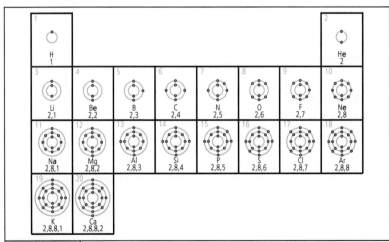

Figure 3.1.3 | The electron arrangements of the first 20 elements

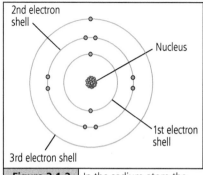

Figure 3.1.2 | In the sodium atom the electrons are arranged in three shells.

KEY POINTS

1 The nucleus is in the centre of all atoms. It contains protons and neutrons.

2 The electrons move at high speed outside the nucleus and are arranged in shells.

3 In a neutral atom the number of electrons equals the number of protons.

4 The first electron shell can hold up to 2 electrons.

5 The second shell can hold up to 8 electrons.

6 The electron arrangement can be written in numbers.

3.2

Protons, neutrons and electrons

Properties of protons, neutrons and electrons

Protons, neutrons and electrons have different masses. They weigh so little that the numbers are difficult to compare. So we compare their masses to each other. This is called the relative mass.

Protons, neutrons and electrons also differ in electric charge. Electric charge can be positive or negative. We also measure the charges relative to each other.

The differences are shown in Table 3.2.1.

Table 3.2.1 Relative masses and charges of protons, neutrons and electrons

Subatomic particle	Where found	Symbol for the particle	Relative mass	Relative charge
Proton	Nucleus	p	1	+1
Neutron	Nucleus	n	1	No charge
Electron	Outside the nucleus	e⁻	0.00054	−1

DID YOU KNOW?

The mass of a proton is only 1.7×10^{-27} kg. This means that there are about 600 000 000 000 000 000 000 000 000 protons in a kilogram of protons!

Electrons have even smaller mass, being over 1000 times lighter than a proton! In some theories of science the electrons are taken as having no mass at all and behaving more like light waves.

Counting subatomic particles

- Atoms of each element have their own symbol to distinguish the element from others. For example:
  - Hydrogen has the symbol H
  - Carbon has the symbol C
  - Lithium has the symbol Li
  - Calcium has the symbol Ca
- For more about symbols see 4.1.
- Atoms of different elements have different numbers of protons. The number of protons is the atomic number (see 3.1).
- The number of protons + the number of neutrons in an atom is called its **mass number**. So if an atom has 11 protons and 12 neutrons, its mass number is 23.

LEARNING OUTCOMES

At the end of this topic you should be able to:

- explain the differences between electrons, protons and neutrons in terms of relative mass, charge and position in the atom
- explain the term mass number
- interpret the notation for atoms and ions showing atomic number, mass number, ionic charge and symbol.

EXAM TIP

Make sure that you know your way around the periodic table to get the most information out of it. The relative atomic mass is usually shown on the periodic table as well as the atomic number.

24

- The number of electrons in a neutral atom equals the number of protons.
- Positively charged **ions** are atoms that have lost one or more electrons.
- Negatively charged ions are atoms that have gained one or more electrons.

A simple notation for atoms

We can show the mass number, atomic number and symbol using the following notation:

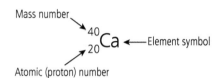

Mass number
$^{40}_{20}Ca$ — Element symbol
Atomic (proton) number

We can extend this to ions as shown below:

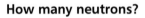

$$^{23}_{11}Na^{+} \qquad ^{32}_{16}S^{2-}$$

How many neutrons?

number of neutrons = mass number − atomic number

= mass number − proton number

So in boron, for example, using the notation above with a mass number of 11:

$$^{11}_{5}B$$

there are 5 protons and 11 − 5 = 6 neutrons.

How many electrons?

- For a negative ion: add the number of charges to the number of electrons in the neutral atom (= number of protons). So for the ion:

$$^{14}_{7}N^{3-}$$

there are 7 + 3 = 10 electrons.

- For a positive ion: subtract the number of charges from the number of electrons in the neutral atom. So for the ion:

$$^{64}_{29}Cu^{2+}$$

there are = 29 − 2 = 27 electrons.

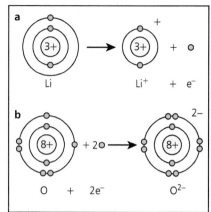

Figure 3.2.1 **a** A lithium atom has lost one electron to form a lithium ion. **b** An oxygen atom has gained two electrons to form an oxide ion.

KEY POINTS

1 Protons have a positive charge, electrons have a negative charge and neutrons are uncharged.

2 Protons and neutrons have (approximately) the same mass. Electrons are much lighter.

3 Mass number is the number of protons + neutrons.

4 Number of neutrons = mass number − atomic number.

5 For negative ions, number of electrons = proton number plus number of charges. For positive ions, number of electrons = proton number minus number of charges.

6 We can write a simple notation for atoms using subscripts and superscripts.

Isotopy

Atoms of the same element always have the same number of protons, i.e. the same atomic number. In most elements, some of the atoms have different numbers of neutrons to others. We call these different forms of atoms **isotopes**.

Isotopes are atoms with the same number of protons but different numbers of neutrons. So isotopes are atoms with the same atomic number but different mass numbers. We usually describe isotopes using the standard notation we used in 3.2 or by writing the mass number after their name, e.g. carbon-14, uranium-235.

The three isotopes of hydrogen are shown in Figure 3.3.1.

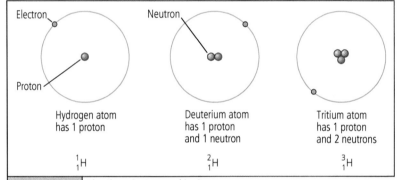

Hydrogen atom has 1 proton

$^{1}_{1}H$

Deuterium atom has 1 proton and 1 neutron

$^{2}_{1}H$

Tritium atom has 1 proton and 2 neutrons

$^{3}_{1}H$

Figure 3.3.1 | The three isotopes of hydrogen

Tritium has three times the mass of hydrogen-1 and deuterium has twice the mass of hydrogen-1. Isotopes of the same element have the same chemical properties but may have different physical properties.

Relative atomic mass

The mass of an atom is so small that you cannot weigh it. To overcome this problem, we have to weigh a sample containing a lot of atoms. But there may be a number of different isotopes among all the atoms we weigh, so the average mass of an atom will be slightly different from the atomic mass.

We define the **relative atomic mass** as the weighted average mass of naturally occurring atoms of an element on a scale where an atom of carbon-12 has a mass of exactly 12 units.

- An average is used because most elements are a mixture of isotopes.
- The 'weighted average' means that you have to take into account the amount of each isotope present.
- The symbol for relative atomic mass is A_r
- A_r of element E $= \dfrac{\text{average mass of isotopes of element E}}{\frac{1}{12} \times \text{mass of one atom of carbon-12}}$

Atomic notation in simple molecules

Molecules such as chlorine and oxygen are diatomic. Their molecules have two atoms. We can show this by including a figure 2 as a subscript at the bottom right of the symbol. Compare the notation for several chlorine molecules with isotopes chlorine-35 and chlorine-37 in their atoms:

a Cl_2

b $^{35}Cl^{35}Cl$ $^{35}Cl^{37}Cl$ $^{37}Cl^{37}Cl$

Figure 3.3.2 **a** The formula for a chlorine molecule, **b** the notation for the isotopes in a chlorine molecule

A chlorine molecule with two atoms of chlorine-35 has a relative mass of 70.

A chlorine molecule with one atom of chlorine-35 and one atom of chlorine-37 has a relative mass of 72.

A chlorine molecule with two atoms of chlorine-37 has a relative mass of 74.

Radioactivity and its uses

Some isotopes, called **radioactive isotopes**, have unstable nuclei, which break down (decay). As the nucleus decays, it gives out tiny particles (called alpha or beta particles) or rays (gamma radiation). The radioactivity from a sample decreases over time. Measuring this rate has found many uses.

Carbon dating

The atmosphere contains carbon dioxide. The carbon in this is mainly carbon-12 (which is non-radioactive) but there is also some carbon-14 (which is radioactive). When an organism dies no new carbon-14 atoms are absorbed into the body. The age of wood or bone from an organism which was once living can be found from the amount of carbon-14 present.

Radiotherapy

Cancer cells divide more rapidly than normal cells. Beta or gamma radiation can be used to kill cancer cells in the affected area.

Radioactive tracers

Specific radioactive isotopes can be injected into the body and their position in the body can be observed using special equipment. One use of tracers is to see how well the thyroid gland is working.

Pacemakers

Heart pacemakers can be powered by 'batteries' of plutonium-238. The heat energy liberated during radioactive decay generates an electric current.

EXAM TIP

You do not need to learn details of the types of radiation. The syllabus only requires you to know three uses of radioactive isotopes.

DID YOU KNOW?

Nuclear power stations use radioactive isotopes such as uranium-235 as a fuel. Heat energy is released in a series of processes. This heat energy is used to boil water. The resulting steam powers turbines to turn generators that generate electricity.

KEY POINTS

1. Isotopes are atoms with the same number of protons but different numbers of neutrons.
2. The relative atomic mass is the weighted average mass of naturally occurring atoms of an element on a scale where an atom of carbon-12 has a mass of exactly 12 units.
3. Radioactive isotopes have unstable nuclei and decay to form different atoms.
4. Radioactive isotopes can be used in carbon dating, radiotherapy, as radioactive tracers, in pacemakers and in energy generation.

4 The periodic table and periodicity

4.1 The periodic table

LEARNING OUTCOMES

At the end of this topic you should be able to:

- describe the historical development of the periodic table
- describe the basis of the arrangement of the periodic table in terms of atomic number and atomic structure
- describe the arrangement of the periodic table in periods and groups.

Early developments

Döbereiner's 'triads'

In 1817, Johann Döbereiner suggested that elements could be grouped together in groups of three (triads). He:

- linked these triads with an increase in their atomic weights (now called atomic masses). For example: chlorine (35), bromine (80) and iodine (127)
- deduced that the middle elements of many of the triads had an atomic weight that was the average of the first and third elements of the triad
- suggested that some triads had similar chemical properties, e.g. lithium, sodium and potassium but others did not.

Newlands' 'law of octaves'

Between 1863 and 1866, John Newlands:

- listed elements in order of their atomic weights
- noted that similar elements were separated by intervals of eight elements (octaves).

Mendeleev's periodic table

Dmitri Mendeleev developed his first **periodic table** of the elements in 1869. He:

- based his reasoning on chemical characteristics
- listed elements in order of atomic weights (masses)
- arranged the elements in **groups** (vertical columns) and **periods** (horizontal rows)
- left gaps in the table where elements had not yet been discovered, so that elements with similar properties, e.g. chlorine, bromine and iodine, fell in the same vertical groups
- showed that there was a gradual change in properties across a period.

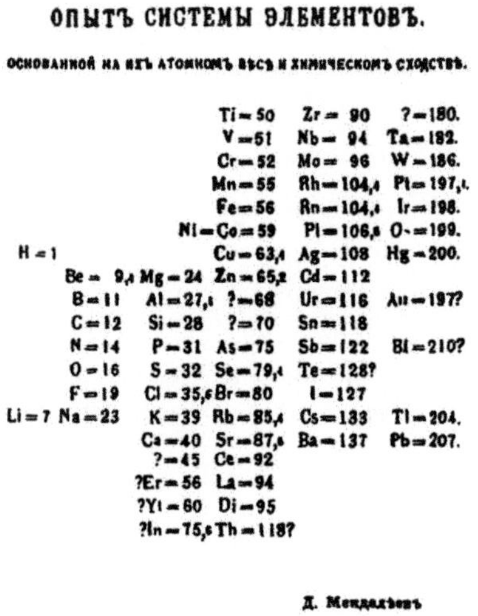

ОПЫТЪ СИСТЕМЫ ЭЛЕМЕНТОВЪ.

ОСНОВАННОЙ НА ИХЪ АТОМНОМЪ ВѢСѢ И ХИМИЧЕСКОМЪ СХОДСТВѢ.

			Ti=50	Zr=90	?=180.
			V=51	Nb=94	Ta=182.
			Cr=52	Mo=96	W=186.
			Mn=55	Rh=104,4	Pt=197,4.
			Fe=56	Rn=104,4	Ir=198.
			Ni=Co=59	Pl=106,6	Os=199.
H=1			Cu=63,4	Ag=108	Hg=200.
	Be=9,4	Mg=24	Zn=65,2	Cd=112	
	B=11	Al=27,4	?=68	Ur=116	Au=197?
	C=12	Si=28	?=70	Sn=118	
	N=14	P=31	As=75	Sb=122	Bi=210?
	O=16	S=32	Se=79,4	Te=128?	
	F=19	Cl=35,5	Br=80	I=127	
Li=7	Na=23	K=39	Rb=85,4	Cs=133	Tl=204.
		Ca=40	Sr=87,6	Ba=137	Pb=207.
		?=45	Ce=92		
		?Er=56	La=94		
		?Yt=60	Di=95		
		?In=75,6	Th=118?		

Д. Менделѣевъ

Figure 4.1.1 Mendeleev's first published periodic table. He developed several forms of the periodic table. The second form has gradually been developed into the periodic table we know today.

The structure of the periodic table

The modern periodic table

Figure 4.1.2 shows the modern periodic table.

The modern extended form of the periodic table has the following features:

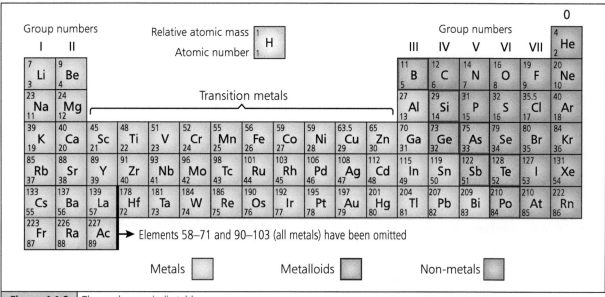

Figure 4.1.2 The modern periodic table

- Elements are arranged in groups numbered I–VII and 0. The elements in Group 0, the noble gases, were discovered after Mendeleev's table was published.
- The elements in Group I have similar chemical properties. The same applies to Groups II, VII and 0.
- The first three periods are called short periods and the others are long periods.
- Across each period there is a gradual change in properties from metallic to non-metallic.
- Across Periods 2 and 3 there is a similar change in physical properties such as boiling point.
- Between the metals and the non-metals are the elements that have some properties of both. These are called metalloids.

The basis of the modern periodic table

The elements in the periodic table are arranged in order of their atomic number. The electron arrangement of an atom, especially the number of outer shell electrons determines the chemical properties of an element.

- Elements in the same group have the same number of outer shell electrons.
- For Groups I–VII the number of outer shell electrons is equal to the group number.
- Elements in Group 0 generally have eight electrons in their outermost shell. Helium, in the first period has two electrons in its outer shell.
- Atoms of elements in the same period have their outermost electrons in the same shell.
- The period number of an element is the number of shells of an element's atom that contain electrons.

Trends in Group II

At the end of this topic you should be able to:

- describe the trends in physical properties of the Group II elements

- describe the reactions of magnesium and calcium with water, air and dilute hydrochloric acid

- describe trends in the reactivity of Group II elements

- explain trends in reactivity of Group II elements in terms of ease of ionisation.

Physical properties of Group II elements

The physical properties of the Group II metals show some general trends down the group.

Table 4.2.1   Physical properties of Group II elements

Element	Melting point (°C)	Density (g cm^{-3})	Radius of atom (nm)
Beryllium (Be)	1280	1.85	0.122
Magnesium (Mg)	650	1.74	0.160
Calcium (Ca)	838	1.55	0.197
Strontium (Sr)	768	2.6	0.215
Barium (Ba)	714	3.5	0.217

Some reactions of Group II elements

Metals in Group II are more reactive going down the group.

Reaction with oxygen

Group II metals burn in air and even more rapidly in oxygen. On descending the group, the metals burn more readily. The reactions are similar, forming the metal oxide.

$$2Ca(s) + O_2(g) \longrightarrow 2CaO(s)$$
calcium   oxygen   calcium
                                    oxide

For more information on writing equations see 6.2.

Reaction with water

Group II metals react with water. The reactivity increases down the group.

Magnesium reacts slowly with cold water:

$$Mg(s) + 2H_2O(l) \longrightarrow Mg(OH)_2(aq) + H_2(g)$$
magnesium   water   magnesium   hydrogen
                                hydroxide

Hot magnesium reacts with steam to form magnesium oxide:

$$Mg(s) + H_2O(g) \longrightarrow MgO(s) + H_2(g)$$

Calcium reacts more rapidly with water than magnesium:

$$Ca(s) + 2H_2O(l) \longrightarrow Ca(OH)_2(aq) + H_2(g)$$
calcium   water   calcium   hydrogen
                             hydroxide

EXAM TIP

Your may be required to analyse data from tables. Remember that a general trend does not have to be one that is going in the same direction without exception. For example, the general trend in melting points of the Group II elements is towards lower melting points as you go down the group. Magnesium is an exception because it has a lower melting point than the trend would suggest.

Reaction with hydrochloric acid

Group II metals react with hydrochloric acid to form hydrogen and salts called chlorides. The reactions are similar. The reactivity increases down the group.

$$Mg(s) + 2HCl(aq) \longrightarrow MgCl_2(aq) + H_2(g)$$

magnesium   hydrochloric   magnesium   hydrogen
            acid   chloride

$$Ca(s) + 2HCl(aq) \longrightarrow CaCl_2(aq) + H_2(g)$$

calcium   hydrochloric   calcium   hydrogen
            acid   chloride

Reactivity and ease of ionisation

The reactivity of the Group II metals is linked to the ease with which they form ions. When they react, their atoms lose their two outermost electrons to form ions.

$$Mg \longrightarrow Mg^{2+} + 2e^-$$

The energy needed to remove an electron from an atom or ion is called the **ionisation energy**. Table 4.2.2 shows that, as you go down the group, the energy needed to remove the two electrons decreases.

Table 4.2.2   Energy needed to remove the two electrons from the outer shell of Group II atoms

Element	Energy needed to remove two electrons from atom (kJ mol^{-1})
Beryllium	2660
Magnesium	2186
Calcium	1740
Strontium	1608
Barium	1468

There are three things which influence the energy required to remove an electron:

- Distance of outer electrons from the nucleus: the further the outer electrons are from the nucleus, the smaller the attraction to the nucleus and the lower the energy needed to remove the outer electrons.
- Nuclear charge: the greater the number of protons in the nucleus, the more energy is required to remove the outer electrons.
- Inner electron shells reduce the amount of nuclear charge felt by the outer electrons. This is called **shielding** or **screening**. The greater the number of inner shells of electrons, the lower the energy needed to remove the outer electrons.

The energy decreases down the group because the increase in the size of the atoms and the increased screening outweigh the effect of increased nuclear charge.

Figure 4.2.1   Magnesium ribbon reacts rapidly with the oxygen in the air.

KEY POINTS

1. There are general trends in some of the physical properties of the Group II elements.

2. The Group II elements react with pure oxygen or oxygen in the air to form oxides.

3. Most Group II elements react with water to form the metal hydroxide and hydrogen.

4. Group II elements react with hydrochloric acid to form metal chlorides and hydrogen.

5. The reactivity of the Group II elements depends on the ease of ionisation of their atoms.

6. The ease of ionisation of atoms depends on the distance from the nucleus, the nuclear charge and the shielding of the outer electrons by inner electron shells.

Trends in Group VII

Physical properties

The Group VII elements are called the **halogens**. They all exist as **diatomic** molecules. This means that they have molecules made up of two atoms. Table 4.3.1 shows some of their physical properties.

Table 4.3.1 Physical properties of the halogens

Halogen	State at 25°C	Colour	Melting point (°C)	Boiling point (°C)
Fluorine (F_2)	Gas	Yellow	−220	−188
Chlorine (Cl_2)	Gas	Yellow-green	−101	−35
Bromine (Br_2)	Liquid	Red-brown	−7	+59
Iodine (I_2)	Solid	Grey-black	+114	+184

- The colours get darker and more intense down the group.
- Bromine vapour is red-brown but iodine vapour is purple and a solution of iodine in aqueous potassium iodide is brown.
- The melting points and boiling points increase down the group.

Displacement reactions

A **displacement reaction** is a reaction in which one type of atom or ion has replaced another in a compound. For example, when an aqueous solution of chlorine (a solution of chlorine in water) is added to aqueous potassium bromide, the chlorine displaces the bromide ion in the potassium bromide:

$$Cl_2(aq) + 2KBr(aq) \longrightarrow 2KCl(aq) + Br_2(aq)$$

chlorine potassium bromide potassium chloride bromine

By adding different halogens to different halides, we can see that a halogen higher in the group has displaced the halogen lower in the group from its halide solution.

Figure 4.3.1 At room temperature, chlorine is a gas, bromine is a liquid and iodine is a solid.

Table 4.3.2 The reactions of the halides with the halogens. The names of the products are given if a reaction occurs. A dash (–) indicates that there is no reaction.

Halogen in aqueous solution	Halide		
	Potassium chloride	Potassium bromide	Potassium iodide
Chlorine	–	potassium chloride + bromine formed	potassium chloride + iodine formed
Bromine	–	–	potassium bromide + iodine formed
Iodine	–	–	–

Explaining the displacement reactions

The halogens get less reactive going down Group VII. This is because of differences in the oxidising power of the halogens. For more information about oxidation see 8.1 and 8.2. We can link this to the ease of the formation of halide ions from halogens.

As we go down the group:

• The radius of the halogen atom increases.

• The oxidising ability of the halogens decreases. A halogen higher in the group is a better oxidising agent than one lower down.

• The oxidising ability decreases like this because it is more difficult to add an electron to a halogen atom to form a negative ion if the halogen atom is larger.

A stronger **oxidising agent** will accept electrons from a weaker oxidising agent. So:

• Chlorine (stronger oxidising agent – better electron acceptor) will displace bromine from a bromide.

• Bromine (weaker oxidising agent – worse electron acceptor) will not displace chlorine from a chloride.

EXAM TIP

It is important to distinguish between halogens and halides. Halogens are diatomic molecules that are elements. Halides are ionic compounds containing fluoride (F^-), chloride (Cl^-), bromide (Br^-) or iodide (I^-) ions. In answering exam questions, however, it is acceptable to write, for example, 'chlorine displaces bromine from a solution of potassium bromide'.

KEY POINTS

1 The colours of the halogens get darker and more intense down the group.

2 The boiling points and melting points of the halogens increase down the group.

3 At room temperature fluorine and chlorine are gases, bromine is a liquid and iodine is a solid.

4 Displacement reactions involve the replacement of one atom or ion by another.

5 The reactivity of the halogens decreases down the group.

6 A more reactive halogen displaces a less reactive one from a halide solution because the more reactive halogen has a greater oxidising power.

7 The easier it is for a halogen atom to accept an electron, the stronger the oxidising power of the halogen.

DID YOU KNOW?

Fluorine is the best oxidant of all the halogens. This is because it has such a small atom with only two electron shells. An additional electron entering its outer shell experiences nearly the full force of the positive nuclear charge. An iodine atom has five electron shells and even though the nuclear charge is higher the nucleus is well screened.

LEARNING OUTCOMES

At the end of this topic you should be able to:

- explain periodicity
- describe trends in Period 3 of the periodic table
- predict properties of unknown elements based on the position of the element in the periodic table.

Trends in Period 3 of the periodic table

As we move from the left to the right in the periodic table, the physical and chemical properties of the elements change. In some instances the change is marked and in others there is a gradual change. **Periodicity** is the regular occurrence of similar properties of the elements in the periodic table so that elements in a given group have similar properties or a trend in properties. Table 4.4.1 shows some of these trends.

Table 4.4.1   Properties across Period 3

	Na	Mg	Al	Si	P	S	Cl	Ar
Electron arrangement	2,8,1	2,8,2	2,8,3	2,8,4	2,8,5	2,8,6	2,8,7	2,8,8
Electron gain or loss (on forming ions)	1e⁻ loss	2e⁻ loss	3e⁻ loss	4e⁻ no ions formed, electrons shared	3e⁻ gain	2e⁻ gain	1e⁻ gain	no loss or gain
State at 25°C	solid	solid	solid	solid	solid	solid	gas	gas
Boiling point (°C)	883	1107	2467	2355	280	445	−35	−186
Electrical conductivity	conductor	conductor	conductor	semiconductor	insulator	insulator	insulator	insulator
Metal or non-metal	metal	metal	metal	metalloid	non-metal	non-metal	non-metal	non-metal

EXAM TIP

The charge on the ion formed from an atom is generally equal to the group number for metals or the group number minus 8 for non-metals. So magnesium in Group II forms the ion Mg^{2+} and the nitride ion derived from nitrogen in Group V is N^{3-}.

- There is a change in metallic to non-metallic character across the period.
- Metals conduct electricity but non-metals do not. Non-metals are **insulators**. The **metalloids** lying between the metals and non-metals have some properties of both metals and non-metals.
- Across the period the boiling point increases then decreases. This reflects the different structures of the elements (see 5.4–5.6).
- Metals tend to lose electrons in forming ions, whereas the non-metals at the right-hand side of the table (apart from elements in Group 0) tend to gain electrons.
- Across the period the ability of the atoms to lose electrons decreases and their ability to gain electrons increases.

There are also periodic changes in chemical properties and reactivity across the period. The chemical properties depend on the number of outer shell electrons in the atoms of the element. For example, in the reaction with water:

- sodium reacts very rapidly and forms an alkaline solution
- magnesium reacts very slowly and forms a slightly alkaline solution
- aluminium only reacts slowly when heated in steam
- silicon, phosphorus and sulfur do not react
- chlorine reacts to form an acidic solution.

Deducing the properties of unknown elements

We can use the trends in the properties of elements to deduce the properties of elements that we know little about.

Example 1

Use the data below to deduce the state and boiling point of astatine and whether or not iodine will react with potassium astatide.

Table 4.4.2   Data about halogens

Halogen	State at 25°C	Boiling point (°C)
Chlorine	Gas	−35
Bromine	Liquid	+59
Iodine	Solid	+184
Astatine	?	?

Astatine is below iodine in Group VII. So continuing the trend:

- Astatine should be a solid.
- Its melting point should be above +184°C. The difference in melting point between chlorine and bromine is 94°C and that between bromine and iodine is 125°C. So continuing the increase, we estimate astatine's boiling point by adding a value of perhaps 150°C. The estimated value is then 184 + 150 = 334°C (actual value = 337°C).
- Potassium astatide will react with iodine to form potassium iodide and astatine. This follows the pattern that the more reactive halogen (iodine) will react with the halide of the less reactive halogen.

Example 2

Predict the properties of selenium (Se) from its position in the section of periodic table shown in Figure 4.4.1.

Using your knowledge of the periodic table by looking at the elements around it, selenium:

- is a non-metal in Group VI of the periodic table
- does not conduct electricity (is an insulator)
- forms ions of type Se^{2-} (since it is in Group VI)
- is a solid at room temperature since S is also a solid.

C	N	O	F
Si	P	S	Cl
Ge	As	Se	Br
Sn	Sb	Te	I

Figure 4.4.1

Ionic bonding

The formation of ions

- Positive ions are formed when an atom loses one or more electrons. For example:

$$Mg \longrightarrow Mg^{2+} + 2e^-$$

- Negative ions are formed when an atom gains one or more electrons. For example:

$$O + 2e^- \longrightarrow O^{2-}$$

- The charge on the ion depends on the number of electrons lost or gained.
- For most metal ions the number of positive charges is the same as the group number. For example, aluminium is in Group III, so its ion is Al^{3+}.
- For most non-metal ions, the negative charge is eight minus the group number. For example, phosphorus is in Group V, so the phosphide ion is P^{3-}.

Forming the noble gas configuration

- When metals combine with non-metals, the electrons in the outer shell of the metal atoms are transferred completely to the non-metal atoms.
- Each non-metal atom usually gains enough electrons to fill its outer shell.
- Each metal atom usually loses its outer shell electrons.
- The ions formed (both metal and non-metal) end up with the electron arrangement of the nearest noble gas (**noble gas configuration**).
- The strong force of attraction between the oppositely charged ions results in an **ionic bond** (see 5.4 for more details).

For example, Figure 5.1.1 shows that:

- The sodium atom has lost one electron. The ion has the electron arrangement of neon.
- The chlorine atom has gained the electron from sodium. The chloride ion has the electron arrangement of argon.

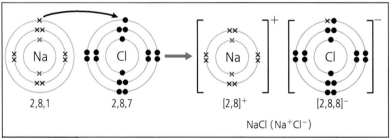

2,8,1   2,8,7   [2,8]$^+$ [2,8,8]$^-$

NaCl (Na$^+$Cl$^-$)

Figure 5.1.1 The sodium atom transfers its outer electron to a chlorine atom, so both ions formed have the electron arrangement of the nearest noble gas.

Dot-and-cross diagrams

Dot-and-cross diagrams help us to keep track of where the electrons have come from when an ionic bond is formed. Dot-and-cross diagrams show:

* the outer electron shells only
* the charge of the ion at the top right outside square brackets.

Figure 5.1.2 shows the dot-and-cross diagram for sodium chloride.

Examples of dot-and-cross diagrams for ions

Magnesium oxide

The two electrons in the outer shell of the magnesium atom are transferred to the outer shell of the oxygen atom. Each ion has the electron arrangement of the nearest noble gas (Figure 5.1.3).

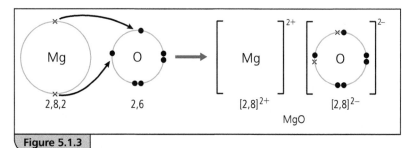

Figure 5.1.3

Calcium chloride

The calcium atom loses its two outer electrons. A single chlorine atom has only space in its outer shell for one electron. So, two chlorine atoms are needed to react with one calcium atom. Each of the chlorine atoms gains one electron (Figure 5.1.4).

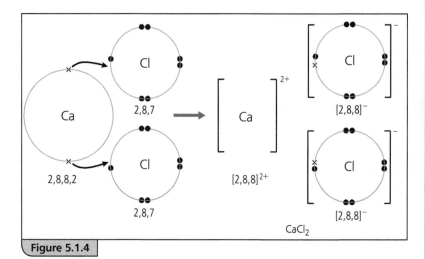

Figure 5.1.4

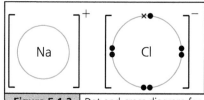

Figure 5.1.2 Dot-and-cross diagram for sodium chloride

KEY POINTS

1. Metal ions are positively charged and are formed by loss of electrons.

2. Non-metal ions are negatively charged and are formed by gain of electrons.

3. Most ions have the noble gas electron arrangement.

4. Ionic bonding involves the complete transfer of one or more electrons from a metal atom to a non-metal atom.

5. Dot-and-cross diagrams for ions show the electron arrangement of the positive and negative ions using dots or crosses to represent the origin of the electrons.

Covalent bonding

At the end of this topic you should be able to:

• describe the formation of covalent bonds

• draw dot-and-cross diagrams to show covalent bonding.

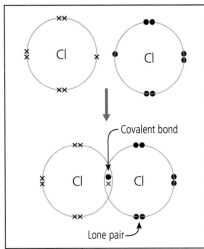

Figure 5.2.1 In a chlorine molecule, each atom shares a pair of electrons, forming a single covalent bond.

DID YOU KNOW?

In a few covalent molecules, one of the atoms may not have the noble gas electron arrangement. An example is boron trichloride, where the boron atom has only six electrons around it. These are called electron-deficient molecules.

What is a covalent bond?

• When two or more non-metals combine they share one or more pairs of electrons.

• A shared pair of electrons is called a **covalent bond**.

• The shared electrons in the covalent bond usually arise from the outer shell of the atoms that combine.

• When some non-metal atoms combine, not all the electrons in the outer shell form covalent bonds. The pairs of electrons not used in covalent bonding are called **lone pairs**.

• In writing displayed formulae, a single covalent bond is shown as a single line between the atoms, e.g. $Cl-Cl$.

Drawing dot-and-cross diagrams for molecules

To draw a dot-and-cross diagram for a molecule:

• Use a dot for electrons of one of the atoms and a cross for the electrons of the other (see Figure 5.2.1).

• If there are more than two types of atom, we can give the electrons other symbols such as a small circle or square.

• The outer electrons are drawn in pairs.

• The electrons are arranged so that, if possible, each atom has the number of outer shell electrons that corresponds to the nearest noble gas configuration. Some of these electrons will be shared and other may not be shared.

Figure 5.2.2 shows how we draw a dot-and-cross diagram for methane.

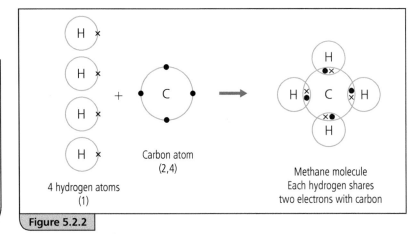

4 hydrogen atoms (1)

Carbon atom (2,4)

Methane molecule
Each hydrogen shares two electrons with carbon

Figure 5.2.2

Molecules with only single bonds

Figure 5.2.3 shows dot-and-cross diagrams for hydrogen chloride, water, ammonia and ethane.

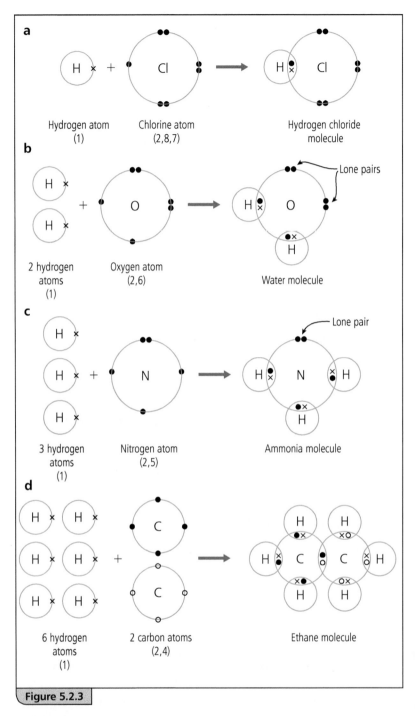

a

Hydrogen atom (1)   Chlorine atom (2,8,7)   Hydrogen chloride molecule

b

2 hydrogen atoms (1)   Oxygen atom (2,6)   Water molecule   Lone pairs

c

3 hydrogen atoms (1)   Nitrogen atom (2,5)   Ammonia molecule   Lone pair

d

6 hydrogen atoms (1)   2 carbon atoms (2,4)   Ethane molecule

Figure 5.2.3

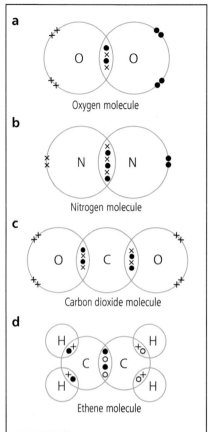

a   Oxygen molecule

b   Nitrogen molecule

c   Carbon dioxide molecule

d   Ethene molecule

Figure 5.2.4

Molecules with multiple bonds

Some atoms are able to share two pairs of electrons. We call this a **double bond**. We can show this by a double line. When drawing the dot-and-cross diagram for an oxygen molecule, each oxygen atom (2,6) needs to gain two electrons to complete its outer shell. It can only do this by sharing two pairs of electrons. A double bond is formed. When three pairs of electrons are shared, as in the nitrogen molecule, a **triple bond** is formed. Figure 5.2.4 shows dot-and-cross diagrams for oxygen, nitrogen, carbon dioxide and ethene.

Ions, molecules and formula units

At the end of this topic you should be able to:

• predict the likelihood of an atom forming ionic or covalent bonds

• write formulae to represent ions, molecules and formula units.

CH_3CH_2OH	H H
	    | |
	H—C—C—O—H
	    | |
	    H H

Simplified structural formula	Displayed formula

Figure 5.3.1 Simplified structural formula and displayed formula of ethanol

DID YOU KNOW?

Atoms can be ordered according to their power of attracting electrons. The ability of an atom that is covalently bonded to another to attract a bonding pair of electrons towards itself is called its *electronegativity*. If there is a small difference in the electronegativity between the atoms, the compound is likely to be covalent. If there is a larger difference in electronegativity, there may be some ionic character in the bond because the bonding pair of electrons is pulled nearer to one atom than the other.

Ionic or covalent?

• Compounds are likely to be ionic when a reactive metal in Group I or II reacts with a reactive non-metal near the top of Group VI or VII. This is because Group I and II elements readily lose electrons and elements near the top of Groups VI and VII generally readily accept electrons.

• Compounds are likely to be covalent when two non-metals react. This is because the power of the atoms to attract the electrons is similar. So neither of the atoms can attract an electron enough to transfer it completely and make an ion.

Three types of chemical formula

• A **molecular formula** gives the number of atoms of each particular element in one molecule of a compound, e.g. HBr, Cl_2, H_2O, C_2H_6O.

• A **structural formula** shows us how the atoms are bonded in a molecule. Simplified structural formulae do not show any bonds except for double and triple bonds but **displayed formulae** show how the bonds are arranged (see Figure 5.3.1).

• An **empirical formula** gives the simplest whole number ratio of atoms or ions in a compound. For example, the empirical formula of ethane, C_2H_6, is CH_3.

Writing formulae for ionic compounds

Since ionic compounds have thousands of positive and negative ions (see 5.4) the **formula unit** for an ionic compound is the empirical formula, e.g. $MgCl_2$, Na_2O.

In an ionic compound:

• The number of positive charges is balanced by the number of negative charges.

• For metal ions in Groups I, II and III, the positive charge on the ion is the same as the group number, e.g. Na^+, Ba^{2+}, Al^{3+}.

• For non-metal ions in Groups V, VI and VII, the negative charge is 8 minus the group number, e.g. Cl^-, S^{2-}, N^{3-}.

• The hydrogen ion is H^+.

• The charges of transition element ions and elements towards the bottom of Groups IV and V may vary and have to be learnt separately (see Table 5.3.1).

• Subscripts are used to show the number of atoms combining, e.g. in P_4O_6, there are four phosphorus atoms and six oxygen atoms.

Table 5.3.1 The charge on some ions

Singly charged	Doubly charged	Triply charged
Silver, Ag^+	Iron(II), Fe^{2+}	Iron(III), Fe^{3+}
Copper(I), Cu^+	Copper(II), Cu^{2+}	
	Zinc, Zn^{2+}	
	Lead(II), Pb^{2+}	

We can deduce the formula for magnesium bromide as follows:

- Write down the ions separately: Mg^{2+} and Br^-.
- Balance the charges: we need two Br^- to balance one Mg^{2+}.
- Write the formula with the metal ion first: $MgBr_2$

Some ions contain more than one type of atom:

$$NH_4^+ \quad OH^- \quad NO_3^- \quad SO_4^{2-} \quad CO_3^{2-} \quad HCO_3^-$$
ammonium　hydroxide　nitrate　sulfate　carbonate　hydrogencarbonate

The formulae of compounds containing these ions are found in the same way by balancing the charges of the ions. Two examples are shown in Figure 5.3.2.

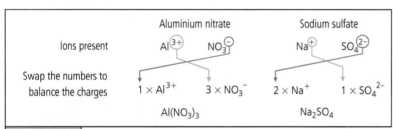

Figure 5.3.2

Writing formulae for covalent compounds

The formulae for compounds can often be found from knowledge of oxidation numbers (see 8.1). As a rough guide we can use the idea of combining powers of different atoms (Table 5.3.2).

So:

- one C atom combines with four H atoms in methane, CH_4
- two atoms of oxygen combine with one atom of carbon in carbon dioxide, CO_2
- one atom of H combines with one atom of Cl to form HCl.

Table 5.3.2 The combining power of non-metal atoms

Atom	Combining power
Carbon, C	4
Chlorine, Cl	1
Hydrogen, H	1
Oxygen, O	2

KEY POINTS

1 Ionic bonds are generally formed between reactive metals and reactive non-metals.

2 When non-metallic atoms combine, covalent bonds are formed.

3 The formula of an ionic compound can be deduced by balancing the charges on the positive and negative ions.

4 The formula of a covalent compound can be found by assigning combining powers (oxidation numbers) to each atom.

Ionic compounds: structure and properties

EXAM TIP

Diagrams of ionic structures often show the ions joined by lines. Remember that these lines do not represent covalent bonds. Ionic forces are not directional.

| Fig 5.4.2 | The shape of these salt crystals shows the way the ions are arranged in the lattice. |

Ionic crystals

The regular structure of a crystal is due to the regular packing of the particles in the crystal. A regularly repeating arrangement of ions, atoms or molecules is called a **crystal lattice**. In ionic lattices there is usually a three-dimensional arrangement of alternating positive and negative ions. This is sometimes called a giant ionic structure.

In an **ionic lattice**:

- the electrostatic attractive forces between the positive and negative ions act in all directions
- these forces are very strong. It takes a lot of energy to overcome them.

The structure of part of a lattice of sodium chloride, NaCl, is shown in Figure 5.4.1. You can see that the ions are packed closely together.

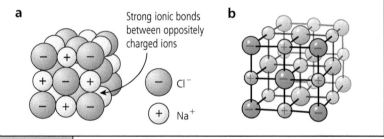

| Figure 5.4.1 | a The close packing of the ions in sodium chloride, b exploded view to show the arrangement of the ions |

Properties of ionic compounds

The properties of ionic compounds, such as sodium chloride, can be explained by their structure and bonding:

- They have high melting points. There are strong attractive forces between the large numbers of positive and negative ions acting in all directions. It needs a lot of energy to overcome these forces to melt the solid.
- They are **brittle**. The crystals split apart when hit in the same direction as the layers of ions. When the layers move slightly, similarly charged ions come close to each other. The large repulsive forces cause the crystal to split.
- They are **hard**. It takes a lot of energy to scratch the surface. This is because the strong attractive forces keep the ions together.
- They are soluble in water. When added to water, the water molecules form weak bonds with the ions on the surface of the crystal. The forces between the ions within the crystal are weakened

and the ions eventually become surrounded by water molecules. The total forces of attraction between the water molecules and the ions are greater than the forces of attraction between the positive and negative ions. So the crystal dissolves (see Figure 5.4.3).

- They do not dissolve in non-polar organic solvents (see 5.6) because either bonds are not formed between the organic solvent and the ions or the bonds are too weak.

- They do not conduct electricity when solid. This is because the ions are not free to move. For a substance to be able to conduct electricity there must be a movement of charged particles. When sodium chloride is molten or dissolved in water, it does conduct electricity. This is because the ions are free to move.

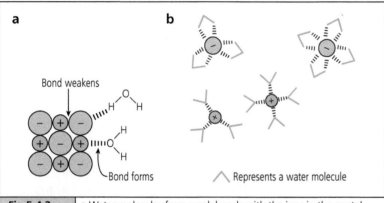

a Water molecules form weak bonds with the ions in the crystal. **b** In a solution, the ions are surrounded by water molecules.

Fig 5.4.3

Uses of ionic compounds

The solubility of sodium chloride makes it useful for:

- manufacturing chlorine and sodium hydroxide by electrolysis of its aqueous solution
- spreading on roads in cold countries to reduce the formation of ice.

The high melting point of ionic compounds, such as magnesium oxide, makes them useful for furnace linings.

KEY POINTS

1   In ionic crystals, the positive and negative ions are arranged in a lattice.

2   Ionic compounds have high melting and boiling points.

3   Ionic compounds are soluble in water but insoluble in non-polar organic solvents.

4   Ionic compounds do not conduct electricity when in the solid state but do conduct when molten or dissolved in water.

5   An aqueous solution of sodium chloride (brine) is used in the production of sodium hydroxide and chlorine. It is spread on roads in cold countries to reduce the formation of ice on road surfaces.

Simple molecular and giant molecular structures

Figure 5.5.1 Part of an iodine lattice

DID YOU KNOW?

Many simple molecular structures containing oxygen or nitrogen bonded to hydrogen are able to dissolve in water. This is because they form a particular type of bond with water called a *hydrogen bond*.

Simple molecular crystals

Iodine and sulfur have a simple **molecular structure**. They can form crystals because the molecules are regularly arranged in a lattice (see Figure 5.5.1).

The properties of iodine and sulfur can be related to their structure:

- They have low melting points because the forces between the molecules are weak. It does not need much energy to overcome these forces and separate the molecules.
- They are soft. When scratched, it does not take much energy to overcome the weak forces between the molecules.
- They do not dissolve easily in water because the water molecules cannot form strong enough bonds with the molecules to separate them from each other.
- They dissolve in non-polar organic solvents because the forces between the solvent molecules and the iodine (or sulfur) molecules are stronger than those between the iodine (or sulfur) molecules themselves. Note, though, that some molecular crystals, such as sucrose, are soluble in water (see 5.6).
- They do not conduct electricity when solid or molten. This is because they have neither ions nor electrons that can move.

Giant molecular structures

Giant molecular structures have a three-dimensional network of covalent bonds. Diamond and graphite are both giant molecular structures made of carbon atoms (see Figure 5.5.2). Different crystalline or molecular forms of the same element are called **allotropes**. In diamond, each carbon atom forms four covalent bonds with other carbon atoms. Each carbon atom can be imagined to be at the centre of a tetrahedron. The network of tetrahedrons extends almost unbroken throughout the whole structure. In graphite, the atoms are arranged in layers of hexagons.

Similarities in properties of diamond and graphite

The properties of diamond and graphite can be explained by their structure and bonding:

- They have high melting points. It needs a lot of energy to break down the network of strong covalent bonds.
- They are insoluble in water and in organic solvents. The network of covalent bonds is too strong to allow solvent molecules to form strong enough bonds with the individual atoms.

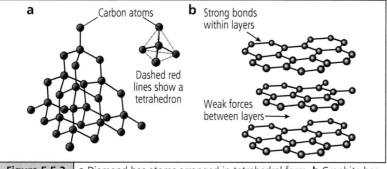

Figure 5.5.2 **a** Diamond has atoms arranged in tetrahedral form. **b** Graphite has a layered structure.

Differences in properties of diamond and graphite

Hardness:

- Diamond is hard: the strong covalent bonding throughout makes it difficult to scratch the surface of the crystal. Diamond is one of the hardest substances known. This makes it ideal to use for the edges of cutting tools such as drilling bits and glass cutters.
- Graphite is soft. The forces between the layers of graphite are weak. So the layers can slide over each other when a force is applied. The layers of graphite flake away easily and so graphite is used as a lubricant and in the 'leads' of pencils.

Electrical conduction:

- Diamond does not conduct electricity. It is a covalent compound with no ions. There are no electrons free to move.
- Graphite conducts electricity. Carbon has four electrons in its outer shell to use in bonding. In graphite, three of the carbon electrons in each atom are used to form covalent bonds. The fourth carbon electron in each atom is free to move around and along the layers. These electrons are called **delocalised electrons**. When a potential difference is applied, these electrons move along the layers.

EXAM TIP

Remember that the forces between the atoms in a molecule are strong because they are covalent bonds but the forces between the molecules are weak.

Figure 5.5.3 Diamonds are hard and long-lasting because of the network of strong covalent bonds in the structure.

KEY POINTS

1. Simple molecules have low melting and boiling points because the forces between the molecules are weak. They are soft.

2. Simple molecular crystals do not conduct electricity. Some dissolve in organic solvents. Others dissolve in water.

3. Diamond and graphite are examples of giant molecular structures.

4. Diamond and graphite have high melting and boiling points.

5. Giant molecular structures are insoluble in both water and organic solvents.

6. Diamond does not conduct electricity but graphite does.

7. Diamond is hard but graphite is soft.

8. Diamond is used for drill tips because it is very hard.

9. Graphite is used as a lubricant because its layers slide over each other.

EXAM TIP

It is a common error to write about strong forces between molecules when asked why giant molecular structures have high melting points. There is a big difference between giant molecules and simple molecules. The best answers refer to strong bonds between the atoms.

Comparing structures

EXAM TIP

Remember that it is the delocalised electrons in a metallic structure that move and conduct electricity, not the ions.

DID YOU KNOW?

Some simple molecular solids, e.g. sucrose, dissolve in water. Water is a polar solvent. Polar solvents have a partial positive charge on one end of their molecule and a negative charge on the other. Solvents that are not charged like this are called non-polar. A useful rule is that polar solvents dissolve polar molecules and non-polar solvents dissolve non-polar molecules. So sucrose (a polar molecule) dissolves in water and iodine (non-polar) dissolves in tetrachloromethane (non-polar).

Metallic bonding

The atoms in a metal are packed closely together and are regularly arranged in layers.

Metal atoms in a lattice tend to lose their outer electrons and become positive ions. The outer electrons are free to move throughout the lattice. They are delocalised.

The **metallic bond** is formed by the attractive forces between the delocalised electrons and the positive ions. Figure 5.6.1 shows metallic bonding.

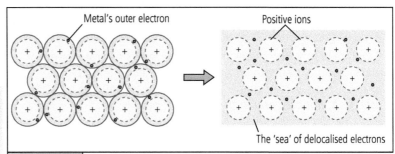

Metal's outer electron   Positive ions

The 'sea' of delocalised electrons

Figure 5.6.1 Metallic bonding arises from attractive forces between metal ions and delocalised electrons.

The strength of metallic bonding increases as:

• the positive charge on the ions increases

• the size of the metal ion decreases

• the number of delocalised electrons increases.

The properties of metals can be related to their structure:

• Many, but not all, metals have high melting points. In metals with high melting points there are strong attractive forces between the positive ions and the delocalised electrons acting in all directions. It needs a lot of energy to overcome these forces to melt the solid.

• They are **malleable** (can be shaped by hitting) and **ductile** (can be drawn into wires). This is because, when a force is applied, the layers slide over each other (see Figure 5.6.2). Metals are not brittle like ionic compounds because in metals, new attractive forces are formed between the delocalised electrons and the atoms in the layers.

• Metals are insoluble in both water and organic solvents but many metals react with water rather than dissolving. In metals that do not react, the metallic bonds are too strong to allow solvent molecules to form strong enough bonds with the individual atoms in order to separate them from each other.

• Metals conduct electricity when solid or molten. This is because the delocalised electrons can easily move through them when a potential difference is applied.

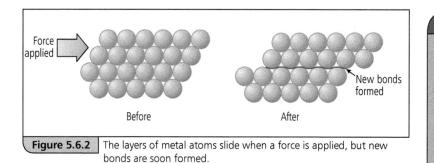

Force applied →

Before   After

New bonds formed

| **Figure 5.6.2** | The layers of metal atoms slide when a force is applied, but new bonds are soon formed. |

Comparing structures

Table 5.6.1 compares ionic, simple molecular, giant molecular and metallic structures.

Table 5.6.1   Properties of ionic, simple molecular, giant molecular and metallic substances

	Ionic structure	Simple molecular structure	Giant molecular structure	Metallic structure
Examples	NaCl, MgBr$_2$	I$_2$, S$_8$, CO$_2$	Carbon, silicon dioxide	Fe, Cu, Sn
Type of bonding	Ionic (strong bonds between + and − ions)	Covalent bonds (strong) between the atoms but weak forces between the molecules	Covalent bonds between the atoms, no weak forces. Graphite is an exception, having weak bonds between its layers.	Metallic bonding (lattice of metal 'ions' within a 'sea' of electrons)
Melting point	High (strong electrostatic force of attraction between + and − ions)	Low (weak forces of attraction between molecules)	High (strong covalent bonding throughout structure)	Most high but a few, e.g sodium and gallium, are low (attractive forces between metal ions and 'sea' of electrons)
Solubility	Soluble in water. Insoluble in non-polar organic solvents.	Non-polar molecules, e.g. iodine, dissolve in non-polar solvents but polar molecules dissolve in polar solvents.	Generally insoluble in polar or non-polar solvents	Those that do not react with water are insoluble in water. Insoluble in non-polar solvents.
Electrical conductivity	Solid does not conduct (ions cannot move). Conducts when molten or in aqueous solution (ions can move).	Does not conduct (no mobile ions or delocalised electrons).	Does not conduct (no ions or delocalised electrons). Exception: graphite (some of the electrons are delocalised).	Conducts (the outer electrons are delocalised).

6 The mole concept

6.1

Moles and molar masses

EXAM TIP

Make sure that you know how to count the atoms or ions in a formula that has brackets. When brackets are used, the small number at the bottom right multiplies what is inside the brackets, e.g. $Cu(NO_3)_2$ has one Cu^{2+} ion and two nitrate ions, NO_3^-. So in total there are $2 \times 1 = 2$ nitrogen atoms and $3 \times 2 = 6$ oxygen atoms per formula unit.

Small masses

The formula of a compound shows the number of atoms of each type present in one molecule or one formula unit. In water:

- Two atoms of hydrogen ($A_r = 1.0$) combine with one atom of oxygen ($A_r = 16.0$).
- So the ratio of mass of hydrogen to oxygen atoms is $2:16$.
- This ratio is the same however much water we have.
- The mass of even $1\,000\,000$ molecules of water is too small to be weighed.
- So we have to scale up a great deal more to get an amount we can weigh accurately.

Relative molecular mass and relative formula mass

In 3.3 we saw that the relative atomic mass (A_r) was defined in terms of the mass of a carbon-12 atom. Values of A_r can be found on the periodic table. When dealing with molecules we use the term **relative molecular mass** (M_r).

- Relative molecular mass is the relative mass of one molecule of a compound on a scale where an atom of the carbon-12 isotope has a mass of exactly 12 units.

We find relative molecular masses by adding up the relative atomic masses of all the atoms in a molecule. So the relative molecular mass of carbon dioxide (CO_2) is found using the A_r values C = 12.0 and O = 16.0:

$$12.0 + (2 \times 16.0) = 44.0$$

For ionic compounds we use the term **relative formula mass**.

- Relative formula mass is the relative mass of one formula unit of a compound on a scale where an atom of the carbon-12 isotope has a mass of exactly 12 units.

We calculate relative formula masses in exactly the same way as relative molecular masses. So the relative formula mass of calcium hydroxide $Ca(OH)_2$ is found by using the A_r values Ca = 40.0, O = 16.0, H = 1.0:

$$40.0 + 2 \times (16.0 + 1.0) = 74.0$$

Note that **relative masses** do not have any units.

The mole and the Avogadro constant

A **mole** (abbreviation: mol) is the relative mass (atomic, molecular or formula mass) in grams. So a mole of calcium atoms has a mass of $40.0\,g$ and a mole of chlorine molecules, Cl_2 ($A_r = 35.5$) has a mass of $2 \times 35.5 = 71\,g$.

- A mole is the amount of substance that has the same number of specified particles (atoms, molecules or ions) as there are atoms in exactly 12 g of the carbon-12 isotope.
- We often refer to the mass of one mole of a substance as its **molar mass** (M).
- Molar mass has a unit of grams per mole usually written as $g\,mol^{-1}$. So the molar mass of sodium is $23.0\,g\,mol^{-1}$.

The number of atoms in a mole of atoms is very large: 6×10^{23} atoms. This number is called the **Avogadro constant** (symbol L). So in 1 mol of sodium there are 6×10^{23} sodium atoms:

- The mole is therefore the amount of substance that contains 6×10^{23} of the specified particles in the substance.

Relating moles to mass

The number of moles of a substance is easily found by dividing the mass of substance in grams by the relative atomic mass for elements or the relative molecular or formula mass for compounds.

$$\text{number of moles} = \frac{\text{mass of substance in grams (g)}}{\text{molar mass (g mol}^{-1})}$$

Example

Deduce the number of moles of sodium hydroxide (NaOH) in 10 g of sodium hydroxide. (A_r values: Na = 23.0, O =16.0, H = 1.0)

Molar mass of NaOH = 23.0 + 16.0 + 1.0 = 40.0

So number of moles $= \dfrac{\text{mass}}{\text{molar mass}} = \dfrac{10}{40} = 0.25\,mol$ NaOH

Avogadro's law

Avogadro's law states that under the same conditions of temperature and pressure, equal volumes of all gases contain the same number of molecules. From this it follows that equal volumes of all gases at the same temperature and pressure contain the same number of moles of gas. At room temperature and pressure (**r.t.p.**), one mole of any gas occupies a volume of $24\,dm^3$ ($1\,dm^3 = 1000\,cm^3$).

KEY POINTS

1. Relative molecular mass is the relative mass of one molecule of a compound on a scale where an atom of the carbon-12 isotope has a mass of exactly 12 units.

2. The mole is the amount of substance that contains 6×10^{23} of the specified particles in the substance.

3. Molar mass is the mass of one mole of a substance.

4. Number of moles $= \dfrac{\text{mass of substance}}{\text{molar mass}}$

5. Avogadro's law states that under the same conditions of temperature and pressure, equal volumes of all gases contain the same number of molecules.

Figure 6.1.1 Amedeo Avogadro was an Italian scientist who deduced that equal volumes of gases contain equal numbers of molecules.

At the end of this topic you should be able to:

- balance molecular symbol equations including the use of state symbols
- balance ionic equations
- state the law of conservation of mass.

EXAM TIP

We use the term 'molecular' equation to distinguish it from an 'ionic' equation (see opposite), even though the compounds in the equation may be ionic, e.g. magnesium oxide.

EXAM TIPS

- When balancing equations, you must not change any of the formulae. The balancing numbers always go at the front of the formula.
- The number in front of a formula multiplies all the way through the formula, e.g. in $2CH_4$ there are 2C atoms and 8H atoms.

The law of conservation of mass

The **law of conservation of mass** states that in a chemical reaction, the mass of the products is equal to the mass of the reactants. In a chemical reaction, some of the bonds in the reactants break and new bonds are made in forming the products. The atoms or ions rearrange themselves so that there is the same number of each type of atom on each side of the equation.

Symbol equations

A full symbol equation (sometimes called a **molecular equation**) is a shorthand way of describing a chemical reaction. When the number of each type of atom in the reactants and products is equal the equation is balanced. Two examples showing a method of balancing an equation are shown below.

The reaction of hydrogen and oxygen to form water

1 Write the formulae for the reactants and products:

$$H_2 + O_2 \longrightarrow H_2O$$

2 Count the number of atoms of each element. You may find using coloured dots helps you.

$$H_2 + O_2 \longrightarrow H_2O$$

There are 2 oxygen atoms on the left but only 1 on the right.

3 Balance the atoms by putting a number in front of one of the reactants or products. In this case it is oxygen that needs balancing. Then count again.

$$H_2 + O_2 \longrightarrow 2H_2O$$

4 Now balance the other atoms. In this case it is hydrogen that needs balancing:

$$2H_2 + O_2 \longrightarrow 2H_2O$$

The reaction of calcium hydroxide with nitric acid

Calcium hydroxide, $Ca(OH)_2$, reacts with nitric acid, HNO_3, to form calcium nitrate $Ca(NO_3)_2$ and water.

1 Write the formulae for the reactants and products:

$$Ca(OH)_2 + HNO_3 \longrightarrow Ca(NO_3)_2 + H_2O$$

2 Count the number of atoms or groups of atoms. Keep the groups of atoms such as OH, SO_4, CO_3, NO_3 as their individual units.

$$Ca(OH)_2 + HNO_3 \longrightarrow Ca(NO_3)_2 + H_2O$$
$$\text{1Ca 2OH} \quad \text{1H 1NO}_3 \qquad \text{1Ca 2NO}_3 \quad \text{2H 1O}$$

3 Balance the nitrate, NO_3.

$$Ca(OH)_2 + 2HNO_3 \longrightarrow Ca(NO_3)_2 + H_2O$$
$$\text{1Ca 2OH} \quad \text{2H 2NO}_3 \qquad \text{1Ca 2NO}_3 \quad \text{2H 1O}$$

4 Balance the hydrogen and oxygen.

$$Ca(OH)_2 + 2HNO_3 \longrightarrow Ca(NO_3)_2 + 2H_2O$$
$$\text{1Ca 2OH} \quad \text{2H 2NO}_3 \qquad \text{1Ca 2NO}_3 \quad \text{4H 2O}$$

Using state symbols

State symbols show us the state of a substance:

(s) = solid,   (l) = liquid,   (g) = gas,   (aq) = aqueous solution

State symbols are written after the formula for each reactant and product, e.g. $Cl_2(g)$ is chlorine gas, $H_2O(l)$ is water, $H_2O(g)$ is steam, $NaCl(aq)$ is aqueous sodium chloride.

Ionic equations

When ionic compounds dissolve in water, the ions separate. An **ionic equation** is a symbol equation that shows only those ions that take part in a reaction. The ions that do not take part are called **spectator ions**. To write an ionic equation:

1 Write down the balanced equation with state symbols. For example:

$$2NaBr(aq) + Cl_2(aq) \longrightarrow 2NaCl(aq) + Br_2(aq)$$

2 Identify the substances that are ionic and write down the ions separately.

$$2Na^+(aq) + 2Br^-(aq) + Cl_2(aq) \longrightarrow 2Na^+(aq) + 2Cl^-(aq) + Br_2(aq)$$

3 Rewrite the equation, deleting the ions that are the same on each side of the equation: in this case the Na^+ ions.

$$2Br^-(aq) + Cl_2(aq) \longrightarrow 2Cl^-(aq) + Br_2(aq)$$

If two solutions are mixed and a precipitate (solid) is formed, you can generally write an ionic equation in the following way:

1 Write the formula of the precipitate as the product.

2 Write down, as reactants, the ions that go to make up the precipitate.

3 Make sure that the equation is balanced.

For example, in the reaction:

$$FeCl_3(aq) + 3NaOH(aq) \longrightarrow Fe(OH)_3(s) + 3NaCl(aq)$$

- The precipitate is $Fe(OH)_3(s)$.
- The ions that go to make up the precipitate are $Fe^{3+}(aq)$ and $OH^-(aq)$.
- The ionic equation is: $Fe^{3+}(aq) + 3OH^-(aq) \longrightarrow Fe(OH)_3(s)$

Figure 6.2.1 The equation for the reaction between calcium carbonate and hydrochloric acid shows all the state symbols:
$CaCO_3(s) + 2HCl(aq)$
$\longrightarrow CaCl_2(aq) +$
$CO_2(g) + H_2O(l)$

EXAM TIP

When writing ionic equations, you need to identify the products that are not ions. These will generally be solids that have precipitated, liquids or gases, e.g. simple molecules such as chlorine or carbon dioxide.

KEY POINTS

1 The law of conservation of mass states that in a chemical reaction, the mass of the products is equal to the mass of the reactants.

2 There is the same number of each type of atom on each side of a chemical equation.

3 Equations are balanced by writing a number in front of particular reactants or products.

4 Ionic equations show only the species that react to form the product(s).

Mole calculations (1)

At the end of this topic you should be able to:

- apply the mole concept to molecular and ionic equations
- calculate the mass of product formed from a given reactant or vice versa.

EXAM TIP

In chemical calculations, it is important to give the answer to the correct number of significant figures that fits the data given.

355.6 rounded to 3 significant figures is 356.

355.6 rounded to 2 significant figures is 360.

The answer given should be the same as the least number of significant figures in the data.

Simple mole calculations

Example 1: mass to moles

How many moles of magnesium chloride, $MgCl_2$, are present in 38.2 g of magnesium chloride? (A_r values: Mg = 24.3, Cl = 35.5)

1 Calculate the molar mass of $MgCl_2$ = 24.3 + (2 × 35.5)
$$= 95.3 \, g \, mol^{-1}$$

2 Use the relationship:

$$\text{number of moles} = \frac{\text{mass (g)}}{\text{molar mass (g mol}^{-1})} = \frac{38.2}{95.3} = 0.401 \, mol$$

Example 2: moles to mass

What mass of calcium nitrate is present in 0.030 mol of calcium nitrate, $Ca(NO_3)_2$? (A_r values: N = 14.0, O = 16.0, Ca = 40.0)

1 Calculate the molar mass of $Ca(NO_3)_2$
$$= 40.0 + 2 \times [14.0 + (3 \times 16.0)] = 164 \, g \, mol^{-1}$$

2 Rearrange the equation in terms of mass:

$$\text{mass (g)} = \text{number of moles (mol)} \times \text{molar mass (g mol}^{-1})$$

3 Substitute the values: 0.030 × 164 = 4.92 g

How much product or reactant?

To find the mass of products formed in a reaction we use:

- the mass of a particular reactant
- the molar mass of this reactant
- the balanced equation.

Example 1 (method 1)

Calculate the maximum mass of iron formed when 798 g of iron(III) oxide, Fe_2O_3, is reduced by excess carbon monoxide, CO. Assume 100% conversion of iron oxide to iron. (A_r values: O = 16.0, C = 12.0, Fe = 55.8)

1 Write the balanced equation for the reaction. You will usually be given this.

$$Fe_2O_3(s) + 3CO(g) \longrightarrow 2Fe(s) + 3CO_2(g)$$

2 Calculate the relevant formula masses. In this case, for Fe_2O_3 and Fe

Fe = 55.8 Fe_2O_3 = (2 × 55.8) + (3 × 16.0) = 159.6

3 Multiply each formula mass in grams by the number of moles in the balanced equation, e.g. 1 mol of Fe_2O_3 produces 2 mol of Fe, so:

159.6 g of Fe_2O_3 produces 2 × 55.8 g = 111.6 g Fe

4 Use simple proportion to calculate the mass of iron produced:

$$\frac{111.6}{159.6} \times 798 = 558\,g\ Fe$$

Example 1 (method 2)

1 Write the balanced equation as before.

2 Calculate the number of moles of $Fe_2O_3 = \dfrac{798}{159.6} = 5.0\,mol$

3 From the equation, 1 mol Fe_2O_3 produces 2 mol Fe.

So 5.0 mol Fe_2O_3 produces 10.0 mol Fe.

4 Calculate the mass of iron from mass = mol [Fe] × M [Fe]

mass of iron = $10.0 \times 55.8 = 558\,g$ Fe

Example 2

Calculate the minimum mass of carbon that reacts with red lead oxide, Pb_3O_4, to form 62.1 g of lead, Pb. Assume 100% conversion of lead oxide to lead. (A_r values: C = 12.0, Pb = 207)

1 The balanced equation is: $Pb_3O_4 + 4C \longrightarrow 3Pb + 4CO$

2 Calculate the number of moles of Pb = $\dfrac{62.1}{207} = 0.300\,mol$

3 From the equation, 3 mol Pb is produced from 4 mol C.

So 0.300 mol lead is produced from 0.400 mol C.

4 So mass of C = mol [C] × M [C]

mass of C = $0.400 \times 12.0 = 4.80\,g$ C

Example 3

We can use a mole calculation to deduce which reagent is in excess:

4.60 g of sodium is reacted with 3.52 g of sulfur to form sodium sulfide, Na_2S. Which reactant is in excess and how many grams of the excess reagent remain? (A_r values: Na = 23.0, S = 32.0)

1 Determine the number of moles of each reactant:

$$mol\ Na = \frac{4.60}{23.0} = 0.200\,mol \qquad mol\ S = \frac{3.52}{32.0} = 0.110\,mol$$

2 Write the equation and determine the ratio of reacting moles.

$2Na + S \longrightarrow Na_2S$ so 2 mol Na react with 1 mol of S

3 To react completely with 0.200 mol of Na, it needs ½ × 0.200 mol S = 0.100 mol.

4 So S is in excess by 0.110 − 0.100 = 0.010 mol

5 Mass of S in excess = mol [S] × M [S]

$$= 0.010 \times 32.0 = 0.320\,g.$$

The reactant which is not in excess in a reaction is called the **limiting reactant**.

EXAM TIP

When doing mole calculations, remember to take into account the number of moles of relevant reactants and products in the balanced equation.

KEY POINTS

1 The chemical equation and relative formula masses can be used to calculate the mass of product formed from a particular reactant or vice versa.

2 A limiting reactant is the one which is not in excess.

Mole calculations (2)

At the end of this topic you should be able to:

- determine percentage composition by mass of an element in a compound
- carry out calculations involving gas volumes at r.t.p. and s.t.p.
- calculate the number of moles in a given volume of gas and vice versa.

Percentage composition by mass

The percentage composition by mass is given by:

$$\% \text{ by mass} = \frac{\text{(sum of the atomic masses of a particular element in a compound)}}{\text{molar mass of the compound}} \times 100$$

Example

Calculate the percentage by mass of nitrogen in ammonium sulfate, $(NH_4)_2SO_4$. (A_r values: H = 1.0, N = 14, O = 16, S = 32)

1 Molar mass of $(NH_4)_2SO_4 = 2 \times [14 + (4 \times 1)] + 32 + (4 \times 16)$

$$= 132 \, g \, mol^{-1}$$

2 In 1 mol of $(NH_4)_2SO_4$ there are 2 mol of N atoms.

So the sum of these atomic masses is $= 14 + 14 = 28$

3 % by mass of $N = \dfrac{28}{132} \times 100 = 21.2\%$

(21% to 2 significant figures)

Using Avogadro's law

In 6.1 we learnt that equal volumes of all gases at the same temperature and pressure have the same number of molecules.

At room temperature and pressure (**r.t.p.**) one mole of any gas occupies $24.0 \, dm^3$. This is called the **molar gas volume** (V_m) at r.t.p. Room temperature and pressure is 20 °C and 1 atmosphere (760 mm mercury) pressure.

At standard temperature and pressure (**s.t.p.**) one mole of gas occupies $22.4 \, dm^3$. This called the molar gas volume at s.t.p. Standard temperature and pressure is 0 °C and 1 atmosphere (760 mm mercury) pressure.

Applying Avogadro's law to the reaction of hydrogen with oxygen to form steam:

$$2H_2(g) + O_2(g) \longrightarrow 2H_2O(g)$$

2 mol	1 mol	2 mol
2 volumes	1 volume	2 volumes
48 dm³	24 dm³	48 dm³

From this we see that if we react, for example, 50 cm³ of hydrogen with 25 cm³ of oxygen, we get 50 cm³ of steam. We can use Avogadro's law in mole calculations because, if there are equal numbers of molecules in the same volume of gas at either r.t.p. or s.t.p., there are also equal numbers of moles.

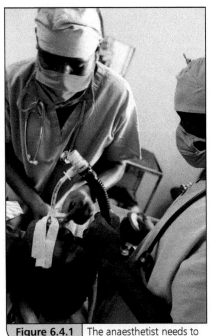

Figure 6.4.1 The anaesthetist needs to know about gas volumes when using equipment to administer gaseous anaesthetics.

Example 1

Calculate the mass of methane ($M = 16\,g\,mol^{-1}$) in $480\,cm^3$ of methane gas at r.t.p.

1 Change volume in cm^3 to volume in dm^3:

$$480\,cm^3 = \frac{480}{1000} = 0.480\,dm^3$$

2 Calculate the number of moles using:

$$\frac{volume\ (dm^3)}{24} = \frac{0.480}{24} = 0.020\,mol$$

3 Calculate mass using:

mass (g) = moles $\times\ M = 0.020 \times 16 = 0.32\,g$ methane

Example 2

Calculate the volume of $3.08\,g$ of carbon dioxide at s.t.p.
(A_r values: C = 12.0, O = 16.0)

1 Calculate moles of CO_2 using:

$$moles = \frac{mass}{molar\ mass} = \frac{3.08}{12.0 + (2 \times 16.0)} = 0.070\,mol$$

2 Calculate the volume using:

volume = moles $\times$ molar volume in dm^3 at s.t.p.

$$= 0.070 \times 22.4 = 1.57\,dm^3 \text{ (to 3 significant figures)}$$

Example 3

Calculate the volume of carbon dioxide formed at r.t.p. when $0.88\,g$ of propane, C_3H_8, is completely burnt in excess oxygen.
(A_r values: H = 1.0, C = 12, O = 16)

1 Calculate the number of moles of propane:

$$\frac{0.88}{(3 \times 12) + (8 \times 1.0)} = 0.020\,mol$$

2 Write the balanced equation for the reaction and identify the relevant mole ratios:

$$C_3H_8 + 5O_2 \longrightarrow 3CO_2 + 4H_2O$$

1 mol   3 mol

3 Calculate the number of moles of CO_2:

$$0.020\,mol\ C_3H_8 \longrightarrow 0.020 \times 3 = 0.060\,mol\ CO_2$$

4 Calculate the volume of CO_2 at r.t.p.:

volume (dm^3) = moles $\times\ V_m = 0.060 \times 24 = 1.4\,dm^3$

(to 2 significant figures)

KEY POINTS

1 The percentage by mass of an element in a compound can be calculated using the relative atomic mass of the element and the relative formula mass of the compound.

2 One mole of any gas occupies $24\,dm^3$ at room temperature and pressure (r.t.p.).

3 One mole of any gas occupies $22.4\,dm^3$ at standard temperature and pressure (s.t.p.).

4 Avogadro's law can be used to calculate the volume of a given mass of gas or to calculate the mass of gas in a given volume.

1 The three states of matter can be converted into one another.

$$\text{Solid} \underset{B}{\overset{A}{\rightleftharpoons}} \text{Liquid} \underset{D}{\overset{C}{\rightleftharpoons}} \text{Gas}$$

a State the name of the changes A, B, C and D.

b Which two of these changes occur with the absorption of energy? Explain your answer using ideas about forces between particles.

2 Describe the arrangement, closeness and motion of the particles in a solid, a liquid and a gas.

3 Define the terms:

a element

b compound

c solvent.

4 Three different mixtures of dyes, A, B and C, were spotted onto a piece of chromatography paper. Two pure dyes, D and E, were also spotted on the same piece of paper.

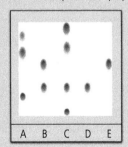

a Which mixture contained the greatest number of different dyes?

b Which dye mixture contained both D and E?

5 Explain the differences in properties between colloids, suspensions and solutions in terms of particle size and light scattering.

6 A crystal of a water-soluble red dye was placed in a beaker of water. After 24 hours, the crystal had disappeared and the red colour had spread throughout the water. Explain these observations using the moving particle theory.

7 Describe the type, number and charge of the subatomic particles present in an atom of $^{35}_{17}Cl$.

8 Write the electron arrangement of:

a an atom of carbon

b an atom of sodium.

9 Define the terms:

a isotopes

b mass number

c relative atomic mass

d allotropes.

10 Potassium chloride has a giant ionic structure but water is a simple molecule.

a State **three** differences in the physical properties of potassium chloride and water.

b Draw dot-and-cross diagrams for potassium chloride. Show the electrons in each electron shell.

c Draw a dot-and-cross diagram for water. Show only the outer electron shells.

11 The diagram shows the structure of diamond and graphite. Both contain carbon atoms.

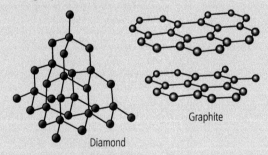

Graphite

Diamond

a Describe **two** other ways in which these structures are similar and **two** ways in which they differ.

b Explain why both diamond and graphite have high melting points.

c Explain why diamond is used for drill tips and why graphite is used as a lubricant.

12 Zinc is a metal but sulfur is a non-metal.

a State **four** differences in the physical properties of zinc and sulfur.

b Draw a diagram to show the metallic bonding in zinc.

13 Write balanced equations including state symbols for the following reactions:

   a solid aluminium chloride + water forming aluminium hydroxide and hydrogen chloride gas

   b calcium carbonate + hydrochloric acid forming calcium chloride, carbon dioxide and water.

   c aqueous lead(II) nitrate, $Pb(NO_3)_2$, + aqueous potassium iodide forming lead(II) iodide, PbI_2, + potassium nitrate.

14 Write ionic equations for these reactions:

   a $Cl_2(aq) + 2NaBr(aq) \longrightarrow Br_2(aq) + 2NaCl(aq)$

   b $CuCl_2(aq) + 2NaOH(aq) \longrightarrow Cu(OH)_2(s) + 2NaCl(aq)$

   c $BaCl_2(aq) + Na_2SO_4(aq) \longrightarrow BaSO_4(s) + 2NaCl(aq)$

15 Calculate the maximum volume of carbon dioxide produced (measured at r.t.p.) when 5.6 g of butane burns in excess air.
(A_r: C = 12, O = 16)

   $C_4H_8 + 6O_2 \longrightarrow 4CO_2 + 4H_2O$

16 Calculate the mass of:

   a 0.50 mol HCl

   b 0.20 mol $Ca(NO_3)_2$

   c 0.015 mol Na_2SO_4

   (A_r: H = 1, C = 12, N = 14, O = 16, Na = 23, S = 32, Cl = 35.5, Ca = 40)

17 Calculate the number of moles of:

   a bromine molecules, Br_2, in 1.2 g Br_2
(A_r: Br = 80)

   b iron atoms in 19.2 g of Fe_2O_3
(A_r: O =16, Fe = 56)

   c chloride ions in 79.17 g $MgCl_2$
(A_r: Mg = 24.3, Cl = 35.5)

18 Define the term *mole*.

19 Iron reacts with excess hydrochloric acid to form iron(II) chloride and hydrogen.

   $Fe + 2HCl \longrightarrow FeCl_2 + H_2$

   Calculate:

   a the maximum mass of $FeCl_2$ formed when 28 g Fe reacts with excess HCl

   (A_r: H = 1, Cl = 35.5, Fe = 56)

   b the minimum mass of Fe needed to produce 10 g hydrogen, H_2.

20 Describe and explain the trend in reactivity of the Group VII elements with aqueous solutions of their sodium halides.

21 When calcium reacts with water, an alkaline solution is formed.

   a Write a balanced equation, including state symbols, for the reaction of calcium with water.

   b Explain why calcium reacts rapidly with water but magnesium reacts very slowly.

22 Describe and explain the trends in the elements of Period 3 in terms of their physical and chemical properties.

23 Describe how you could separate the components of the following mixtures. In each case explain the theory behind the separation method.

   a a mixture of salt (sodium chloride) and sand

   b a mixture of two miscible liquids A and B, where A has a boiling point of 140 °C and B has a boiling point of 165 °C.

24 State **three** differences between a mixture of iron and sulfur and a compound of iron and sulfur.

25 Draw dot-and-cross diagrams for:

   a an oxygen molecule

   b the ionic compound calcium fluoride, CaF_2.

   In each case, show only the outer shell electrons.

26 Write formulae for the following ionic compounds:

   a aluminium sulfate

   b magnesium nitride (the symbol for the nitride ion is N^{3-})

   c iron(III) oxide (the symbol for an iron(III) ion is Fe^{3+})

   d magnesium nitrate.

27 Is carbon disulfide, CS_2, an ionic or covalent compound? Give a reason for your answer.

7.1   Acids and bases

At the end of this topic you should be able to:

• define acid, acid anhydride, alkali, base and salt

• explain acids and bases in terms of replaceable hydrogen and proton transfer.

Figure 7.1.1   All these household products contain acids.

EXAM TIP

The sign $\longrightarrow$ is used when the reaction goes to completion. For strong acids and bases, the reaction always goes to completion. The sign $\rightleftharpoons$ is used when the reaction does not go to completion and both reactants and products are present (see 7.2). This applies to weak acids and bases.

What are acids and bases?

Acids usually have a sour taste, change blue litmus to red, and are corrosive. The commonest inorganic acids are hydrochloric acid, $HCl(aq)$, sulfuric acid, $H_2SO_4(aq)$ and nitric acid, $HNO_3(aq)$. A simple definition of an acid is that it is a substance that neutralises a **base** to form a salt and water. For example:

$$2HCl(aq) + CaO(s) \longrightarrow CaCl_2(aq) + H_2O(l)$$
$$\text{acid} \qquad\quad \text{base} \qquad\qquad \text{salt} \qquad\quad \text{water}$$

Acids have one or more **replaceable hydrogen** atoms. The hydrogen is replaced by a metal or ammonium ion, NH_4^+. In the reaction above, the hydrogen in the acid is replaced by the calcium ion.

• Monobasic acids have one replaceable hydrogen atom, e.g. HCl.

• Dibasic acids have two replaceable hydrogen atoms, e.g. sulfuric acid:

$$H_2SO_4(aq) + CaO(s) \longrightarrow CaSO_4(aq) + H_2O(l)$$

• Tribasic acids, e.g. H_3PO_4, have three replaceable hydrogen atoms.

A base is a substance that neutralises an acid to form a salt and water. Bases are often oxides and hydroxides of metals.

A base that is soluble in water is called an **alkali**. The hydroxides of the Group I metals, e.g. NaOH, and aqueous ammonia, $NH_3(aq)$, are alkalis.

Salts

A **salt** is a compound formed when the hydrogen in an acid is replaced by a metal or ammonium ion.

• Chloride salts are formed from hydrochloric acid. For example, calcium chloride:

$$2HCl(aq) + Ca(OH)_2(aq) \longrightarrow CaCl_2(aq) + 2H_2O(l)$$

• Sulfates are formed from sulfuric acid. For example, sodium sulfate:

$$H_2SO_4(aq) + 2NaOH(aq) \longrightarrow Na_2SO_4(aq) + 2H_2O(l)$$

• Nitrates are formed from nitric acid. For example, potassium nitrate:

$$HNO_3(aq) + KOH(aq) \longrightarrow KNO_3(aq) + H_2O(l)$$

Proton transfer in acids and bases

When an acid dissolves in water, it ionises (splits up into ions). Hydrogen ions are formed. The equation below shows hydrogen chloride gas ionising in water (aq).

$$HCl(g) + (aq) \longrightarrow H^+(aq) + Cl^-(aq)$$

When an alkali dissolves in water, it ionises and forms hydroxide ions:

$$NaOH(s) + (aq) \longrightarrow Na^+(aq) + OH^-(aq)$$

• We can define acids and bases in terms of the transfer of hydrogen ions.
• In talking about acids and bases, a hydrogen ion is called a proton.
• An acid is a proton donor – it gives one or more protons to a base.
• A base is a proton acceptor – it takes one or more protons from an acid.
• Hydrochloric acid is an acid because when it dissolves in water, it donates a proton to water:

$$\underset{\text{acid}}{HCl(g)} + \underset{\text{base}}{H_2O(l)} \longrightarrow H_3O^+(aq) + Cl^-(aq)$$

H⁺ donated

• Ammonia is a base because it accepts a proton from water:

$$\underset{\text{base}}{NH_3(g)} + \underset{\text{acid}}{H_2O(l)} \rightleftharpoons NH_4^+(aq) + OH^-(aq)$$

H⁺ donated

You can see that water can act as either an acid or a base according to what is dissolved in it. A substance that can act as an acid or a base is described as **amphoteric**.

Equations for the ionisation of some acids

We can simplify the equations for the ionisation of acids by ignoring the water. For example:

$$H_2SO_4(l) \longrightarrow 2H^+(aq) + SO_4^{2-}(aq)$$

Acid anhydrides

An **acid anhydride** is a compound that forms an acid when it reacts with water. For example, carbon dioxide forms carbonic acid and sulfur dioxide forms sulfurous acid:

$$CO_2(g) + H_2O(l) \rightleftharpoons H_2CO_3(aq)$$
$$SO_2(g) + H_2O(l) \rightleftharpoons H_2SO_3(aq)$$

KEY POINTS

1 An acid neutralises a base to form a salt and water.

2 A base neutralises an acid to form a salt and water.

3 The hydrogen in an acid can be replaced by a metal or ammonium ion.

4 An alkali is a base that is soluble in water.

5 Acids are proton donors and bases are proton acceptors.

6 An acid anhydride is a compound that forms an acid when it reacts with water.

EXAM TIP

In organic acids such as C_2H_5COOH (see 13.5), not all the hydrogen in the molecule ionises. Remember it is only the H in the COOH group which ionises. It is this H that is replaceable.

Acidity and alkalinity

The pH scale

The **pH scale** is a scale of numbers from 0 to 14 (Figure 7.2.1). It is used to show how acidic or alkaline a solution is.

• A pH below 7 is acidic.

• A pH above 7 is alkaline.

• A pH of exactly 7 is neutral.

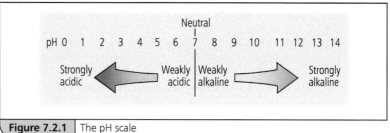

Figure 7.2.1 | The pH scale

Finding the pH

Using universal indicator

Universal indicator is a mixture of coloured compounds that shows a range of colours depending on the pH (Figure 7.2.2). The universal indicator is dipped in the solution under test and the colour is matched against a colour chart showing the pH corresponding to different colours.

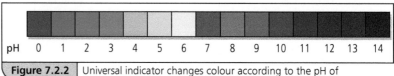

Figure 7.2.2 | Universal indicator changes colour according to the pH of the solution.

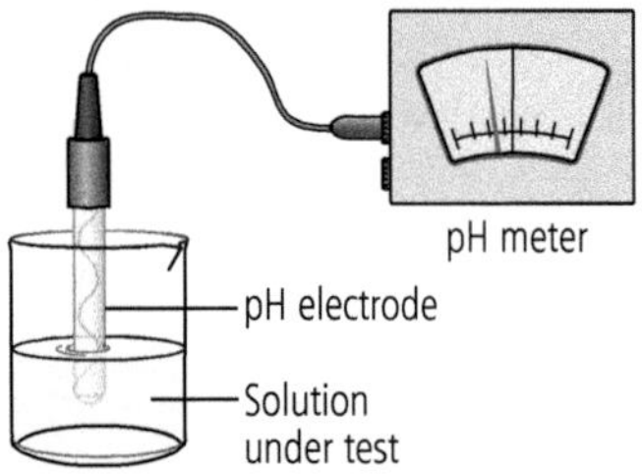

Using a pH meter

We can use a pH electrode connected to a pH meter to measure the pH of a solution directly (Figure 7.2.3). A pH meter gives a more accurate value of pH than universal indicator.

The litmus test

Litmus is an **acid–base indicator**. An acid–base indicator is a coloured compound or mixture of coloured compounds that changes colour over a specific pH range. Litmus is blue in alkaline solutions and red in acidic solutions. It changes colour around pH 7.

Figure 7.2.3 | A pH meter can be used to find the exact pH of a solution.

pH meter
pH electrode
Solution under test

- Acids turn damp blue litmus red.
- Alkalis turn damp red litmus blue.

Concentrated or dilute?

A concentrated solution of an acid contains more particles of acid per dm³ than a dilute solution (see Figure 7.2.4). It does not tell us anything about how well the acid ionises.

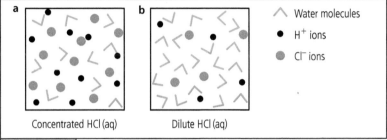

∧	Water molecules
●	H⁺ ions
●	Cl⁻ ions

Figure 7.2.4 **a** A concentrated solution of acid, **b** a dilute solution of acid

Strong and weak acids and bases

Strong acids and **strong bases** ionise completely in solution. Hydrochloric, sulfuric and nitric acids are strong acids, e.g.:

$$HCl(aq) \longrightarrow H^+(aq) + Cl^-(aq)$$

Group I hydroxides are strong bases, e.g.:

$$NaOH(aq) \longrightarrow Na^+(aq) + OH^-(aq)$$

Weak acids and **weak bases** ionise only partially in solution. There are many more molecules of un-ionised acid or base present than there are ions. We use the double arrow ($\rightleftharpoons$) to show that both products and reactants are present in what we call an equilibrium reaction.

Organic acids such as ethanoic acid, CH_3OOH, are weak acids.

$$CH_3COOH(aq) \rightleftharpoons H^+(aq) + CH_3COO^-(aq)$$

Ammonia is an example of a weak base.

$$NH_3(g) + H_2O(l) \rightleftharpoons NH_4^+(aq) + OH^-(aq)$$

Table 7.2.1 compares the pH values of typical weak acids and bases at two different concentrations. At the same concentration, strong acids have a greater concentration of H⁺ ions and a lower pH than weak acids. For a given concentration, the stronger the acid is, the lower the pH.

Table 7.2.1 pH values of strong and weak acids and bases

Concentration (mol dm⁻³)	pH of strong acid	pH of weak acid	pH of strong base	pH of weak base
1.0	0	2.4	14	11.6
0.1	2	3.4	12	10.6

DID YOU KNOW?

The equations for weak acids (and weak bases) dissolving in water are examples of equilibrium reactions. In these reactions, the concentrations of acid molecules and ions formed remain constant at constant temperature. Adding more hydrogen ions will alter the position of this equilibrium so that more un-ionised acid is formed.

KEY POINTS

1 The pH scale is used to show the degree of acidity or alkalinity of a solution.

2 Solutions with pH below 7 are acidic, and solutions above pH 7 are alkaline.

3 Universal indicator can be used to find the pH of a solution.

4 Blue litmus turns red in acid. Red litmus turns blue in alkali.

5 Strong acids are completely ionised in solution. Weak acids are partially ionised in solution.

The reaction of some acids and bases

At the end of this topic you should be able to:

- describe oxides as acidic, basic, amphoteric or neutral
- describe some reactions of non-oxidising acids
- distinguish between normal salts and acid salts
- describe the reaction of bases with ammonium salts
- explain how nitrogen is removed from the soil when lime is added with fertilisers to the soil.

DID YOU KNOW?

Although carbon monoxide, CO, is sometimes classified as a neutral oxide, it can also be classified as a very weak acidic oxide because it does react with water under high pressure to give methanoic acid.

DID YOU KNOW?

Nitric acid does not always react with metals to form a salt and water. This is because it is a good oxidising agent (see 8.2). It oxidises metals to metal salts and releases oxides of nitrogen.

Four different types of oxide

- **Acidic oxides** react with alkalis to form a salt and water. Many of them also react with water to form acids. They are all oxides of non-metals.

$$CO_2(g) + 2NaOH(aq) \longrightarrow Na_2CO_3(aq) + H_2O(l)$$

- **Basic oxides** react with acids to form a salt and water. Group I and some Group II oxides react with water to form hydroxides.

$$CuO(s) + H_2SO_4(aq) \longrightarrow CuSO_4(aq) + H_2O(l)$$

$$Li_2O(s) + H_2O(l) \longrightarrow 2LiOH(aq)$$

- **Amphoteric oxides** react with both acids and alkalis. Aluminium oxide reacts with acids to form aluminium salts and water, and with alkalis to form aluminates.

$$Al_2O_3(s) + 6HCl(aq) \longrightarrow 2AlCl_3(aq) + 3H_2O(l)$$

$$Al_2O_3(s) + 2NaOH(aq) \longrightarrow 2NaAlO_2(aq) + H_2O(l)$$
$$\text{sodium aluminate}$$

Similarly zinc oxide reacts with acids to form zinc salts and water, and with alkalis to form zincates, e.g. Na_2ZnO_2.

- **Neutral oxides** do not react with acids or alkalis. Nitrogen(I) oxide, N_2O, and nitrogen(II) oxide, NO, are neutral oxides.

Reactions of acids

Reaction with metals

Most acids react with reactive metals to form a salt and hydrogen.

Full equation: $\quad Mg(s) + 2HCl(aq) \longrightarrow MgCl_2(aq) + H_2(g)$

Ionic equation: $\quad Mg(s) + 2H^+(aq) \longrightarrow Mg^{2+}(aq) + H_2(g)$

Reaction with carbonates and hydrogencarbonates

Acids react with carbonates to form a salt, carbon dioxide and water.

Full equation:
$$Na_2CO_3(s) + H_2SO_4(aq) \longrightarrow Na_2SO_4(aq) + CO_2(g) + H_2O(l)$$

Ionic equation:
$$CO_3^{2-}(s) + 2H^+(aq) \longrightarrow \qquad CO_2(g) + H_2O(l)$$

Acids react with hydrogencarbonates in a similar way.

Full equation: $\quad KHCO_3(s) + HCl(aq) \longrightarrow KCl(aq) + CO_2(g) + H_2O(l)$

Ionic equation: $HCO_3^-(s) + H^+(aq) \longrightarrow \qquad CO_2(g) + H_2O(l)$

Reaction with bases

Acids react with oxides to form a salt and water.

Full equation: $CuO(s) + 2HCl(aq) \longrightarrow CuCl_2(aq) + H_2O(l)$

Ionic equation: $O^{2-}(s) + 2H^+(aq) \longrightarrow \qquad\qquad H_2O(l)$

Acids react with hydroxides to form a salt and water.

Full equation: $NaOH(aq) + HNO_3(aq) \longrightarrow NaNO_3(aq) + H_2O(l)$

Ionic equation: $OH^-(aq) + H^+(aq) \longrightarrow \qquad\qquad H_2O(l)$

Acid salts

In **acid salts** the replaceable hydrogen in the acid has only been partially replaced by one or more metal atoms. Acid salts are formed from dibasic or tribasic acids.

Normal salt formation:
$$H_2SO_4(aq) + 2NaOH(aq) \longrightarrow Na_2SO_4(aq) + 2H_2O(l)$$

Acid salt formation:
$$H_2SO_4(aq) + NaOH(aq) \longrightarrow NaHSO_4(aq) + H_2O(l)$$

You can see that the mole ratio of alkali to acid is lower for the acid salt.

The reaction of bases with ammonium salts

Bases react with ammonium salts to release ammonia especially if gently heated. For example:

$$NH_4Cl(s) + NaOH(aq) \longrightarrow NH_3(g) + NaCl(aq) + H_2O(l)$$

This type of reaction is sometimes a problem for farmers:

- Farmers add fertilisers to the soil to help crops grow. The nitrogen in the fertiliser is incorporated into plant protein.
- Fertilisers such as ammonium sulfate and ammonium chloride are slightly acidic. Crops do not grow well if the soil is too acidic.
- So farmers add lime to the soil to neutralise the acidity.
- Lime reacts with water in the soil to form calcium hydroxide. Solid calcium hydroxide is called slaked lime.

$$CaO(s) + H_2O(l) \longrightarrow Ca(OH)_2(aq)$$

- Lime or slaked lime reacts with ammonium salts in the fertilisers to produce ammonia.
  Full equation:
  $$2NH_4Cl(s) + Ca(OH)_2(aq) \longrightarrow 2NH_3(g) + CaCl_2(aq) + 2H_2O(l)$$
  Ionic equation:
  $$NH_4^+(s) + OH^-(aq) \longrightarrow NH_3(g) + H_2O(l)$$
- Ammonia is a gas, so it escapes into the atmosphere. This results in a loss of nitrogen from the soil.
- Plant growth may suffer because of the lack of nitrogen.

KEY POINTS

1 Acidic oxides react with bases, and basic oxides react with acids. In both cases a salt and water is formed.

2 Many acids react with reactive metals to form a salt and hydrogen.

3 Carbonates and hydrogencarbonates react with acids to form a salt, water and carbon dioxide.

4 Basic oxides and the hydroxides of reactive metals react with acids to form a salt and water.

5 In acid salts the replaceable hydrogen in the acid has been only partially replaced by one or more metal atoms.

6 Nitrogen is lost from the soil as ammonia gas when lime is added with fertilisers to the soil.

Uses of acids and carbonates

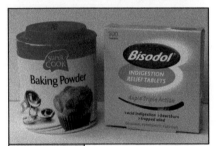

Figure 7.4.1 | These products contain sodium hydrogencarbonate.

Figure 7.4.2 | Pepper sauce is a favourite condiment with many people throughout the Caribbean. Vinegar is an important ingredient.

Uses of carbonates

Antacids

Indigestion (heartburn) is caused by the production of excess hydrochloric acid in the stomach. Many antacids contain magnesium carbonate, calcium carbonate, magnesium hydroxide or sodium hydrogencarbonate to neutralise the excess acid.

Baking powder

Baking powder is used to make cakes rise. It contains two solids: sodium hydrogencarbonate and a salt of a weak acid, tartaric acid. When added to the liquid in the cake mix, these two compounds dissolve and react to form carbon dioxide. The carbon dioxide makes the cake rise.

Fire extinguishers

Dry foam fire extinguishers contain sodium hydrogencarbonate and nitrogen under pressure. When the valve is opened, the pressure is reduced and the sodium hydrogencarbonate foam is formed. This decomposes in the heat to form carbon dioxide. The foam containing carbon dioxide extinguishes the fire by preventing oxygen in the air from reaching it.

Natural acids

Methanoic acid

Methanoic acid, HCOOH, is found naturally in ants, especially fire ants, as well as in stinging nettles. The ants bite their prey to immobilise them. But we can also get bitten by ants. Methanoic acid is a weak acid but is a powerful skin irritant. A household remedy for an ant bite is to dab the bite with a dilute solution of ammonia (a weak base).

Vinegar

Vinegar is made by fermenting plant material. During the fermentation, ethanoic acid, CH_3COOH, a weak acid, is produced. This gives vinegar its sharp taste. Vinegar is used to preserve some types of food (pickling) because the low pH prevents bacterial growth.

Lactic acid

Lactic acid is present in milk. It also builds up in our muscles under extreme exercise. Our muscle cells use oxygen for respiration. When we exercise very energetically, oxygen cannot get to the muscles fast enough. In the absence of oxygen, the muscle cells respire anaerobically (respiration in the absence of oxygen) so our muscle cells keep working for a while. Under these conditions lactic acid is produced in the muscles. Too much lactic acid in the muscles produces cramps. When we stop exercising, the lactic acid can be converted to glucose in the liver.

Lime juice

Lime juice contains organic acids such as citric acid. A household use of lime juice is the removal of rust stains from clothes. The stain is soaked in the juice. The acid reacts with the iron oxide to form colourless compounds that can be removed by washing. Because lime juice is only weakly acidic, it does not 'burn' the clothes.

Vitamin C

Vitamin C (ascorbic acid) is essential for some of the chemical reactions in our cells. It is an antioxidant and is essential for the healing of wounds and promotion of healthy connective tissue in the body. Citrus fruits such as limes, oranges and lemons and raw green vegetables are good sources of vitamin C.

Vitamin C is easily destroyed by oxidation. This oxidation is increased by heating, exposure to air and alkaline conditions. So cooking vegetables, especially above pH 7, reduces the amount of vitamin C drastically. Some people add sodium hydrogencarbonate to vegetables when cooking them. This improves their texture and appearance. Sodium hydrogencarbonate is slightly alkaline.

So the vitamin C content of the vegetables is reduced.

Determining the vitamin C content of fruit juice

The vitamin C content of heated and unheated fruit juice can be compared. The method for determining the amount of vitamin C uses the oxidation–reduction indicator DCPIP, which is blue when oxidised and colourless when reduced.

1 Pipette a known volume of fruit juice into a flask.

2 Add 1% DCPIP solution from a burette, drop by drop, to the solution in the flask and shake the flask gently.

3 The end point is reached when the blue colour of the DCPIP does not fade when it has been added to the solution.

Figure 7.4.3 Limes are cultivated in several areas of the Caribbean. In the days when sailing ships were used to transport cargoes from one continent to another, limes were carried on board to prevent sailors getting scurvy.

Figure 7.4.4 West Indian cherries are the richest source of vitamin C known.

KEY POINTS

1 Antacids contain bases such as magnesium carbonate and magnesium hydroxide to neutralise excess stomach acid.

2 Sodium hydrogencarbonate foam extinguishes fires because it decomposes when heated to produce carbon dioxide.

3 Some examples of acids in living systems are methanoic acid, ethanoic acid, lactic acid, citric acid and ascorbic acid.

4 Vinegar can be used to preserve food and lime juice can be used to remove rust stains.

5 Vitamin C in fruit and vegetables is destroyed by heating and under alkaline conditions.

6 The vitamin C content of fruit juice can be determined using the indicator DCPIP.

DID YOU KNOW?

Some toothpastes contain insoluble carbonates or hydroxides that are added as abrasives to help clean the surface of the teeth. These also have a side-effect of reacting with excess acid in the mouth, which may damage the surface layer of enamel on the teeth. Fluoride ions are also added to toothpaste to strengthen the enamel. Some scientists think that the fluoride ions may replace some of the hydroxide groups in the structure of the tooth.

Solubility rules and salt preparation

Solubility rules

Many salts are soluble in water but others are not. If a solid is obtained when solutions of two soluble compounds are mixed, the reaction is called a **precipitation reaction**. The solid obtained is the **precipitate**. In order to make salts by precipitation we have to know which compounds are soluble in water and which are insoluble. Some rules for predicting solubility (solubility rules) are given in Table 7.5.1.

Table 7.5.1   Some rules for predicting solubility

Soluble compounds	Insoluble compounds
All salts of Group I elements	
All nitrates and ammonium salts	
Most chlorides, bromides and iodides	Chlorides, bromides and iodides of silver and lead
Most sulfates	Sulfates of calcium, barium and lead
Group I hydroxides and carbonates	Most hydroxides and carbonates
Group I and II oxides react with water	Most metal oxides

Preparing salts by precipitation

This is how you can make an insoluble salt, for example, lead chloride.

1 Identify the ions present in the salt: lead and chloride.

2 Identify two soluble salts containing these ions, e.g. lead nitrate and sodium chloride.

3 Add one of the solutions to the other.

4 Filter off the precipitate, then wash the precipitate with distilled water and dry it (Figure 7.5.1).

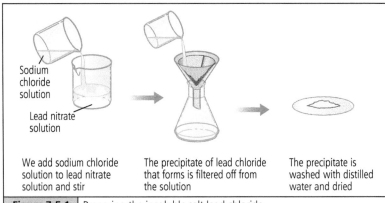

Sodium chloride solution

Lead nitrate solution

We add sodium chloride solution to lead nitrate solution and stir

The precipitate of lead chloride that forms is filtered off from the solution

The precipitate is washed with distilled water and dried

Figure 7.5.1   Preparing the insoluble salt lead chloride

Preparing salts by direct combination

We can react two elements together to form a salt. To do this we usually react a metal with a non-metallic element. For example, we can prepare sodium chloride by burning sodium in chlorine gas (Figure 7.5.2).

$$2Na(s) + Cl_2(g) \longrightarrow 2NaCl(s)$$

We can purify the sodium chloride by recrystallisation.

Preparing salts by replacing hydrogen ions

We can make soluble salts by reacting metals or metal oxides with acids. The metal ions replace the hydrogen ions in the acid.

$$Zn(s) + 2HCl(aq) \longrightarrow ZnCl_2(aq) + H_2(g)$$

$$CuO(s) + H_2SO_4(aq) \longrightarrow CuSO_4(aq) + H_2O(l)$$

The method (Figure 7.5.3) is:

1 Add the metal or metal oxide to the acid in a beaker. The metal or metal oxide should be in excess.

2 Warm the flask gently to make sure reaction is complete.

3 Filter off the excess metal or metal oxide. The filtrate is a solution of the salt.

4 Evaporate the water from the filtrate until the crystallisation point is reached. (Crystals start to form on the side of the evaporating basin.)

5 Filter off the crystals and wash them carefully with the minimum amount of water.

6 Dry the crystals between sheets of filter paper.

Figure 7.5.2 | When sodium burns in chlorine, sodium chloride can be seen on the side of the jar as a white powder.

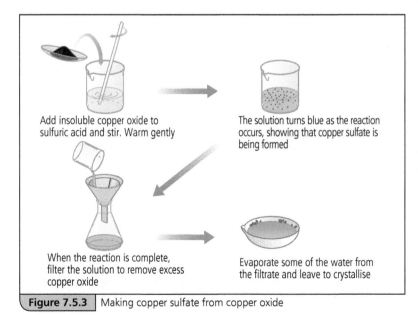

Add insoluble copper oxide to sulfuric acid and stir. Warm gently

The solution turns blue as the reaction occurs, showing that copper sulfate is being formed

When the reaction is complete, filter the solution to remove excess copper oxide

Evaporate some of the water from the filtrate and leave to crystallise

Figure 7.5.3 | Making copper sulfate from copper oxide

We can also make soluble salts by reacting an acid with an alkali using a titration method (see 7.6).

Acid–base titrations

At the end of this topic you should be able to:

- describe neutralisation reactions using indicators
- describe acid–base titrations
- describe how to prepare salts by replacement of hydrogen in an acid directly or indirectly by a metal or ammonium ion using a titration technique.

EXAM TIP

You cannot use universal indicator in an accurate acid–base titration because it changes colour gradually and you cannot see a sharp colour change on adding a drop of acid to the alkali at the end point.

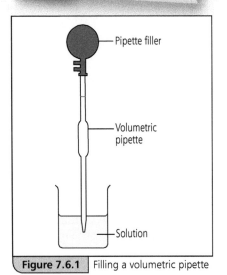

Figure 7.6.1 Filling a volumetric pipette

Labels: Pipette filler, Volumetric pipette, Solution

Neutralisation reactions

The reaction between an acid and a base is called a **neutralisation reaction**. The products are a salt and water. For example:

$$KOH(aq) + HCl(aq) \longrightarrow KCl(aq) + H_2O(l)$$

We can see how the pH changes by adding an acid drop by drop to a solution of potassium hydroxide to which some universal indicator has been added:

1 The indicator is blue-purple as the start (high pH).

2 As the acid is added the indicator colour changes to blue, then to blue-green (pH is decreasing in the alkaline region).

3 When the acid has completely neutralised the alkali, the indicator is green (pH 7).

4 When the acid is in excess, the indicator changes from yellow and as more and more acid is added, it turns red (pH is below 7 and decreasing further).

We can use a procedure called **titration** to determine the amount of substance present in a given volume of solution of acid or alkali. We add the acid gradually to the alkali until the alkali has been neutralised. We use an acid–base **indicator** to find out when the acid has just reacted completely with the alkali. The point where this happens is called the **end point** of the titration. At the end point, the colour of the indicator suddenly changes.

If we want to find out the amount of substance present in a given volume of solution of potassium hydroxide, we:

1 Measure a known volume of potassium hydroxide solution (alkali) into a titration flask using a volumetric pipette (see Figure 7.6.1).

2 Add an indicator solution to the alkali in the flask.

3 Fill a clean burette with the acid (after having washed the burette with a little of the acid). The acid in the burette has a known concentration (amount of substance present in a given volume).

4 Set up the apparatus shown in Figure 7.6.2 and record the initial burette reading.

5 Slowly add the acid from the burette to the flask. Swirl the flask all the time to make sure that the contents are mixed.

6 When the indicator changes colour (the end point), record the final burette reading. This is the rough titration. The final burette reading minus the initial burette reading is called the **titre**.

7 Repeat steps 1 to 6 but this time when you are near the end point, add the acid drop by drop.

8 Repeat the process until you have two titres that are not more than 0.1 cm³ apart.

Typical results are shown in Table 7.6.1.

Table 7.6.1

	Rough titre	1st accurate titre	2nd accurate titre	3rd accurate titre
Final burette reading (cm³)	21.6	21.1	20.8	21.1
Initial burette reading (cm³)	0.0	0.2	0.1	0.3
Titre (cm³)	21.7	20.9	20.7	20.8

Preparing soluble salts by titration

We can make a soluble salt by titrating alkalis such as Group I hydroxides or aqueous ammonia with an acid. The titration is first carried out using an indicator, then repeated without the indicator, using the volume of acid that was shown by the titration to just neutralise the alkali. This method is especially useful for making ammonium salts:

$$2NH_3(aq) + H_2SO_4(aq) \longrightarrow (NH_4)_2SO_4(aq)$$

Figure 7.6.3 shows the method.

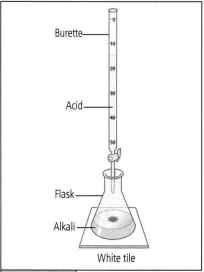

Figure 7.6.2 | Titrating an alkali with an acid

EXAM TIP

When taking readings from burettes and graduated pipettes, the reading should be taken from the bottom of the meniscus (the concave part of the surface of the solution).

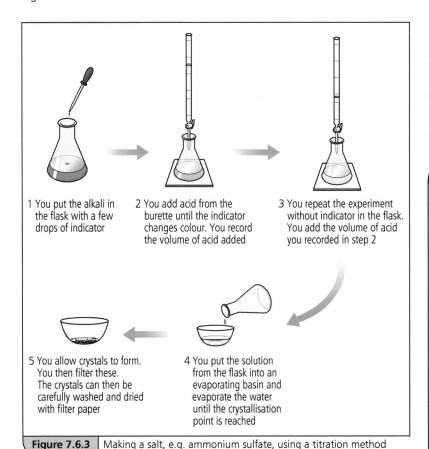

1 You put the alkali in the flask with a few drops of indicator

2 You add acid from the burette until the indicator changes colour. You record the volume of acid added

3 You repeat the experiment without indicator in the flask. You add the volume of acid you recorded in step 2

4 You put the solution from the flask into an evaporating basin and evaporate the water until the crystallisation point is reached

5 You allow crystals to form. You then filter these. The crystals can then be carefully washed and dried with filter paper

Figure 7.6.3 | Making a salt, e.g. ammonium sulfate, using a titration method

KEY POINTS

1 The reaction of an acid with a base is a neutralisation reaction.

2 The concentration of an acid or alkali can be found using an acid–base titration.

3 An indicator is used to show the end point of an acid–base titration.

4 A titration method can be used to prepare salts of Group I metals from their hydroxides or to prepare ammonium salts.

Neutralisation, salts and solution concentration

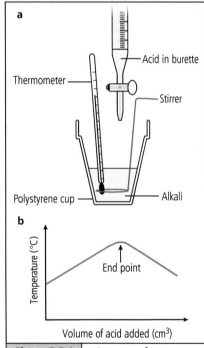

Figure 7.7.1 **a** Apparatus for thermometric titration, **b** typical graph of results

Figure 7.7.2 Some foods containing preservatives

Thermometric titrations

When an acid neutralises an alkali, energy is released. This energy heats up the reaction mixture. We can use the change in temperature of a solution when we add an acid to an alkali to determine what volume of acid of known concentration is needed to neutralise an alkali. This is called a **thermometric titration**. The procedure is shown in Figure 7.7.1(a):

1 Place a measured volume of alkali in an insulated container e.g. a polystyrene drinking cup.

2 Record the initial temperature of the alkali.

3 Add acid of known concentration from a burette in small measured amounts.

4 After each addition of acid, stir the solution in the cup and record its temperature.

The end point of the reaction, when the acid has just neutralised the alkali, is shown by the break in the curve of a graph of temperature against volume of acid added (Figure 7.7.1(b)).

The uses of some salts

In 7.4 we learned about the use of sodium hydrogencarbonate in baking powder. Many other salts have particular uses:

Calcium carbonate is used to make cement. Limestone rock (which is calcium carbonate) is mixed with clay and heated in a furnace. It is then mixed with calcium sulfate and the mixture is crushed.

Calcium sulfate is also used as a food additive to promote healthy bones, teeth and nails. It is also used to make plaster of Paris. This can be used to make casts to keep broken bones in place. Magnesium sulfate (Epsom salts) is used in bath salts to refresh the skin. It can also be used as a laxative.

Some salts are used in food preservation:

• Sodium chloride is used to preserve food. It withdraws water from any microorganisms present by osmosis. Brine (a solution of sodium chloride) is often used in pickling.

• Sodium nitrate and sodium nitrite are used to preserve meats and help maintain the colour of the food.

• Sodium benzoate is used as a preservative in fruit juices and acidic foods. It reduces bacterial and fungal growth below pH 5.

Solution concentration

Molar concentration is the number of moles of solute dissolved in a solvent to make $1\,dm^3$ of a solution. Its units are $mol\,dm^{-3}$.

$$\text{concentration (mol dm}^{-3}) = \frac{\text{number of moles of solute (mol)}}{\text{volume of solution (dm}^3)}$$

In calculations involving solutions we also need to remember:

- to change mass in grams to moles
- to change cm^3 to dm^3 by dividing the volume in cm^3 by 1000
- that moles of solute (mol) = concentration (mol dm^{-3}) × volume (dm^3).

Worked example 1

Calculate the concentration of a solution of sodium hydroxide ($M_r = 40$) containing 0.60 g NaOH in 200 cm^3 solution.

1 Convert grams to moles: $\frac{0.60}{40} = 0.015\,\text{mol}$

2 Change cm^3 to dm^3: 200 cm^3 = 0.20 dm^3

3 Calculate concentration: $\frac{0.015}{0.20} = 0.075\,\text{mol dm}^{-3}$

Worked example 2

Calculate the mass of calcium chloride ($M_r = 111$) in 50 cm^3 of a 0.20 mol dm^{-3} solution of calcium chloride.

1 Change cm^3 to dm^3: 50 cm^3 = 0.050 dm^3

2 Calculate number of moles: 0.20 × 0.05 = 0.01 mol

3 Convert moles to grams: 0.01 × 111 = 1.1 g (to 2 significant figures)

Mass concentration

We can also express concentrations in terms of mass. **Mass concentration** is the number of grams of solute dissolved in a solvent to make 1 dm^3 of a solution. Its units are g dm^{-3}.

$$\text{mass concentration} = \frac{\text{mass of solute (g)}}{\text{volume of solution (dm}^3)}$$

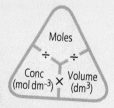

Solution concentration and titrations

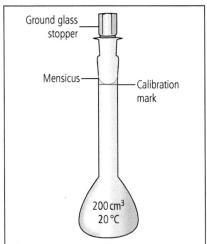

Figure 7.8.1	A volumetric flask is used to make standard solutions.

Making a standard solution

We need to make sure that the acid (or alkali) we use in the burette has the correct concentration by titrating it with a primary standard. A **standard solution** has a known accurate concentration at a specified temperature and pressure (usually at s.t.p.). Although standard conditions are 25 °C and 1 atmosphere pressure, most glassware is calibrated at 20 °C. For accurate work in many branches of chemistry a **standard concentration** contains one mole of substance in 1 dm³ of solution under standard conditions. This is the type of standard solution used in electrochemistry. We can form solutions of other concentrations by diluting the standard.

To make 200 cm³ of a solution of sodium hydroxide of known concentration we use a volumetric flask (see Figure 7.8.1):

1 Weigh out the required amount of sodium hydroxide and tip the solid into a beaker.

2 Add enough water to dissolve the sodium hydroxide.

3 Wash out the volumetric flask with pure water then pour the solution from the beaker into the flask, using a funnel.

4 Wash out the beaker several times with pure water and add the washings through the funnel to the flask.

5 Fill the volumetric flask with pure water so that the bottom of the meniscus is on the calibration mark.

6 Put the stopper on the flask and shake the flask gently.

Calculations from titration results

In every titration calculation we need to know four of the following five points:

- the balanced equation for the reaction
- the concentration of the solution in the burette
- the volume of the titre
- the concentration of the solution in the titration flask
- the volume of the solution in the titration flask.

In titration calculations we usually need to deduce the concentration of solution in the titration flask.

Example 1

25.0 cm³ of potassium hydroxide solution is exactly neutralised by 12.3 cm³ of sulfuric acid of concentration 0.200 mol dm⁻³. Calculate the concentration, in mol dm⁻³ of the potassium hydroxide solution.

$$2KOH(aq) + H_2SO_4(aq) \longrightarrow K_2SO_4(aq) + 2H_2O(l)$$

We use the following procedure:

1 Calculate the number of moles of reagent for which both concentration and volume are known. This is the acid.

moles (mol) = concentration (mol dm⁻³) × volume (dm³)

$$\text{moles acid} = 0.200 \times \frac{12.3}{1000} = 2.46 \times 10^{-3}\,\text{mol}$$

2 Use the mole ratio in the balanced equation to calculate the number of moles of KOH.

$2\,\text{mol KOH} : 1\,\text{mol } H_2SO_4$

So moles KOH = $2 \times 2.46 \times 10^{-3} = 4.92 \times 10^{-3}\,\text{mol KOH}$

3 Calculate the concentration of KOH using:

$$\text{concentration (mol dm}^{-3}) = \frac{\text{number of moles of solute (mol)}}{\text{volume of solution (dm}^{-3})}$$

$$\text{concentration of KOH} = 4.92 \times 10^{-3} \times \frac{1000}{25.0} = 0.197\,\text{mol dm}^{-3}$$

Figure 7.8.2 The results from a titration can be used to calculate the concentration of an acid or alkali.

Example 2

The equation for the reaction of calcium hydroxide with hydrochloric acid is:

$$Ca(OH)_2(aq) + 2HCl(aq) \longrightarrow CaCl_2(aq) + 2H_2O(l)$$

0.148 g of calcium hydroxide ($M_r = 74.0$) was completely dissolved in water. Calculate the volume of 0.150 mol dm⁻³ hydrochloric acid required to just neutralise the calcium hydroxide.

1 Calculate the moles of calcium hydroxide:

$$\frac{0.148}{74.0} = 2.00 \times 10^{-3}\,\text{mol } Ca(OH)_2$$

2 Use the mole ratio in the balanced equation to calculate the number of moles of acid:

$1\,\text{mol } Ca(OH)_2 : 2\,\text{mol HCl}$

So moles HCl = $2 \times (2 \times 10^{-3}) = 4.00 \times 10^{-3}\,\text{mol HCl}$

3 Calculate the volume of HCl using:

$$\text{volume (dm}^3) = \frac{\text{number of moles of solute (mol)}}{\text{concentration of solution (mol dm}^{-3})}$$

$$\text{volume of HCl} = \frac{4.0 \times 10^{-3}}{0.150} = 0.0267\,\text{dm}^3$$

EXAM TIP

When carrying out mole calculations involving concentrations, remember the units of volume you are using throughout the calculation – you may need to convert cm³ to dm³ at an appropriate point so that the units of concentration are mol dm⁻³.

KEY POINTS

1 A standard solution is prepared by weighing out a fixed amount of solid and making it up to a fixed volume in a volumetric flask.

2 Standard concentration refers to one mole of substance in 1 dm³ of solution under standard conditions.

3 The concentration of an acid or alkali can be found from the results of a titration using the relationship between concentration, number of moles reacting and volume of solution in dm³, as well as the mole ratio in the equation for the reaction.

8 Oxidation and reduction reactions

8.1

Oxidation and reduction

LEARNING OUTCOMES

At the end of this topic you should be able to:

- identify oxidation and reduction reactions in terms of oxygen loss or gain, or electrons transfer
- deduce oxidation number from formulae.

What are oxidation–reduction reactions?

Simple definitions of oxidation and reduction are:

- **Oxidation** is the gain of oxygen by a substance.
- **Reduction** is the loss of oxygen by a substance.

When copper oxide reacts with hydrogen both oxidation and reduction are occurring at the same time:

$$CuO(s) + H_2(g) \longrightarrow Cu(s) + H_2O(l)$$

- Hydrogen is gaining oxygen atoms from the copper oxide. We say that the hydrogen has been oxidised.
- Copper oxide is losing oxygen to the hydrogen. We say that the copper oxide has been reduced.
- Oxidation and reduction have occurred at the same time.

Reactions where oxidation and reduction occur at the same time are called **oxidation–reduction** reactions or **redox** reactions.

Electron transfer in redox reactions

We can extend our definition of oxidation and reduction to include reactions that do not involve oxygen:

- Oxidation is loss of electrons.
- Reduction is gain of electrons.

Figure 8.1.1 An oxidation–reduction reaction takes place when jet fuel burns.

Magnesium reacts with chlorine to form the ionic compound magnesium chloride:

$$Mg(s) + Cl_2(g) \longrightarrow MgCl_2(s)$$

- Each magnesium atom loses two electrons. Magnesium atoms have been oxidised to magnesium ions:

$$Mg \longrightarrow Mg^{2+} + 2e^-$$

- Each chlorine atom in the chlorine molecule gains one electron. Chlorine has been reduced to chloride ions:

$$Cl_2 + 2e^- \longrightarrow 2Cl^-$$

Equations like this showing the oxidation and reduction reactions separately are called **half equations**.

Another example is the displacement reaction:

$$Cl_2(aq) + 2I^-(aq) \longrightarrow 2Cl^-(aq) + I_2(aq)$$

- Chlorine has gained electrons from iodine. Chlorine has been reduced.

Reduction: $Cl_2 + 2e^- \longrightarrow 2Cl^-$ \qquad Oxidation: $2I^- \longrightarrow I_2 + 2e^-$

DID YOU KNOW?

We can also define oxidation and reduction in terms of hydrogen loss or gain. Gain of hydrogen is reduction and loss of hydrogen is oxidation. This definition is especially useful in the chemistry of organic compounds.

Oxidation numbers (oxidation states)

We can extend our definition of oxidation and reduction to include redox reactions involving covalent compounds. We do this by using oxidation numbers.

An **oxidation number** (abbreviation OxNo) is a number given to each atom or ion in a compound to show the degree of oxidation. There are rules for applying oxidation numbers:

1 OxNo refers to a single atom or ion in a compound.

2 The OxNo of each atom in an element is 0, e.g. each Cl in $Cl_2 = 0$, $Zn = 0$.

3 The OxNo of an ion arising from a single atom = charge on the ion, e.g. $Cl^- = -1$, $O^{2-} = -2$, $Mg^{2+} = +2$, $Al = +3$.

4 The OxNo of an oxygen atom in a compound is -2 (but in peroxides, it is -1).

5 The OxNo of a hydrogen atom in a compound is $+1$ but when combined with a metal alone, it is -1, e.g. in HCl, NH_3 and H_2SO_4, $H = +1$ but in CaH_2, $H = -1$.

6 The sum of all the OxNos of atoms or ions in a compound is zero, e.g. in Al_2O_3:

$$2Al^{3+} = 2 \times (+3) = +6 \quad \text{and} \quad 3O^{2-} = 3 \times (-2) = -6$$

7 The sum of the OxNos in a compound ion such as SO_4^{2-} or $NO_3^- = $ the charge on the ion, e.g. sum of oxidation number of $S + 4O$ in $SO_4^{2-} = -2$.

Applying oxidation number rules to compounds

The atoms of many elements in Groups IV, V and VI and transition elements have variable OxNos. So we have to work these out, using the OxNos we know.

Example 1

Deduce the OxNo of Fe in the ionic compound, $FeCl_3$.

• Applying rule 3: $Cl^- = -1$ so $3Cl^- = -3$
• Applying rule 6: $Fe + (-3) = 0$ So OxNo of Fe in $FeCl_3 = +3$.

Example 2

Deduce the OxNo of S in H_2SO_4.

• Applying rules 4 and 5: $O = -2$ and $H = +1$
• Applying rule 6:
  $2H + S + 4O = 0$ So $2 \times (+1) + S + 4 \times (-2) = 0$
• So sum of OxNos of
  $2H + 4O = +2 + (-8) = -6$ So OxNo of $S = +6$.

DID YOU KNOW?

Oxidation number depends on a property called the *electronegativity* of an element. If we ignore the Group 0 elements, electronegativity increases across a period and decreases down a group in the periodic table. The most electronegative element is fluorine. The more electronegative element is given the more negative (or less positive) oxidation number. So in the compound ClF, F has the OxNo -1 and Cl is $+1$.

KEY POINTS

1 Oxidation is addition of oxygen or loss of electrons.

2 Reduction is loss of oxygen or gain of electrons.

3 In an oxidation–reduction reaction (redox reaction) both oxidation and reduction occur at the same time.

4 Oxidation number (OxNo) tells us the degree of oxidation or reduction of an atom or ion in a compound.

5 Oxidation number rules allow us to deduce the oxidation number of atoms or ions that are variable.

Oxidising and reducing agents

At the end of this topic you should be able to:

- identify oxidation and reduction reactions from changes in oxidation number
- distinguish between oxidising and reducing agents
- describe examples of compounds that can act as both an oxidising agent and a reducing agent.

EXAM TIP

When identifying which atoms gets oxidised and reduced, you need to identify the atoms which change in oxidation number. Oxygen and hydrogen in compounds as both reactants and products do not usually change their oxidation numbers. But they do if H_2 or O_2 are reactants or products. For example in the reaction:

$$CuO + H_2 \longrightarrow Cu + H_2O$$

oxygen does not change in OxNo because it is still in a compound but H_2 is oxidised.

Changes in oxidation number

Oxidation and reduction can be defined in terms of changes of OxNo of a specific atom or ion during a reaction.

- Oxidation is an increase in oxidation number.
- Reduction is a decrease in oxidation number.

When tin reacts with nitric acid, the oxidation numbers change as shown:

$$Sn(s) + 4HNO_3(aq) \longrightarrow SnO_2(s) + 4NO_2(g) + 2H_2O(l)$$

OxNos   0   +5   +4   +4

(reduction from HNO₃ to NO₂; oxidation from Sn to SnO₂)

The tin (Sn) is oxidised because its OxNo increases from 0 to +4.

The nitric acid (HNO_3) gets reduced because the OxNo of the N decreases from +5 to +4.

When copper oxide reacts with ammonia, the oxidation changes are:

$$3CuO(s) + 2NH_3(g) \longrightarrow 3Cu(s) + N_2(g) + 3H_2O(l)$$

OxNos   +2   −3   0   0

(reduction from CuO to Cu; oxidation from NH₃ to N₂)

The copper is reduced because its OxNo decreases from +2 to 0.

The ammonia (NH_3) gets oxidised because the OxNo of the N increases from −3 to 0.

Atoms or ions with variable OxNos exist in different oxidation states. For example, Fe^{3+} has a higher oxidation state than Fe^{2+}.

Figure 8.2.1 Some sunglasses get darker or lighter because of redox reactions involving silver ions.

Oxidising and reducing agents

During a reaction:

- An **oxidising agent** gains electrons and gets reduced. The OxNo of a particular atom or ion in the oxidising agent decreases.
- A **reducing agent** loses electrons and gets oxidised. The OxNo of a particular atom or ion in the reducing agent increases.

In the reaction between aqueous chlorine and aqueous potassium bromide:

$$Cl_2(aq) + 2KBr(aq) \longrightarrow Br_2(aq) + 2KCl(aq)$$

OxNos   0   −1   0   −1

Ionic equation: $Cl_2(aq) + 2Br^-(aq) \longrightarrow Br_2(aq) + 2Cl^-(aq)$

The bromide ion is the reducing agent because each ion loses an electron and its OxNo increases from −1 to 0.

- Chlorine is an oxidising agent because each chlorine atom gains an electron and the OxNo decreases from 0 to −1.

In the reaction between potassium iodide and hydrogen peroxide (H_2O_2) in acid solution:

$$2KI(aq) + H_2O_2(aq) + H_2SO_4(aq) \longrightarrow I_2(aq) + K_2SO_4(aq) + 2H_2O(l)$$

     −1   −1   0   −2

OxNos

Ionic equation: $2I^-(aq) + H_2O_2(aq) + 2H^+(aq) \longrightarrow I_2(aq) + 2H_2O(l)$

- Potassium iodide is a reducing agent because it loses electrons and its OxNo increases from −1 to 0.
- Hydrogen peroxide is an oxidising agent because it gains electrons and the OxNo of oxygen decreases from −1 to −2 (see rule 4 in 8.1).

Some compounds can act as both oxidising and reducing agents according to the nature of the other reactants and conditions. We have seen how hydrogen peroxide oxidises iodide ions to iodine. Hydrogen peroxide also reduces chlorine to chloride ions:

$$Cl_2(aq) + H_2O_2(aq) \longrightarrow 2HCl(aq) + O_2(g)$$

OxNos   0   −1   −1   0

The chlorine is reduced because its OxNo decreases and the peroxide is oxidised because the OxNo of the O atoms increases.

KEY POINTS

1. Increase in oxidation number is oxidation and decrease in oxidation number is reduction.
2. An oxidising agent gains electrons and gets reduced in a reaction.
3. A reducing agent loses electrons and gets oxidised in a reaction.
4. Hydrogen peroxide can act as an oxidising agent or a reducing agent depending on the other reactant.

Using oxidising and reducing agents

EXAM TIP

When using iron(II) sulfate to test for oxidising agents, the colour change from Fe^{2+} (aq) to Fe^{3+} (aq) is not obvious in dilute solutions. In order to make this more obvious, add excess sodium hydroxide. This gives a rust-coloured precipitate if Fe^{3+} ions are present (see 19.1).

DID YOU KNOW?

Breathalysers to detect the alcohol level in breath formerly used potassium dichromate(VI) to determine the amount of alcohol in the breath. The alcohol in the breath reduced the orange dichromate(VI) ion to the green Cr^{3+} ion. Modern breathlysers use an electronic system to monitor alcohol levels in the breath accurately.

Tests for oxidising agents

Tests for common oxidising and reducing agents involve the observation of a colour change in the solution under test. Many of these tests require the test solution to be acidic, so a few drops of sulfuric acid are added to the reaction mixture when appropriate.

Potassium iodide is a reducing agent that is used to test for oxidising agents. When potassium iodide is added to an acidified solution of an oxidising agent such as hydrogen peroxide, aqueous chlorine or potassium manganate(VII), the solution turns brown because iodine is formed. Table 8.3.1 below shows the oxidation number changes and colour changes for two compounds used to test for oxidising agents.

Table 8.3.1   Tests for oxidising agents

Reducing agent used (in acidic solution)	Oxidation number changes	Colour change
Potassium iodide (I^- ion)	$I^- (-1) \longrightarrow I_2 (0)$	Colourless (I^-) to brown (I_2)
Iron(II) sulfate (Fe^{2+} ion)	$Fe^{2+} (+2) \longrightarrow Fe^{3+} (+3)$	Pale green (Fe^{2+}) to yellow-brown (Fe^{3+})

Tests for reducing agents

Potassium manganate(VII) is an oxidising agent that is used to test for reducing agents. When acidified potassium manganate(VII) is added to a reducing agent such as zinc, iron(II) sulfate, sodium sulfite (Na_2SO_3) or hydrogen peroxide, its colour changes from purple to colourless. Table 8.3.2 shows the oxidation number changes and colour changes for two compounds used to test for reducing agents.

Table 8.3.2   Tests for reducing agents

Oxidising agent used (in acidic solution)	Oxidation number changes	Colour change
Potassium manganate(VII) (MnO_4^- ion)	$MnO_4^- (Mn = +7) \longrightarrow Mn^{2+} (+2)$	Purple (MnO_4^- ion) to colourless (Mn^{2+})
Potassium dichromate(VI) ($Cr_2O_7^{2-}$ ion)	$Cr_2O_7^{2-} (Cr = +6) \longrightarrow Cr^{3+} (+3)$	Orange ($Cr_2O_7^{2-}$) to green (Cr^{3+})

Oxidation and reduction in everyday life

Oxidation–reduction reactions play an important part in everyday life. For example, the effects of rusting (the oxidation of iron to form hydrated iron oxide), cost many economies millions of pounds every year. For more information about rusting see 15.6.

The action of bleach

Bleaches are added to clothes to remove stains. Many bleaches contain the chlorate(I) ion (ClO^-). When added to stained cloth, the bleach oxidises the stain or dye to a colourless form which is then washed out. The chlorate(I) ion behaves as an oxidising agent in this reaction with the dye:

coloured dye + chlorate(I) ions $\longrightarrow$ colourless dye + chloride ions
(reduced form)   (oxidised form)

Sulfites and sulfur dioxide in food preservation

Many bacteria and fungi need oxygen to survive and multiply. Sulfites such as sodium hydrogensulfite ($NaHSO_3$) are reducing agents. They prevent the growth of microbes in foods such as fish and fruit by preventing oxidation and inhibiting enzyme action. Sulfites also prevent fats from getting rancid. Sulfur dioxide is added to fruit squashes to prevent bacterial action. It is also added to wine to prevent the ethanol oxidising to ethanoic acid.

Browning of fruits

Browning of cut fruits is caused by oxidation reactions. In the presence of oxygen, enzymes in the broken cells change small colourless molecules called phenols to polymers (see 14.2) which are coloured. Sulfites prevent this oxidation by inhibiting enzyme action.

Figure 8.3.1 | Ships' hulls rust easily in the presence of water and air.

KEY POINTS

1 Potassium iodide or iron(II) sulfate are used to test for oxidising agents.

2 Potassium dichromate(VI) or potassium manganate(VII) are used to test for reducing agents.

3 Tests for oxidising and reducing agents depend on the observation of specific colour changes.

4 Bleaches are oxidising agents that oxidise stains to a colourless form.

5 Sulfites and sulfur dioxide are reducing agents. They prevent the oxidation of foods such as fish and fruit by preventing oxidation reactions.

9 Electrochemistry

9.1 Conductors and insulators

LEARNING OUTCOMES

At the end of this topic you should be able to:

• describe investigations leading to the classification of substances as conductors or non-conductors

• distinguish between metallic and electrolytic conduction

• classify electrolytes as strong or weak based on conductivity.

Conductors and insulators

Conductors are substances that have a low resistance to the passage of electricity. They allow an electric current to pass through them easily. They can be:

• solids, e.g. metals or graphite
• liquids, e.g. molten zinc chloride or molten metals
• solutions, e.g. a solution of sodium chloride in water or solutions of acids.

| Figure 9.1.1 | Overhead power lines are made of metals that are good conductors of electricity. |

Insulators resist the flow of electricity. They are poor conductors of electricity. Most insulators used to prevent the flow of electricity are solids e.g. plastics or ceramics.

We can test to see whether a substance is a conductor or insulator by using one or other of the circuits shown in Figure 9.1.2.

• If the substance placed between crocodile clips is a conductor the lamp (bulb) will light when the switch is closed. The ammeter will show a reading.

• If the substance between the crocodile clips is an insulator, the lamp will not light when the switch is closed. The ammeter will not show a reading.

• The higher the ammeter reading, the better the conductor is.

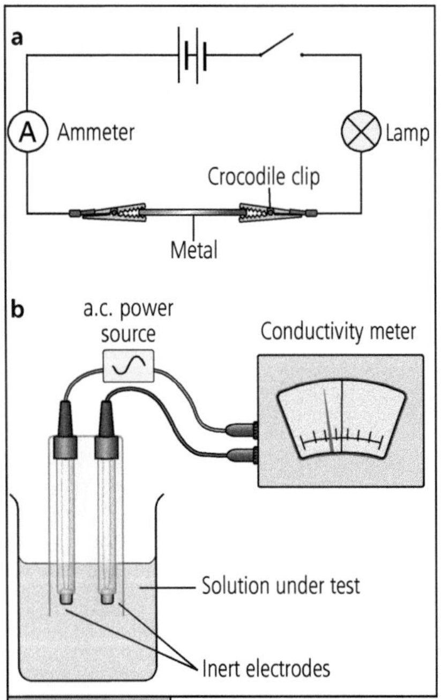

Metallic and electrolytic conduction

• **Metallic conduction** is due to the movement of mobile (delocalised) electrons through the metal lattice (see 5.6) when a potential difference is applied. The metal atoms in the lattice do not move. They remain unchanged.

• **Electrolytic conduction** is due to the movement of ions in a liquid or in solution when a potential difference is applied. In electrolytic conduction there is often a change in the molten ionic

a

Ammeter (A) — Lamp ⊗

Crocodile clip

Metal

b

a.c. power source

Conductivity meter

Solution under test

Inert electrodes

| Figure 9.1.2 | Circuit **a** is used to test the conductivity of solids. In circuit **b** a conductivity meter is used to test the conductivity of liquids or solutions. |

compound or aqueous solution of ions. For example, molten zinc chloride decomposes to zinc and chlorine:

$$ZnCl_2 \text{ (l)} \longrightarrow Zn(s) + Cl_2(g)$$

Electrolytes

An **electrolyte** is a molten ionic compound or a solution containing ions that conducts electricity.

Strong electrolytes

Strong electrolytes have a high concentration of ions in the electrolyte. Examples of strong electrolytes are:

- molten ionic compounds, e.g. molten lead bromide, $PbBr_2(l)$
- aqueous solutions of ionic compounds (soluble salts), e.g. sodium chloride, $NaCl(aq)$, copper sulfate, $CuSO_4(aq)$
- strong acids (acids that are completely ionised in aqueous solution), e.g. sulfuric acid, $H_2SO_4(aq)$, hydrochloric acid, $HCl(aq)$
- strong alkalis (alkalis that are completely ionised in aqueous solution), e.g. sodium hydroxide, $NaOH(aq)$.

Weak electrolytes have a relatively low concentration of ions in the electrolyte. Examples of weak electrolytes are:

- weak acids (acids that are only partially ionised in aqueous solution), e.g. ethanoic acid, $CH_3COOH(aq)$, methanoic acid, $HCOOH(aq)$
- weak alkalis (alkalis that are only partially ionised in aqueous solution), e.g. aqueous ammonia, $NH_3(aq)$.

The strength of an electrolyte can be tested using a conductivity meter such as that shown in Figure 9.1.2. A power source using alternating current must be used to prevent electrolysis of the solution. The greater the strength of the electrolyte, the higher is the reading on the conductivity meter.

KEY POINTS

1. Conductors have a low resistance to the passage of electricity whereas insulators have a high resistance to the passage of electricity.
2. The conductivity in metals is due to the movement of electrons.
3. Electrolytic conduction is due to the movement of ions.
4. An electrolyte is a molten ionic compound or a solution of ions that conducts electricity.
5. Strong electrolytes have a high concentration of ions and weak electrolytes have a low concentration of ions in the electrolyte.
6. Molten ionic compounds, aqueous solutions of salts and strong acids and alkalis are strong electrolytes.
7. Weak acids and alkalis are weak electrolytes.

EXAM TIPS

- It is important that you make the distinction between metallic and electrolytic conduction in terms of the particles which move. Do not be swayed by the 'electro' in electrolytic. Electrolytic conduction involves moving ions and metallic conduction involves moving electrons.
- It is important to realise that the electrons in metals and the ions in electrolytes do not move in a particular direction on their own. A potential difference has to be applied to get them to move in a particular direction.

Electrolysis

At the end of this topic you should be able to:

• define electrolysis, anode, cathode, cation and anion

• identify ions present in electrolytes

• predict the electrode to which an ion will drift

• identify oxidation reactions at the electrodes.

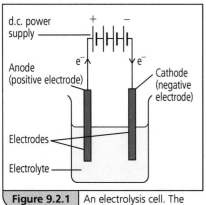

d.c. power supply

Anode (positive electrode)

Cathode (negative electrode)

Electrodes

Electrolyte

Figure 9.2.1 An electrolysis cell. The direction of travel of the electrons in the external circuit is shown by e^-.

DID YOU KNOW?

Pure water also contains a very low concentration of hydrogen and hydroxide ions in equal amounts. This is because water undergoes self-ionisation:

$$H_2O(l) \rightleftharpoons H^+(aq) + OH^-(aq)$$

Terms used in electrolysis

Electrolysis is the decomposition of a compound by an electric current. Electrolysis takes place in an **electrolysis cell**, which can be a beaker or can be one of the electrodes. The beaker contains the electrolyte. The different parts of an electrolysis cell are shown in Figure 9.2.1.

• The **electrodes** are rods that conduct electric current to and from the electrolyte. They are made from either graphite or a metal.

• The **anode** is the positive electrode.

• The **cathode** is the negative electrode.

Identifying the ions in electrolytes

In solid salts, the particles are already present as ions. Electrolysis can only occur when the salt is molten so that the ions separate from each other and are free to move:

$$NaCl(s) \longrightarrow Na^+(l) + Cl^-(l)$$

$$PbBr_2(s) \longrightarrow Pb^{2+}(l) + 2Br^-(l)$$

When salts dissolve in water, they separate into their ions. For example:

$$KCl(s) \longrightarrow K^+(aq) + Cl^-(aq)$$

$$CuSO_4(s) \longrightarrow Cu^{2+}(aq) + SO_4^{2-}(aq)$$

In water, acids form hydrogen ions and negative ions:

$$HCl(g) \longrightarrow H^+(aq) + Cl^-(aq)$$

In water, alkalis form hydroxide ions:

$$NaOH(s) \longrightarrow Na^+(aq) + OH^-(aq)$$

• Positive ions are called **cations**. So H^+, Pb^{2+} and Cu^{2+} are cations.

• Negative ions are called **anions**. So Cl^-, SO_4^{2-} and OH^- ions are anions.

Electrode reactions

Which way do the ions drift?

We can predict the direction in which cations and anions drift during electrolysis. Unlike charges attract and like charges repel. So:

• positively charged ions (cations) move towards the negative electrode (cathode) during electrolysis

• negatively charged ions (anions) move towards the positive electrode (anode) during electrolysis.

Oxidation–reduction reactions at the electrodes

When the ions reach the electrodes, oxidation–reduction reactions occur. The ions gain or lose electrons. We say they are **discharged**. The nature of the ion discharged depends on the types of ion present in the electrolyte. The position of the ion in the electrochemical series (see 9.3) and its concentration play an important part in determining which ion is discharged. For example, in an aqueous solution of sodium chloride, the ions present are $Na^+(aq)$ and $Cl^-(aq)$ from the sodium chloride and $H^+(aq)$ and $OH^-(aq)$ from the ionisation of water.

Some examples of oxidation–reduction reactions at the electrodes are:

At the cathode (see Figure 9.2.2(a)):

- Cations gain electrons from the cathode:

$$Zn^{2+}(aq) + 2e^- \longrightarrow Zn(s)$$

$$2H^+(aq) + 2e^- \longrightarrow H_2(g)$$

- Gain of electrons is reduction. Reduction always happens at the cathode.
- If metals are formed, they are usually deposited either as a layer on the cathode or form a separate layer at the top or bottom of the electrolysis cell. Gases formed bubble off from the cathode.

At the anode (see Figure 9.2.2(b)):

- Anions lose electrons to the anode:

$$2Br^-(aq) \longrightarrow Br_2(l) + 2e^-$$

$$4OH^-(aq) \longrightarrow O_2(g) + 2H_2O(l) + 4e^-$$

- Loss of electrons is oxidation. Oxidation always happens at the anode.
- Gases formed bubble off at the anode. Liquids form a layer if they are immiscible with the electrolyte or dissolve in the electrolyte.

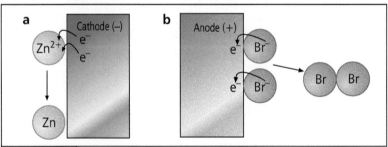

Figure 9.2.2   **a** Positive ions gain electrons at the cathode. **b** Negative ions lose electrons at the anode.

Equations such as:

$$Zn^{2+}(aq) + 2e^- \longrightarrow Zn(s)$$

and $$2Br^-(aq) \longrightarrow Br_2(l) + 2e^-$$

are called half equations. They show the oxidation and reduction parts of the reaction separately.

We can put two half equations together to form the overall equation. For the electrolysis of zinc bromide the full equation will be:

$$ZnBr_2(l) \longrightarrow Zn(s) + Br_2(l)$$

The electrochemical series and electrode products

At the end of this topic you should be able to:

- predict chemical reactions making use of the electrochemical series
- describe how the concentration of electrolyte, type of electrode and position of ions in the electrochemical series affect the products of electrolysis.

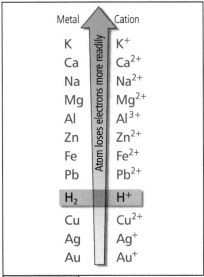

Figure 9.3.1 The electrochemical series

EXAM TIP

We can also look at the electrochemical series in terms of how easy it is for the cations to accept electrons. The lower the metal cation is in the series, the easier it is for the cation to accept an electron and form atoms.

The electrochemical series

We can place metals in order of reactivity by reacting metals with different metal salts. The order of reactivity, with the most reactive at the top is called the **electrochemical series** (Figure 9.3.1). Hydrogen is also included in this series to show which metals displace hydrogen from acids (see 'Displacement of hydrogen' below).

As we go up the electrochemical series the metals:

- increase in reactivity
- lose electrons more readily, so form positive ions more readily
- become stronger reducing agents.

Explaining displacement reactions

A metal higher in the electrochemical series can displace a metal below it from a solution of its ions. We can use the electrochemical series to predict whether or not a reaction is likely to happen.

Example 1

Will magnesium react with aqueous copper(II) sulfate?

- Magnesium is higher than copper in the electrochemical series.
- So magnesium loses electrons and forms ions more readily than copper. Magnesium is a better reducing agent.
- Copper ions are better at accepting electrons than magnesium ions.
- So the reaction taking place should be one in which magnesium atoms lose electrons and copper ions gain electrons.

When excess magnesium ribbon is added to a solution of copper(II) sulfate, the blue colour of the copper sulfate disappears and a pink deposit of copper is seen.

$$Mg(s) + CuSO_4(aq) \longrightarrow MgSO_4(aq) + Cu(s)$$

Ionic equation: $Mg(s) + Cu^{2+}(aq) \longrightarrow Mg^{2+}(aq) + Cu(s)$

Example 2

Will silver react with aqueous zinc chloride?

- Silver is lower than zinc in the electrochemical series.
- Zinc loses electrons and forms ions more readily than silver. Zinc is the better reducing agent.
- So no reaction takes place. Zinc ions cannot accept electrons from silver because silver is less good at releasing electrons than zinc.

Displacement of hydrogen

Only metals above hydrogen in the electrochemical series react with acids to produce hydrogen gas. This is because:

- metals above hydrogen are more reactive than hydrogen
- they lose electrons and form positive ions more readily than hydrogen forms H^+ ions
- hydrogen ions are better at accepting electrons than zinc ions
- hydrogen ions are converted to hydrogen gas:

$$2H^+(aq) + 2e^- \longrightarrow H_2(g)$$

Therefore zinc reacts, for example, with hydrochloric acid:

$$Zn(s) + 2H^+(aq) \longrightarrow Zn^{2+}(aq) + H_2(g)$$

What affects the electrode products?

Solutions often contain more than one type of anion or cation. For example, aqueous sodium chloride contains the ions $Na^+(aq)$, $H^+(aq)$, $Cl^-(aq)$ and $OH^-(aq)$ (see 9.2).

On electrolysis, only one type of cation or anion is discharged. This is called **preferential discharge of ions**. There are three factors determining this:

- The position of the ion in the electrochemical series. Ions lower in the electrochemical series are discharged in preference to the ones above them. So, if Cu^{2+} and H^+ ions are present, Cu^{2+} ions are discharged at the cathode. We can also arrange anions in a discharge series (see Figure 9.3.3). So in concentrated aqueous sodium chloride, Cl^- ions are discharged in preference to OH^- ions.

- The concentration of the solution. For anions, the most concentrated ion tends to get discharged in preference to the less concentrated ion. So, Cl^- ions are discharged in preference to OH^- ions when a concentrated aqueous solution of sodium chloride is electrolysed. But if the sodium chloride solution is dilute, the OH^- ion is discharged in preference. Then oxygen is formed, not chlorine.

- Inert or inactive electrodes. Graphite or platinum electrodes do not take part in the chemical reaction. Active electrodes, such as copper electrodes dipping into aqueous copper sulfate, do take part in the reaction.

KEY POINTS

1. The electrochemical series shows the order of reactivity of metals, with the most reactive at the top.

2. A metal higher in the electrochemical series can displace a metal below it from a solution of its ions.

3. The higher the metal in the reactivity series, the easier it is for the metal to lose electrons and form ions.

4. If more than one type of anion or cation is present in a solution undergoing electrolysis, only one of the ions is discharged (preferential discharge).

5. Preferential discharge depends on the position of the ion in the electrochemical series, the concentration of the solution and whether or not the electrode is inactive or active.

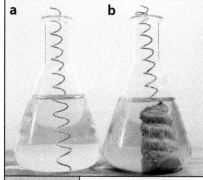

Figure 9.3.2 **a** There is no reaction of copper with zinc chloride. **b** Copper reacts with silver nitrate and crystals of silver form on the copper.

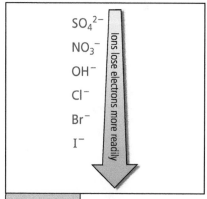

SO_4^{2-}
NO_3^-
OH^-
Cl^-
Br^-
I^-

Ions lose electrons more readily

Figure 9.3.3 Discharge series for anions

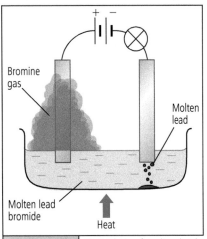

Figure 9.4.1	Electrolysis of molten lead bromide

EXAM TIP

The electrolysis of dilute sulfuric acid can be thought of as the 'electrolysis of water'. The acid is added to improve the conductivity of the water because pure water is a poor conductor.

Electrolysis of fused metal halides

- At the cathode, metal ions gain electrons forming a metal.
- At the anode, halide ions lose electrons and form a halogen.

When molten lead bromide is electrolysed (Figure 9.4.1), the electrode reactions are:

At the cathode: $Pb^{2+}(l) + 2e^- \longrightarrow Pb(l)$

At the anode: $2Br^-(l) \longrightarrow Br_2(g) + 2e^-$

When molten sodium chloride is electrolysed, the electrode reactions are:

At the cathode: $Na^+(l) + e^- \longrightarrow Na(l)$

At the anode: $2Cl^-(l) \longrightarrow Cl_2(g) + 2e^-$

In both these cases inert electrodes are used and the electrolyte is used up.

Electrolysis of dilute sulfuric acid

Dilute sulfuric acid, $H_2SO_4(aq)$, is electrolysed using inert platinum electrodes (Figure 9.4.2). The ions present in dilute sulfuric acid are $H^+(aq)$, $SO_4^{2-}(aq)$ and $OH^-(aq)$.

- At the cathode, H^+ ions gain electrons, forming hydrogen:
  $$2H^+(aq) + 2e^- \longrightarrow H_2(g)$$
- At the anode, OH^- ions (from the water) are preferentially discharged. This is because OH^- ions are lower in the discharge series than SO_4^{2-} ions. The OH^- ions lose electrons and form oxygen and water:
  $$4OH^-(aq) \longrightarrow O_2(g) + 2H_2O(l) + 4e^-$$

During the electrolysis, as the H^+ and OH^- ions are removed, more water ionises. The acid gets more concentrated as the amount of water in the acidic solution decreases.

Electrolysis of aqueous sodium chloride

When aqueous sodium chloride is electrolysed using inert graphite electrodes (Figure 9.4.3), the product at the anode depends on the concentration of chloride ions.

With concentrated aqueous sodium chloride

The ions present are $Na^+(aq)$, $H^+(aq)$, $Cl^-(aq)$ and $OH^-(aq)$.

- At the cathode, H^+ ions are preferentially discharged. This is because they are lower in the electrochemical series than Na^+ ions.
  $$2H^+(aq) + 2e^- \longrightarrow H_2(g)$$

- At the anode, Cl^- ions are preferentially discharged. This is because Cl^- ions are present in high concentration. The concentration effect has more influence than the position of the Cl^- and OH^- ions in the discharge series.

$$2Cl^-(aq) \longrightarrow Cl_2(g) + 2e^-$$

During the electrolysis, the H^+ and Cl^- ions get used up leaving Na^+ and OH^- ions in solution at the end of the electrolysis: a solution of sodium hydroxide.

With dilute aqueous sodium chloride

- At the cathode, H^+ ions are preferentially discharged. This is because they are lower in the electrochemical series than Na^+ ions.

$$2H^+(aq) + 2e^- \longrightarrow H_2(g)$$

- At the anode, OH^- ions are preferentially discharged. This is because Cl^- ions are present at a low concentration and the position of the ions in the discharge series has more influence that the concentration of the Cl^- ion.

$$4OH^-(aq) \longrightarrow O_2(g) + 2H_2O(l) + 4e^-$$

During the electrolysis, the H^+ and OH^- ions get used up, leaving Na^+ and Cl^- ions in solution. Water is used up and the solution becomes more concentrated.

Electrolysis of aqueous copper sulfate

With graphite electrodes (inert electrodes)

The ions present are $Cu^{2+}(aq)$, $H^+(aq)$, $SO_4^{2-}(aq)$ and $OH^-(aq)$.

- At the cathode, Cu^{2+} ions are preferentially discharged. This is because they are lower in the electrochemical series than H^+ ions.

$$Cu^{2+}(aq) + 2e^- \longrightarrow Cu(s)$$

- At the anode, OH^- ions (from the water) are preferentially discharged. This is because OH^- ions are lower in the discharge series than SO_4^{2-} ions. The OH^- ions lose electrons and form oxygen and water.

$$4OH^-(aq) \longrightarrow O_2(g) + 2H_2O(l) + 4e^-$$

The ions left in solution are H^+ and SO_4^{2-} The solution becomes acidic and the concentration of copper sulfate in solution decreases.

With copper electrodes (active electrodes)

- At the cathode, the reaction is the same as with inert electrodes.
- At the anode, copper gets oxidised because the electrode is an active electrode. Electrons are removed from the copper to form copper ions which go into solution: $Cu(s) \longrightarrow Cu^{2+}(aq) + 2e^-$

The copper cathode gets thicker as copper is deposited. The copper anode gets thinner as copper is removed. The concentration of copper sulfate in solution remains the same.

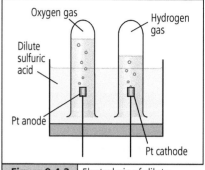

Figure 9.4.2 Electrolysis of dilute sulfuric acid

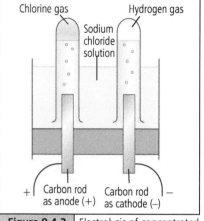

Figure 9.4.3 Electrolysis of concentrated aqueous sodium chloride

KEY POINTS

1 Electrolysis of fused halides produces a metal at the cathode and a halogen at the anode.

2 Electrolysis of dilute sulfuric acid produces hydrogen at the cathode and oxygen at the anode.

3 Electrolysis of aqueous sodium chloride produces hydrogen at the cathode. The anode product is chlorine with concentrated NaCl or oxygen with dilute NaCl.

4 Electrolysis of aqueous copper sulfate produces copper at the cathode. The anode product is oxygen if inert electrodes are used or copper if active electrodes are used.

Electrolysis calculations

At the end of this topic you should be able to:

- define the Faraday constant
- calculate the masses and volumes of substances liberated during electrolysis
- use the relationship $Q = It$

Charge transfer in electrolysis

The mass of a substance produced at the electrodes (or consumed at a reactive anode) during electrolysis is proportional to:

- the electric current (in amperes)
- the time (in seconds) over which a constant current passes.

The **electric charge** in coulombs (C), transferred in electrolysis is given by:

$$Q = I \times t$$

charge (coulombs, C)   current (amperes, A)   time (seconds, s)

The Faraday constant, F

The **Faraday constant** (symbol F) is the quantity of electric charge carried by one mole of electrons or one mole of singly charged ions. Its approximate value is 96 500 coulombs per mole ($C\,mol^{-1}$).

- When we electrolyse silver nitrate solution using silver electrodes, silver is deposited at the cathode.

$$Ag^+(aq) + e^- \longrightarrow Ag(s)$$

One Faraday (96 500 C) is required to deposit 1 mol of silver. This is the same amount of electricity that is required to remove 1 mol of silver from a silver anode.

- When we electrolyse copper sulfate solution using copper electrodes, copper is deposited at the cathode.

$$Cu^{2+}(aq) + 2e^- \longrightarrow Cu(s)$$

In this case, it requires 2 Faradays ($2 \times 96\,500$ C) to deposit 1 mol of copper. This is because 2 mol of electrons are needed to produce 1 mol of copper atoms from 1 mol of copper(II) ions.

The Faraday constant is named after Michael Faraday (1791–1867). Faraday was one of the great experimental scientists of his day and was famous for his lectures. His laws of electrolysis are:

1st law: The mass of any product liberated in electrolysis is proportional to the quantity of electricity which has passed.

2nd law: When the same quantity of electricity is passed through a number of electrolytes in series, the masses of products liberated are in the ratio of their equivalent weights. (Here equivalent weights means molar masses divided by the numerical charges on the ions.)

Electrolysis calculations

Mass of substance deposited during electrolysis

Example

Calculate the mass of lead deposited at the cathode during electrolysis when a current of 2.5 A flows through molten lead bromide for 10 minutes. ($A_r = 207$, $F = 96\,500\,C\,mol^{-1}$)

1 From the half equation, deduce the number of moles of electrons needed to deposit 1 mol of substance:

$$Pb^{2+}(l) + 2e^- \longrightarrow Pb(l)$$

So 2 mol of electrons are required per mole of lead.

2 Use the Faraday constant to deduce the number of coulombs needed to deposit 1 mol of lead:

$$= 2F = 2 \times 96\,500 = 193\,000\,C\,mol^{-1}$$

3 Calculate the charge transferred during the electrolysis:

$$Q = It$$

So $Q = 2.5 \times 10 \times 60 = 1500\,C$

4 Calculate the mass by simple proportion, using the relative atomic mass:

207 g are deposited by 193 000 C.

So mass deposited by $1500\,C = \dfrac{1500 \times 207}{193\,000}$

$$= 1.6\,g \text{ lead}$$

If you are asked to calculate the mass of metal lost from the anode, the calculation is exactly the same.

Volume of gas formed during electrolysis

Example

A dilute solution of sulfuric acid is electrolysed for exactly 1 hour using a current of 0.20 A. Calculate the volume of oxygen released at the anode at r.t.p. ($F = 96\,500\,C\,mol^{-1}$)

1 From the half equation, deduce the number of moles of electrons transferred to produce 1 mol of substance:

$$4OH^-(aq) \longrightarrow O_2(g) + 2H_2O(l) + 4e^-$$

So 4 mol of electrons are transferred per mole of oxygen.

2 Use the Faraday constant to deduce the number of coulombs transferred to produce 1 mol of oxygen:

$$= 4F = 4 \times 96\,500$$

$$= 386\,000\,C\,mol^{-1}$$

3 Calculate the charge transferred during the electrolysis:

$$Q = It$$

So $Q = 0.20 \times 1 \times 60 \times 60$

$$= 720\,C$$

4 Calculate the volume by simple proportion, using the relationship that 1 mol of gas at r.t.p. occupies $24\,dm^3$:

$24\,dm^3$ of gas released by 386 000 C.

So volume released by $720\,C = \dfrac{720 \times 24}{386\,000}$

$$= 0.0448\,dm^3$$

$$= 45\,cm^3 \text{ (to 2 significant figures)}$$

KEY POINTS

1 The Faraday constant is the quantity of electric charge carried by 1 mol of electrons or 1 mol of singly charged ions.

2 Electric charge (in coulombs) = current (in amperes) × time (in seconds).

3 The value of the Faraday constant is $96\,500\,C\,mol^{-1}$.

4 The masses or volumes of the products of electrolysis can be found using the number of electrons required per mole of product, the value of the Faraday constant and the quantity of charge passed.

Applications of electrolysis

Extracting metals using electrolysis

Many metals can be extracted by reducing their oxides with carbon at high temperatures. Carbon can be placed in the electrochemical series between aluminium and zinc.

• Metals oxides below carbon in the electrochemical series can be reduced by carbon. For example:

$$2Fe_2O_3(s) + 3C(s) \longrightarrow 4Fe(l) + 3CO_2(g)$$

• Metals above carbon in the electrochemical series are extracted using electrolysis. The oxides of metals such as aluminium, magnesium and sodium cannot be reduced because carbon is not a strong enough reducing agent. It cannot release electrons as well as the metals higher in the series.

Purification of metals

Many metals can be purified by electrolysis.

• The impure metal is the anode.
• A thin sheet of pure metal is the cathode.
• The electrolyte is a soluble salt of the pure metal.

In the purification of copper (Figure 9.6.1):

• the copper atoms at the anode lose electrons and form Cu^{2+} ions

$$Cu(s) \longrightarrow Cu^{2+}(aq) + 2e^-$$

• the anode becomes thinner and the impurities fall to the bottom of the cell as an anode sludge
• the copper ions at the cathode gain electrons and form Cu atoms

$$Cu^{2+}(aq) + 2e^- \longrightarrow Cu(s)$$

• the cathode becomes thicker because the pure metal is deposited on it.

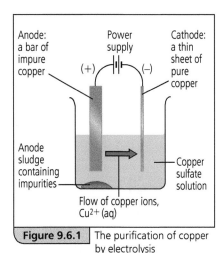

Figure 9.6.1 The purification of copper by electrolysis

Electroplating

Electroplating involves coating of the surface of one metal with a layer of another, usually less reactive, metal. We electroplate articles because it:

• makes them more resistant to corrosion, e.g. chromium plating, nickel plating
• improves their appearance, e.g. plating with silver.

Figure 9.6.2 shows the apparatus required for electroplating.

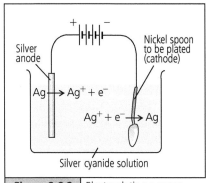

Figure 9.6.2 Electroplating a spoon with silver

In electroplating:

- the anode is the pure metal
- the cathode is the object to be electroplated (usually a metal)
- the electrolyte is a soluble salt of the pure metal at the anode.

In silver plating, Ag^+ ions are formed at the anode from Ag atoms. The Ag^+ ions accept electrons from the cathode and become silver atoms. These form the layer (silver plating) on the cathode.

Anodising

Anodising is the process of increasing the thickness of an unreactive oxide layer on the surface of a metal. It is used to reduce the reactivity of metals, such as nickel or aluminium, so that they can be used under a variety of conditions to increase corrosion resistance and reduce wear. The apparatus used for anodising aluminium is shown in Figure 9.6.3.

- The anode is the metal. When anodising aluminium, the thin oxide layer normally present on the surface of the metal is first removed by reaction with sodium hydroxide.
- The cathode is usually unreactive, e.g. carbon.
- The electrolyte is sulfuric acid.

During the reaction, the sulfuric acid is electrolysed to form oxygen and hydrogen.

- Oxygen gas is produced at the anode:
$$4OH^-(aq) \longrightarrow O_2(g) + 2H_2O(l) + 4e^-$$
- The oxygen gas reacts with the anode and forms a thick oxide layer:
$$4Al(s) + 3O_2(g) \longrightarrow 2Al_2O_3(s)$$

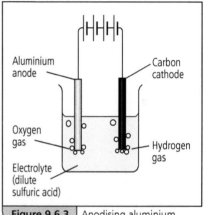

Figure 9.6.3 Anodising aluminium

KEY POINTS

1 Metals below carbon in the electrochemical series can be extracted from their oxides by reduction with carbon.

2 Metals above carbon in the electrochemical series are extracted using electrolysis.

3 Metals can be purified by electrolysis using an impure metal anode and pure metal cathode.

4 Electroplating is used to coat the surface of one metal with a layer of another metal.

5 In electroplating, the pure metal is the anode and the object to be plated, the cathode.

6 Anodising is used to increase the thickness of oxide layer on the surface of a metal. The metal to be anodised is the anode and the electrolyte is sulfuric acid.

10 Rates of reaction

10.1 Following the course of a reaction

At the end of this topic you should be able to:

- define rate of reaction
- describe how to carry out experiments on rate of reaction involving measurement of gas volume, measurement of mass and the use of titrations and changes in light transmission.

Rate of reaction

Rate of reaction is the change in concentration of a reactant or product with time at a stated temperature. The units of rate of a reaction are $mol\,dm^{-3}\,s^{-1}$.

$$\text{rate of reaction } (mol\,dm^{-3}\,s^{-1}) = \frac{\text{change in concentration of reactant or product } (mol\,dm^{-3})}{\text{time taken for this change (s)}}$$

We cannot measure concentration directly, so when carrying out experiments on rates of reaction we measure something that is proportional to concentration, e.g. mass, volume of gas, colour intensity or electrical conductivity.

Following the course of a reaction

The rate of reaction changes with temperature, concentration and particle size of reactants that are solids. So when carrying out experiments to determine rate, we have to make sure that only one of these factors is varied at a time.

- Effect of temperature on rate: keep the concentration and particle size of reactants that are solids constant.
- Effect of concentration on rate: keep the temperature and particle size of solid reactants constant.
- Effect of particle size on rate: keep the concentration and temperature constant.

Measuring the volume of gas given off

The volume of gas given off is measured at time intervals using a gas syringe or upturned measuring cylinder initially full of water. The reaction of magnesium with hydrochloric acid can be followed in this way.

$$Mg(s) + 2HCl(aq) \longrightarrow MgCl_2(aq) + H_2(g)$$

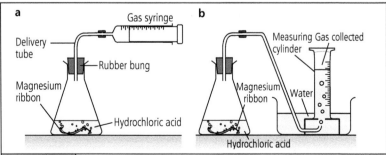

Figure 10.1.1 Measuring the rate of the reaction of magnesium with hydrochloric acid **a** using a gas syringe, **b** using a measuring cylinder

Measuring change in mass

If a gas is given off in a reaction mixture, the mass of the reaction mixture decreases. The decrease in mass is measured at measured time intervals, for example, the reaction in Figure 10.1.2.

$$CaCO_3(s) + 2HCl(aq) \longrightarrow CaCl_2(aq) + CO_2(g) + H_2O(l)$$

Measurement of rate by sampling

Small samples are removed from the reaction mixture at time intervals and analysed by titration. The reaction of potassium iodide with dilute acidified hydrogen peroxide can be followed in this way.

$$2KI(aq) + 2HCl(aq) + H_2O_2(aq) \longrightarrow 2H_2O(l) + I_2(aq) + 2KCl(aq)$$

The reactants are colourless. As the reaction proceeds, the solution gets a deeper and deeper brown due to the increased concentration of iodine. The method is:

1 Take fixed volumes of samples at particular times.

2 Immediately after each sample has been taken, pipette the sample into sodium carbonate solution to stop the reaction continuing.

3 Titrate each sample with standard sodium thiosulfate solution.

4 The end point of the titration is when the brown colour of the iodine disappears.

5 Repeat this process with each sample.

Measuring the time taken for a solid to obscure a cross

When sodium thiosulfate reacts with hydrochloric acid, a suspension of sulfur is formed.

$$Na_2S_2O_3(aq) + 2HCl(aq) \longrightarrow 2NaCl(aq) + S(s) + SO_2(g) + H_2O(l)$$

The suspension of sulfur gets denser and denser until it obscures a cross placed below the reaction flask (Figure 10.1.3). The time taken for this to happen is recorded. The experiment is then repeated varying only one of the factors, e.g. changing only the temperature.

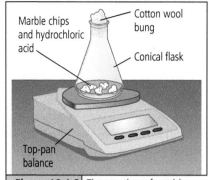

Figure 10.1.2 The reaction of marble chips with hydrochloric acid is accompanied by a decrease in the mass of the contents of the flask.

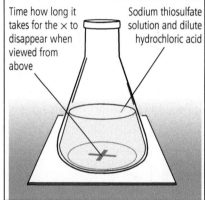

Figure 10.1.3 The reaction of sodium thiosulfate with hydrochloric acid is followed by timing how long it takes for the cross to 'disappear' when viewed from above.

KEY POINTS

1 Rate of reaction is the change in concentration of a reactant or product with time at a stated temperature.

2 When carrying out experiments to determine rate, we have to make sure that only one factor is varied at a time.

3 The progress of some reactions can be followed by measuring how volume of gas or mass changes with time.

4 The progress of some reactions can be followed by taking samples at various times throughout the reaction and then titrating the samples.

5 When a suspension of solid is formed in a reaction, the progress of the reaction can be followed by timing how long it takes for a cross below the reaction mixture to be obscured.

DID YOU KNOW?

Sodium thiosulfate is used in titrations to deduce the concentration of iodine because it reacts with iodine to form colourless products. The end point of the titration can be made clearer if a few drops of starch solution are added. The colour change at the end point is from blue-black to colourless.

Determining rates of reaction

At the end of this topic you should be able to:

- use data to deduce the effect of various factors on rate of reaction
- interpret graphical representation of data obtained in studying rates of reaction
- describe how rate of reaction changes as a reaction proceeds
- describe the general shape of graphs of concentration against time, concentration against 1/time and rate against time.

Graphs showing progress of reaction

Excess magnesium reacts with dilute hydrochloric acid of concentration $0.4\,mol\,dm^{-3}$.

$$Mg(s) + 2HCl(aq) \longrightarrow MgCl_2(aq) + H_2(g)$$

The concentration of the hydrochloric acid falls as the volume of hydrogen gas released rises. Typical results are given in Table 10.2.1.

Table 10.2.1

Concentration of acid $(mol\,dm^{-3})$	0.4	0.3	0.2	0.1	0.05	0.0	0.0
Volume of H_2 (cm^3)	0	48	96	144	168	192	192
Time (s)	0	15	43	100	180	500	600

- When we plot concentration of reactant (in this case acid) against time, we get a downward curve. The curve gets less steep as the reaction proceeds. So the reaction is getting slower as it proceeds (Figure 10.2.1(a)).
- When we plot volume of product (hydrogen) against time we get an upward curve. The curve gets less steep as the reaction proceeds. So, again, the reaction is getting slower is it proceeds (Figure 10.2.1(b)).

How does rate change as a reaction proceeds?

Although rate is defined in terms of concentration, we can plot something that changes proportionally to concentration against time, e.g. volume of gas, mass, colour or electrical conductivity. When excess calcium carbonate reacts with hydrochloric acid, we can plot either the volume of carbon dioxide released against time (Figure 10.2.2(a)) or the change in mass of the reaction mixture against time (Figure 10.2.2(b)).

$$CaCO_3(s) + 2HCl(aq) \longrightarrow CaCl_2(aq) + CO_2(g) + H_2O(l)$$

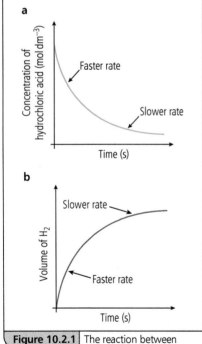

Figure 10.2.1 The reaction between magnesium and hydrochloric acid can be recorded as **a** a decrease in concentration of acid with time, **b** an increase in volume of H_2 gas with time.

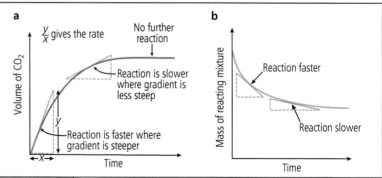

Figure 10.2.2 Curves for **a** CO_2 increase v. time, **b** mass decrease v. time

In both graphs we can see that:

- The gradient *y/x* gives the rate at a particular point where a tangent has been drawn to the curve.
- The gradient (slope) decreases as the reaction proceeds.
- The rate decreases as the reaction proceeds.

Figure 10.2.3 shows how we can find:

- how long it takes for a reaction to produce a given volume of gas
- the volume of gas produced at a given time
- when the reaction has finished.

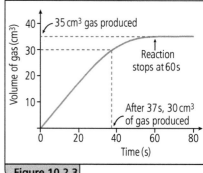

Figure 10.2.3

Analysing the sodium thiosulfate–acid reaction

In this reaction, we measure the time taken for the cross to be obscured by the precipitate of sulfur (see 10.1). We can see how rate changes with concentration of acid by doing several experiments using different concentrations of acid at constant temperature.

A graph of concentration against $\dfrac{1}{\text{time taken for the cross to be obscured}}$ is then plotted (see Figure 10.2.4).

Rate is inversely proportional to time. So from this graph, we can see that the rate of reaction (proportional to 1/time) is proportional to the concentration of the acid.

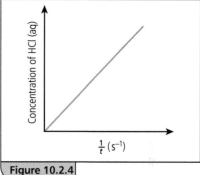

Figure 10.2.4

> **DID YOU KNOW?**
>
> A plot of concentration against rate does not always produce a straight line. The line may be an upward curve. The exact shape of the line or curve depends on the reaction and whether or not a particular reactant is in excess.

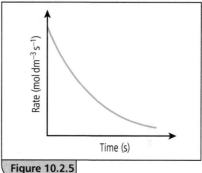

Figure 10.2.5

Rate–time graphs

When we plot rate of reaction against time, the graph is usually a curve. At the beginning of the reaction, the rate is highest but as the reaction proceeds the rate gets slower and slower (Figure 10.2.5).

> **KEY POINTS**
>
> 1 As a reaction proceeds the rate of reaction decreases.
>
> 2 Rate of reaction can be deduced by drawing tangents at particular points on the curve of a concentration–time graph.
>
> 3 A graph of mass change against time for a reaction that produces a gas is a downward curve.
>
> 4 Rate of reaction is proportional to 1/time.
>
> 5 A plot of concentration against 1/time shows how the rate of reaction changes with increase in concentration.

EXAM TIP

In some graphs the concentration appears to be proportional to the time early on in the reaction. You can easily calculate the initial rate of reaction by taking the initial gradient of the graph.

How concentration and surface area affect rates of reaction

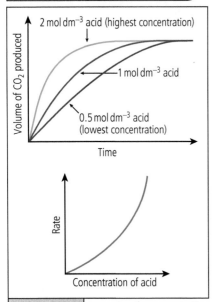

Increasing the concentration of acid increases the rate of reaction between calcium carbonate and hydrochloric acid.

The effect of concentration on rate of reaction

Increasing the concentration of reactants generally increases the rate of a reaction (keeping everything else constant). In the reaction of calcium carbonate with excess hydrochloric acid:

$$CaCO_3(s) + 2HCl(aq) \longrightarrow CaCl_2(aq) + CO_2(g) + H_2O(l)$$

increasing the concentration of hydrochloric acid, increases the rate of reaction (Figure 10.3.1). The final volume of carbon dioxide released is the same in each experiment because the hydrochloric acid is in excess (the calcium carbonate is the limiting reagent).

Using data to deduce how concentration affects rate

Increasing the concentration of reactants (at constant temperature) generally increases the rate of a reaction. However, not all reactants behave in this way. Table 10.3.1 compares the rate of reaction of formation of iodine from iodide ions (I^-) and hydrogen peroxide (H_2O_2) in acid solution (H^+) when different concentrations of reactants are used.

Table 10.3.1 Reaction rates of iodide ions (I^-) and hydrogen peroxide (H_2O_2) in acid solution (H^+)

Experiment number	Relative rate of reaction	Concentration of H_2O_2 (mol dm^{-3})	Concentration of I^- (mol dm^{-3})	Concentration of H^+ (mol dm^{-3})
A	1	0.1	0.1	0.1
B	2	0.2	0.1	0.1
C	2	0.1	0.2	0.1
D	1	0.1	0.1	0.2

You can see that:

- doubling the concentration of H_2O_2, doubles the rate (comparing A and B)

- doubling the concentration of I^- doubles the rate (comparing A and C)

- doubling the concentration of H^+ has no effect (comparing A and D).

Explaining the effect of concentration on rate of reaction

- Increasing the concentration, decreases the distance between the particles. There are more particles per dm^3.

- So there are more collisions per second between the particles.

- So there is a greater chance of the particles reacting (Figure 10.3.2).

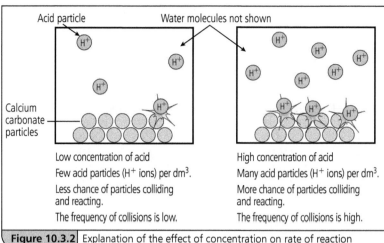

Figure 10.3.2 Explanation of the effect of concentration on rate of reaction

EXAM TIP

Remember, that if the same mass of marble chips is taken, the combined surface area of all the particles from large chips is less than that of the combined surface area of all the small chips.

The effect of surface area on rate of reaction

When marble chips (calcium carbonate) react with hydrochloric acid, the reaction rate depends on the particle size of the marble chips (everything else being kept the same). The greater the surface area of the marble, the greater is the number of particles exposed to the acid to react. Breaking up the marble into smaller pieces exposes more surfaces, resulting in more particles being available to react (see Figure 10.3.3). So, with the same mass of marble, smaller pieces react faster than larger pieces.

The explanation for the increasing rate of reaction with decreasing size of solid particles is similar to that for concentration. There are more particles available to react with the acid. So there are more collisions per second and therefore the rate of reaction is faster.

Combustible powders

Some industrial processes cause fine powders to get into the air. These can be sawdust from sawmills, particles of flour from flour mills, tiny particles of metal from metal-working or coal dust from coal mining. The fine powders are extremely combustible (burn readily in air) because they have a very large surface area compared with their volume. A lit match or spark from a machine can cause them to explode.

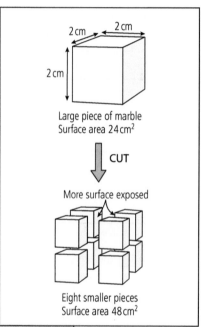

Figure 10.3.3 Cutting up marble

Large piece of marble
Surface area 24 cm^2

CUT

More surface exposed

Eight smaller pieces
Surface area 48 cm^2

KEY POINTS

1 Increasing the concentration of a reagent generally increases the rate of reaction.

2 Rate increases as the concentration of reactant increases because the frequency of collisions of the reacting particles increases.

3 Increasing the surface area of a solid increases the rate of reaction.

4 For the same total mass, smaller particles have a larger surface area than larger particles.

5 Finely divided substances may explode in the air because they have a large surface area for their volume.

DID YOU KNOW?

The first verifiable explosion in a flour mill happened on 14 December 1785 in Torino, Italy.

10.4

How temperature and catalysts affect rates of reaction

LEARNING OUTCOMES

At the end of this topic you should be able to:

- describe how temperature affects the rate of reaction
- explain in simple terms how temperature affects the rate of reaction
- describe how catalysts affect the rate of reaction
- use data to deduce the effect of factors on rate of reaction.

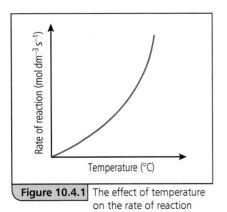

Figure 10.4.1 The effect of temperature on the rate of reaction

EXAM TIP

When answering questions about rates of reaction it is important that you use comparative words or phrases, e.g. 'rate of reaction gets fastER the highER the temperature' instead of 'the reaction is fast at high temperatures'.

The effect of temperature on reaction rate

Table 10.4.1 shows how changing the temperature changes the rate of reaction between sodium thiosulfate and hydrochloric acid (see 10.1). The time taken to obscure a cross at different temperatures was recorded using the same concentration of thiosulfate and acid each time.

Table 10.4.1

Temperature (°C)	Time to obscure cross (s)	1/time (s^{-1})
20	47	0.021
30	23	0.043
40	12	0.083
50	6	0.167

As the temperature increases, the time taken for the cross to be obscured decreases. The third column (1/time) is proportional to the rate of reaction. So as the temperature increases, the rate of reaction increases. The rate approximately doubles as the temperature rises by 10 °C.

Explaining the effect of temperature on rate of reaction

In order to react when they collide, particles must have a minimum amount of energy. This is called the **activation energy**. At a low temperature only a small proportion of the particles have this energy. So the reaction is slow. The effect of temperature on reaction rate can be explained in the following way:

- Increasing the temperature increases the average kinetic energy of the particles. The particles move faster and more energetically.
- The higher the temperature, the more energetic are the collisions between the reactant particles.
- The higher the temperature, the greater is the proportion of reactant particles having energy above or equal to the activation energy.
- The number of collisions per unit time leading to a reaction is increased. So the rate increases.

The effect of catalysts on rate of reaction

A **catalyst** is a substance that speeds up a chemical reaction without getting used up.

- The catalyst is not used up in the reaction. Its mass is the same at the end as at the start of the reaction.
- Only a tiny amount of catalyst is needed to increase the rate of reaction by a vast amount.

98

- The chemical composition of the catalyst at the end of the reaction is the same as that at the beginning.

Catalysts can be:

- solids, e.g. manganese(IV) oxide or copper(II) oxide can be used to speed up the decomposition of hydrogen peroxide
- catalysts that work in solution, e.g. hydrogen ions (H⁺) are used to speed up many reactions in solution.

Figure 10.4.2 shows the effect of various catalysts on the decomposition of hydrogen peroxide. In the absence of a catalyst hydrogen peroxide decomposes only very slowly.

$$2H_2O_2(l) \longrightarrow 2H_2O(l) + O_2(g)$$

The reaction can be followed by measuring the volume of oxygen given off with time at constant temperature.

We can see from Figure 10.4.2 that:

- hydrogen peroxide does not decompose over the time-scale of the experiment
- manganese(IV) oxide and lead(IV) oxide are good catalysts
- copper(II) oxide is a less effective catalyst than manganese(IV) oxide or lead(IV) oxide.

Enzymes

Enzymes are biological catalysts. They are proteins that catalyse reactions in the cells of all organisms. Examples of enzyme-catalysed reactions include:

- the browning reaction when some fruits are cut
- the production of ethanol by fermentation.

Figure 10.4.3 shows how increasing the temperature affects the rate of a typical enzyme-catalysed reaction.

- Below 40°C, the rate increases as the temperature increases.
- The optimum rate of reaction is about 40°C.
- Above 40°C, the rate decreases as the temperature increases.

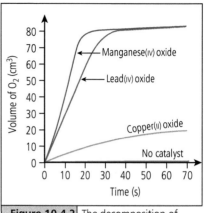

Figure 10.4.2 The decomposition of hydrogen peroxide is catalysed by various metal oxides.

DID YOU KNOW?

Most enzymes do not catalyse reactions efficiently above 40°C because the structure of the enzyme protein changes so that the reactants cannot bind properly to the surface of the enzyme. At temperatures above about 60°C the enzyme structure is irreversibly changed. We say that the enzymes are 'denatured'.

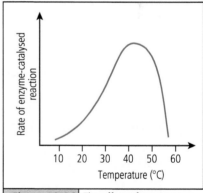

Figure 10.4.3 The effect of temperature on the rate of an enzyme-catalysed reaction

KEY POINTS

1 The rate of a chemical reaction increases with temperature.

2 The activation energy is the minimum energy the reactant particles must have to react when they collide.

3 Increasing the temperature increases the proportion of reactant particles having energy greater than the activation energy.

4 A catalyst is a substance that speeds up a chemical reaction without getting used up.

5 Enzymes are biological catalysts.

11 Energetics

11.1 Exothermic and endothermic changes

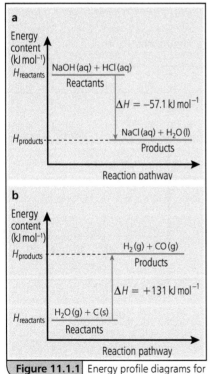

Figure 11.1.1 Energy profile diagrams for **a** an exothermic reaction, **b** an endothermic reaction

Exothermic and endothermic reactions

An **exothermic reaction** is a reaction that releases energy to the surroundings. The temperature of the surroundings increases. Examples of exothermic changes:

• the reactions of acids with metals

• the neutralisation reactions of acids with bases

• the combustion of fuels

• dissolving alkali metal hydroxides, e.g. sodium hydroxide, in water.

An **endothermic reaction** is a reaction that absorbs energy from the surroundings. The temperature of the surroundings decreases. Examples of endothermic changes include:

• the thermal decomposition of carbonates

• dissolving potassium nitrate or ammonium nitrate in water.

Enthalpy changes

An **enthalpy change** is the heat energy exchanged between a chemical reaction and its surroundings at constant pressure. The symbol for enthalpy change is ΔH. The unit for enthalpy change is $kJ\,mol^{-1}$.

Figure 11.1.1 shows **energy profile diagrams** for an exothermic and an endothermic reaction. The heat energy content (enthalpy, H) of the reactants and products is shown on the vertical axis. The reaction pathway is shown on the horizontal axis. The reaction pathway shows the course of the reaction as you go from reactants to products. You can see that the enthalpy change is the energy difference between the heat energy content of the products and reactants.

enthalpy change = energy of products − energy of reactants

For an exothermic reaction:

• the energy of the reactants is higher than the energy of the products

• so energy is released to the surroundings

• (energy of products − energy of reactants) is a negative value

• so ΔH is negative, e.g.

$$NaOH(aq) + HCl(aq) \longrightarrow NaCl(aq) + H_2O(l) \quad \Delta H = -57.1\,kJ\,mol^{-1}$$

For an endothermic reaction:

• the energy of the reactants is lower than the energy of the products

• so energy is absorbed from the surroundings

- (energy of products − energy of reactants) is a positive value
- so ΔH is positive, e.g.

$$H_2O(g) + C(s) \rightleftharpoons H_2(g) + CO(g) \qquad \Delta H = +131\,kJ\,mol^{-1}$$

Activation energy and the effect of catalysts

In order for particles to react when they collide, they must have a minimum amount of energy. This is called the **activation energy** (see 10.4). Activation energy is always endothermic because it is the energy that the particles must acquire before they are able to collide successfully and react. So we sometimes call the activation energy the 'energy barrier' for the reaction. We can extend our energy profile diagrams to include activation energy (see Figure 11.1.2).

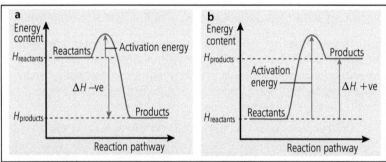

Figure 11.1.2 Energy profile diagrams including activation energy for **a** an exothermic reaction, **b** an endothermic reaction

A **catalyst** is a substance that speeds up the rate of reaction but remains unchanged at the end of the reaction (see 10.4). Catalysts speed up a reaction because they lower the energy barrier to the reaction by decreasing the activation energy. In Figure 11.1.3 we see that the activation energy for the catalysed reaction, E_a(catalysed), is much lower than for the uncatalysed reaction, E_a(uncatalysed). Note that the activation energy arrow goes from the reactants to the highest point on the curve.

EXAM TIP

Make sure that the arrows in energy profile diagrams point the correct way. Show the arrows for activation energy and ΔH for an endothermic reaction pointing upwards ($\uparrow$). Show the arrow for ΔH for an exothermic reaction pointing downwards ($\downarrow$).

KEY POINTS

1 Exothermic reactions release energy to the surroundings. Endothermic reactions absorb energy from the surroundings.

2 The enthalpy change of a reaction, ΔH, is the energy exchanged between a chemical reaction and its surroundings at constant pressure.

3 Energy profile diagrams show the energy content of the reactants and products plotted against the reaction pathway.

4 For an exothermic reaction the value of ΔH is negative. For an endothermic reaction the value of ΔH is positive.

5 Activation energy is the minimum amount of energy that particles must have in order to react when they collide.

6 Catalysts are substances that speed up a reaction without being chemically changed.

7 Catalysts speed up a reaction by lowering its activation energy.

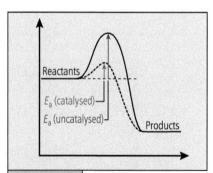

Figure 11.1.3 Energy profile diagrams for an exothermic reaction with and without a catalyst. E_a(catalysed) is the activation energy for the catalysed reaction. E_a(uncatalysed) is the activation energy for the uncatalysed reaction.

11.2 Energy changes by experiment

EXAM TIP

Remember that definitions involving energy changes are always compared under standard conditions. Standard conditions are 1 atmosphere pressure (760 mm mercury pressure) and 25°C.

Types of enthalpy change

We describe enthalpy changes (heat changes) according to the type of chemical reaction taking place. Three examples are:

Heat of neutralisation, ΔH_n: The enthalpy change when one mole of water is formed by the reaction of an acid with an alkali under standard conditions. For example, the neutralisation of the strong alkali sodium hydroxide with the strong acid hydrochloric acid:

$$NaOH(aq) + HCl(aq) \longrightarrow NaCl(aq) + H_2O(l) \quad \Delta H_n = -57.1 \, kJ \, mol^{-1}$$

Heat of solution, ΔH_{sol}: The enthalpy change when one mole of a solute is dissolved in a solvent to form an infinitely dilute solution under standard conditions. By 'infinitely dilute' we mean a solution in which no further heat change occurs on further dilution. For example, when sodium hydroxide dissolves in excess water:

$$NaOH(s) + aq \longrightarrow NaOH(aq) \qquad \Delta H_{sol} = -470 \, kJ \, mol^{-1}$$

Heat of reaction, ΔH_r: The enthalpy change when the molar amounts of reactants shown in the equation react to give products under standard conditions. For example, when a metal reacts with an acid:

$$Mg(s) + 2HCl(aq) \longrightarrow MgCl_2(aq) + H_2(g) \quad \Delta H_r = -106.7 \, kJ \, mol^{-1}$$

We can use the general term 'heat of reaction' for any reaction whose equation is given.

Energy changes from experiments

We measure the enthalpy (heat energy) change using a piece of apparatus called a **calorimeter**. A simple calorimeter can be a polystyrene cup, a copper can or a vacuum flask. Figure 11.2.1 shows a simple calorimeter.

When carrying out experiments to calculate energy changes we need to know:

• the amounts of reactants in moles
• the volume of solvent
• the temperature change during the reaction.

Finding the heat of neutralisation by experiment

To find the enthalpy change of neutralisation of sodium hydroxide by hydrochloric acid:

1 Place a known volume of $1.0 \, mol \, dm^{-3}$ aqueous sodium hydroxide in a polystyrene cup (calorimeter).

2 Record the temperature of the aqueous sodium hydroxide.

3 Add the same volume of $1.0 \, mol \, dm^{-3}$ hydrochloric acid to the cup.

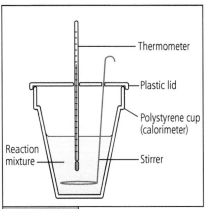

Thermometer

Plastic lid

Polystyrene cup (calorimeter)

Reaction mixture

Stirrer

Figure 11.2.1 A polystyrene cup can be used as a calorimeter to measure enthalpy changes.

The acid should be at the same starting temperature as the sodium hydroxide.

4 Stir the reaction mixture and record the highest temperature reached.

Finding the heat of solution by experiment

A similar method is used to find the heat of solution of sodium hydroxide experimentally (Figure 11.2.2).

1 Place a known volume of water in the polystyrene cup (calorimeter).

2 Record the temperature of the water.

3 Add a known mass of sodium hydroxide to the water.

4 Stir the reaction mixture and record the highest temperature.

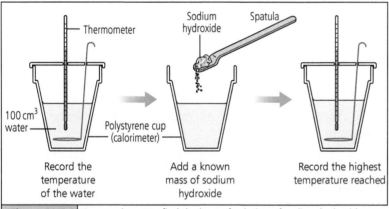

Figure 11.2.2 An experiment to find the heat of solution of sodium hydroxide

When alkali metal hydroxides dissolve in water, the reaction is always exothermic. The value of ΔH is negative.

When salts dissolve in water, the energy change can be exothermic or endothermic, depending on the salt. When potassium nitrate or ammonium nitrate dissolves in water, heat is absorbed. The value of ΔH is positive (endothermic). The temperature of the solution decreases. So in these cases we have to measure the lowest temperature obtained rather than the highest.

Finding the heat of reaction of a metal with acid

If we want to find the heat of reaction of magnesium with hydrochloric acid, the method is similar to the method used to find the heat of solution.

1 Place a known volume, e.g. $100\,cm^3$, of $2.0\,mol\,dm^{-3}$ hydrochloric acid (an excess) in the polystyrene cup (calorimeter).

2 Record the temperature of the hydrochloric acid.

3 Add a known mass of magnesium, e.g. $0.4\,g$, to the hydrochloric acid.

4 Stir the reaction mixture and record the highest temperature.

KEY POINTS

1 Heat of neutralisation is the enthalpy change when one mole of water is formed by the reaction of an acid with an alkali under standard conditions.

2 Heat of solution is the enthalpy change when one mole of a solute is dissolved in a solvent to form an infinitely dilute solution under standard conditions.

3 Heat of reaction is the enthalpy change when the molar amounts of reactants shown in the equation react to give products under standard conditions.

4 Energy changes can be measured experimentally using the temperature rise of a known amount of reactants and known volume of solution.

5 Thermometric titrations can be used to determine the end point of an acid–alkali titration.

At the end of this topic you should be able to:

- calculate energy changes from experimental results
- calculate enthalpy changes from data derived from experiments
- understand enthalpy changes in terms of bond making and bond breaking.

Heat losses to the surroundings are the major error in experiments involving exothermic reactions using calorimeters. Heat is lost by conduction to the calorimeter, thermometer and stirrer, by convection to the air and by radiation from the walls of the calorimeter. Using a vacuum flask as a calorimeter reduces most of these heat losses.

When a reaction occurs between two different compounds, the compounds do not separate into individual atoms. Sometimes one particular bond breaks and then forms a new bond with a different atom. Sometimes a bond starts forming as another one breaks. The way this happens is called the mechanism of the reaction.

Energy changes from experimental results

The energy transferred as heat from the experiments described in 11.2 is calculated using the equation:

$$q = m \times c \times \Delta T$$

where:

q is the energy transferred in joules (J)

m is the mass of solution in grams (g)

c is the specific heat capacity in joules per gram per °C ($J g^{-1} °C^{-1}$)

ΔT is the change in temperature.

In using this equation we make the following assumptions:

- The solution has the same specific heat capacity as water ($4.2 J g^{-1} °C^{-1}$).
- The density of a dilute solution is the same as that of water ($1.0 g cm^{-3}$).
- The change in temperature, ΔT, assumes that there are no heat losses to the surroundings.

Calculating the energy change

Example 1

When 25 cm³ of hydrochloric acid of concentration $1.0 mol dm^{-3}$ is added to 25 cm³ of potassium hydroxide of concentration $1.0 mol dm^{-3}$, the temperature rises from 21.1 °C to 27.3 °C. Calculate the heat of neutralisation for this reaction.

$$KOH(aq) + HCl(aq) \longrightarrow KCl(aq) + H_2O(l)$$

1 mass of solution (assuming density = $1.0 g cm^{-3}$)
$$= 25 g + 25 g = 50 g$$

2 specific heat capacity = $4.2 J g^{-1} °C^{-1}$

3 temperature change = $(27.3 - 21.1) °C = 6.2 °C$

4 heat energy released $q = m \times c \times \Delta T$
$$= 50 \times 4.2 \times 6.2 = 1302 J$$

5 number of moles of acid $= \dfrac{\text{concentration} \times \text{volume}}{1000}$
$$= \dfrac{1.0 \times 25}{1000} = 0.025 mol$$

6 1302 J of energy is released by 0.025 mol HCl

7 So for 1 mol of HCl (and 1 mol of water formed) energy released is

$$1302 \times \frac{1}{0.025} = 52080 J$$

So $\Delta H_n = -52 kJ mol^{-1}$ (to 2 significant figures)

Example 2

When 0.5 g of sodium hydroxide, NaOH, is dissolved completely in 200 cm³ of water, the temperature of the solution rose from 21.4 °C to 28.4 °C. Calculate the heat of solution of sodium hydroxide. (Molar mass of NaOH = 40 g mol⁻¹)

1 mass of solution (assuming density = 1.0 g cm⁻³) = 200 g

2 specific heat capacity = 4.2 J g⁻¹ °C⁻¹

3 temperature change = (28.4 − 21.4) °C = 7.0 °C

4 heat energy released $q = m \times c \times \Delta T$

$q = 200 \times 4.2 \times 7.0 = 5880$ J

5 number of moles of NaOH = $\dfrac{\text{mass taken}}{\text{molar mass}} = \dfrac{0.5}{40} = 1.25 \times 10^{-2}$ mol

6 5880 J of energy is released by 1.25×10^{-2} mol NaOH

7 So for 1 mol of NaOH energy released is

$5880 \times \dfrac{1}{1.25 \times 10^{-2}} = 470\,400$ J

So $\Delta H_{sol} = -470$ kJ mol⁻¹ (to 2 significant figures)

Bond making and bond breaking

- An input of energy is needed to break bonds. So bond breaking is endothermic.
- Energy is released when bonds are formed. So bond making is exothermic.
- In an endothermic reaction, more energy is needed to break the bonds in the reactants than is given out, making new bonds in the products.
- In an exothermic reaction, more energy is released on forming new bonds in the products than is needed to break the bonds in the reactants.

Bond energy calculations

- The energy needed to break a covalent bond between two particular atoms is called the **bond energy**, e.g. $E(H{-}H) = 436$ kJ mol⁻¹, $E(O{=}O) = 498$ kJ mol⁻¹, $E(O{-}H) = 464$ kJ mol⁻¹. We can use bond energies to calculate the energy change in a reaction.
- For example, consider the reaction:

$$2H_2(g) \quad + \quad O_2(g) \quad \longrightarrow \quad 2H_2O(g)$$

bonds broken in reactants	bonds formed in products
(endothermic, ΔH positive)	(exothermic, ΔH negative)
$2 \times E(H{-}H) + E(O{=}O)$	$4 \times E(O{-}H)$
$2 \times 436 + 498$	4×464
bonds broken = $+1370$ kJ mol⁻¹	bonds formed = -1856 kJ mol⁻¹

The exothermic change is greater by $(1856 - 1370)$ kJ = 486 kJ mol⁻¹.

So the enthalpy change is −486 kJ mol⁻¹.

EXAM TIP

The energy released when sulfuric acid is neutralised by sodium hydroxide is −112.6 kJ. In this reaction 2 mol of water are produced.

$$2NaOH + H_2SO_4 \longrightarrow Na_2SO_4 + 2H_2O$$

So the heat of neutralisation (which is per mole of water formed) is half this value: −56.3 kJ mol⁻¹

KEY POINTS

1 The heat energy given out in a reaction can be calculated using the equation
$q = m \times c \times \Delta T$

2 In calculating enthalpy changes from experimental results we assume that:
- the solution has the same specific heat capacity as water
- the density of a dilute solution is the same as that of water
- there are no heat losses from the apparatus.

3 Bond breaking is endothermic. Bond making is exothermic.

4 The energy required to break a bond between two atoms in a covalent compound is called the bond energy.

5 The overall enthalpy change in a reaction depends on the difference in the bond energies of particular bonds in the reactants and products.

Objectives A7–11

1 Calculate the concentration in mol dm^{-3} of a solution containing 2 g of sodium hydroxide, NaOH, in 50 cm^3 of solution.
(A_r: H = 1, O = 16, Na = 23)

2 Calculate the mass of potassium nitrate, KNO_3, in 20 cm^3 of a solution of potassium nitrate of concentration 0.40 mol dm^{-3}.
(A_r: N = 14, O = 16, K = 39)

3 A solution of potassium hydroxide of unknown concentration was titrated with sulfuric acid.
$$2KOH + H_2SO_4 \longrightarrow K_2SO_4 + 2H_2O$$
It required 15 cm^3 of 0.10 mol dm^{-3} sulfuric acid to neutralise 25 cm^3 of the potassium hydroxide solution.
Calculate:
a the number of moles of sulfuric acid used in the titration
b the concentration of the aqueous potassium hydroxide
c the mass of potassium hydroxide present in 20 cm^3 of potassium hydroxide.

4 Define the terms acid and base in terms of:
a pH   b proton transfer.

5 What is meant by the terms
a weak acid   b strong base?
Give an example of each and illustrate your answers with relevant equations.

6 Describe how you would prepare pure dry crystals of the soluble salt potassium chloride from potassium hydroxide using a titration method.

7 Lead iodide is an insoluble salt. Describe how you would prepare a pure dry sample of lead iodide.

8 State the difference between an acidic oxide, a basic oxide, an amphoteric oxide and a neutral oxide, giving an example of each.

9 Write a balanced equation for the reaction of sodium hydroxide with ammonium sulfate.

10 Explain why lime and fertilisers containing ammonium salts should not be added to the

soil at the same time, especially if the ground is moist.

11 State a use for each of the following compounds:
a calcium carbonate   b sodium chloride
c calcium sulfate   d sodium benzoate.

12 Describe how you could determine the end point of a neutralisation reaction without using pH changes or an acid–base indicator.

13 Define oxidation and reduction in terms of:
a oxidation number   b electrons.

14 Deduce the oxidation number of:
a Fe in $FeCl_3$ b P in P_2O_5
c S in Na_2SO_3 d N in the NO_3^- ion
e S in Na_2S.

15 Identify the oxidising and reducing agents in the following equations.
a $Cl_2 + 2NaI \longrightarrow I_2 + 2NaCl$
b $CO + ZnO \longrightarrow Zn + CO_2$
c $H_2O_2 + 2I^- + 2H^+ \longrightarrow 2H_2O + I_2$

16 Answer these questions about the equations in Question 15.
a Which species in equation **15a** gets oxidised? Give a reason for your answer.
b Which species in equation **15b** gets reduced? Give a reason for your answer.
c Which species in equation **15c** does not change in oxidation number?

17 A dilute aqueous solution of LiCl is electrolysed using carbon electrodes.
a Explain why an aqueous solution of LiCl conducts electricity but solid LiCl does not conduct.
b State the names of the products formed at the
  i anode   ii cathode
in this electrolysis and write half equations for these reactions.
c At which electrode is oxidation taking place? Explain your answer.

18 Electrolysis of a concentrated solution of sodium chloride produces chlorine at the anode and hydrogen at the cathode.

  a Explain why hydrogen is formed at the cathode and not sodium.

  b Explain why chlorine is formed at the anode and not oxygen.

19 Describe and explain the differences in the electrolysis of aqueous copper(II) sulfate using inert (graphite) electrodes and active (copper) electrodes.

20 During the electrolysis of copper(II) sulfate solution, copper is deposited at the cathode. Calculate the mass of copper deposited when a current of 0.2 amps flows for 1 h 25 min.

  (A_r: Cu = 63.5; F = 96 500 C mol^{-1})

21 Calculate the volume of oxygen, at r.t.p., produced at the anode when acidified water is electrolysed for 40 min using a current of 2.5 amps.

  (Hint 1: Water ionises slightly to form OH$^-$ and H$^+$ ions.

  Hint 2: $4OH^- \longrightarrow O_2(g) + 2H_2O(l) + 4e^-$)

22 Define: a rate of reaction   b catalyst.

23 Large marble chips (calcium carbonate) were reacted with 1.0 mol dm^{-3} hydrochloric acid at 24 °C. The course of the reaction was followed by measuring the volume of carbon dioxide given off.

  a Draw a labelled diagram of the apparatus that could be used.

  b Describe one other way of measuring the course of this reaction that does not involve measuring the volume of carbon dioxide.

  c Describe how the following would affect the speed of this reaction. In each case, assume all other factors are kept the same.

    i Using 0.05 mol dm^{-3} hydrochloric acid

    ii Using smaller marble chips

    iii Carrying out the reaction at 22 °C

  d Sketch a curve to show how the volume of carbon dioxide changes with time. Use this curve to explain how the rate of reaction changes with time.

24 Zinc reacts with aqueous copper(II) sulfate.

  $Zn(s) + CuSO_4(aq) \longrightarrow ZnSO_4(aq) + Cu(s)$
  $\Delta H = -212 \, kJ \, mol^{-1}$

  a Is this reaction exothermic or endothermic? Give a reason for your answer by referring to the information in the equation.

  b Explain your answer to part **a** using ideas about bond making and bond breaking.

  c Draw a labelled energy profile diagram for this reaction.

25 The heat of solution is the energy change when 1 mol of a substance is dissolved in excess solvent under standard conditions.

  a Describe how you would carry out an experiment to calculate the heat of solution of potassium nitrate in water.

  b When calculating the heat of solution using the relationship

    energy = mass × specific heat capacity
    × temperature change

    what assumptions would you make?

26 Iron(II) sulfate contains can be used to test for oxidising agents. Suggest how iron(II) sulfate can be used to show that potassium manganate(VII) is an oxidising agent.

27 Define the terms:

  a electrode   b cation   c electrolysis.

28 A spoon made from nickel can be electroplated with silver.

  a Draw a labelled diagram to show the apparatus used to electroplate a nickel spoon with silver.

  b Write the half equations for the reactions occurring at i the anode ii the cathode.

  c Give **two** reasons why articles are electroplated.

29 Write equations for the following reactions:

  a The reaction of copper oxide, CuO, with sulfuric acid.

  b The reaction of calcium hydroxide with hydrochloric acid.

  c The reaction of sodium hydrogencarbonate with hydrochloric acid.

Section A Practice exam questions

1 Which of the following best describes a mixture of clay and water?

  a   Solution

  b   Suspension

  c   Colloid

  d   Homogeneous

2 Which of the following is a common use of carbon-14?

  a   To make a nuclear bomb

  b   To generate electricity

  c   To determine the age of animal and plant remains

  d   To provide a power source for heart pacemakers

3 Which of the following is the electron arrangement of the Group II element that will react most vigorously with dilute hydrochloric acid?

  a   2,8,8,2

  b   2

  c   2,8,2

  d   2,2

4 Element X has an atomic number of 7. Which of the following statements is/are true of element X?

    I   Atoms of element X can engage in ionic bonding.

    II   Atoms of element X can engage in metallic bonding.

    III Atoms of element X can engage in covalent bonding.

  a   I only

  b   I and II only

  c   I and III only

  d   I, II and III

5 Which of the following is the best definition of a standard solution?

  a   A solution whose concentration is accurately known

  b   A solution whose concentration is determined through volumetric analysis

  c   A solution obtained following titration

  d   A solution that is added into the burette during a titration

6 Which of the following is the percentage composition by mass of oxygen in copper(II) sulfate?

(A_r: Cu = 64; S = 32; O = 16)

  a   10%

  b   16%

  c   40%

  d   64%

7 Which of the following is **not** used in food preservation?

  a   Sodium nitrite

  b   Sodium chloride

  c   Sodium benzoate

  d   Sodium carbonate

8 When substance Y is added to a solution of acidified potassium manganate(VII), the solution changes from purple to colourless. When substance Y is added to a solution of an iron(II) salt, the solution changes from pale green to yellow.

Which of the following is substance Y?

  a   Acidified $K_2Cr_2O_7$

  b   Acidified H_2O_2

  c   Dilute HNO_3

  d   Conc. H_2SO_4

9 a Name the processes which best describe the following observations:

   i Steven notices that water has collected on the underside of the lid used to cover a pot of hot soup.

   ii Blue crystals of copper(II) sulfate slowly turn water from colourless to blue.

   iii Mothballs decrease in size without becoming liquid. *(3)*

  b What method would you use to separate and retain the following substances?

   i Water from rum

   ii Pure water from tap water

   iii Barium sulfate from sodium chloride solution *(4)*

  c Distinguish between the following pairs:

   i Element and compound

   ii Atom and ion

   iii Cation and anion

   iv Electrons in a potassium atom and electrons in a potassium ion *(8)*

10 Calcium carbonate can undergo a variety of reactions. Examine the flowchart below and use it to answer the questions which follow.

calcium oxide + carbon dioxide

↑ Heat

| Solid calcium carbonate | + X(aq) ⟶ CaCl₂(aq) + A + B
+
H_2SO_4(aq)

↓

Salt + A + B

  a Write a balanced chemical equation with state symbols to represent the heating (thermal decomposition) of calcium carbonate. *(2)*

  b Name products A and B. *(2)*

  c Suggest the name of reactant X. *(1)*

  d i Name the salt formed when calcium carbonate reacts with H_2SO_4(aq). *(1)*

   ii Predict the major observations that will be recorded during this reaction. *(3)*

   iii Explain using your knowledge of salt preparation, why the actual percentage yield of the salt is only 1% while the percentage yield for $CaCl_2$ is 85%. *(5)*

  e Give **one** industrial use of calcium carbonate. *(1)*

11 Redox reactions are used on a large scale in the industrial preparation of substances. One industrial process that occurs because of redox reactions is electrolysis.

  a Define the term redox reaction. *(1)*

  b Below is an ionic equation representing a redox reaction:

$$Cu(s) + 2Ag^+(aq) \longrightarrow Cu^{2+}(aq) + 2Ag(s)$$

   i Identify the reducing agent in this reaction and explain your answer in terms of oxidation numbers. *(3)*

   ii Given that an excess of silver solution was added to 5 g of copper, calculate the mass of silver that would be formed from this reaction.

   (A_r: Cu = 64; Ag = 108) *(3)*

12 a 26.50 cm³ of 0.5 mol dm⁻³ sulfuric acid were needed to neutralise 25.00 cm³ of potassium hydroxide. Use this information to calculate the molar concentration of potassium hydroxide solution. *(5)*

  b i 25 cm³ of 2.64 mol dm⁻³ hydrochloric acid is reacted with 50 cm³ of 1.32 mol dm⁻³ sodium hydroxide solution in a polystyrene cup. Given that the temperature rose from 25 °C to 37 °C, calculate the heat of neutralisation. (Specific heat capacity of water = 4.18 J g⁻¹ °C⁻¹) *(5)*

   ii How does this value compare with the expected value? *(1)*

   iii List **two** assumptions which would have been made during this experiment. *(2)*

12 Organic chemistry: an introduction

12.1 Organic structures

LEARNING OUTCOMES

At the end of this topic you should be able to:

- understand that carbon atoms can form single and double bonds
- describe the structures of organic carbon compounds in terms of branched chains, unbranched chains and rings
- write condensed and displayed formulae for simple organic compounds
- understand the term functional group.

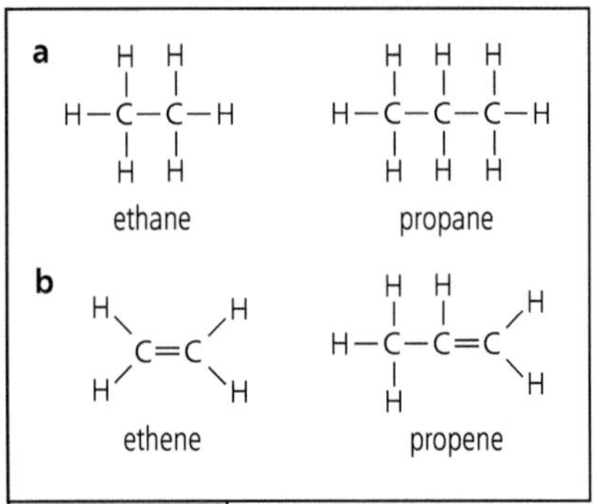

Figure 12.1.1 **a** Ethane and propane are saturated compounds. **b** Ethene and propene are unsaturated compounds.

DID YOU KNOW?

About 200 years ago, a Swedish chemist called Jöns Berzelius divided chemicals into two main groups: organic and inorganic. Most organic compounds burn or char (go black) when heated. Most inorganic chemicals melt or decompose.

Organic compounds

Organic compounds are the basis of all living things. All organic compounds contain carbon atoms. They usually contain hydrogen atoms and may contain other atoms, e.g. oxygen, nitrogen or halogen atoms.

Saturated or unsaturated?

The electronic structure of carbon is 2,4. So a carbon atom can share four electrons with other atoms. For the electronic structure of the carbon compounds ethane and ethene, see Figures 5.2.3 and 5.2.4. Organic compounds may be classified according to the type of bonds they contain.

- Compounds with only single bonds in their molecules are called **saturated compounds**. Examples are ethane and propane (see Figure 12.1.1(a)).
- Compounds containing double or triple bonds (in addition to single bonds) are called **unsaturated compounds**. Examples are ethene and propene (see Figure 12.1.1(b)).

Three different types of structure

We may also classify organic compounds according to their structure as **unbranched chains**, **branched chains** and **ring** structures. Figure 12.1.2 shows the structures of unbranched, branched and ring hydrocarbons. **Hydrocarbons** are compounds containing only carbon and hydrogen atoms.

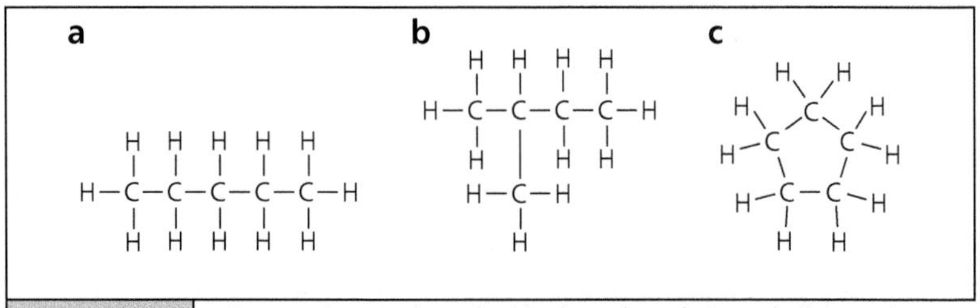

Figure 12.1.2 **a** Pentane is an unbranched hydrocarbon, **b** 2-methylbutane is a branched hydrocarbon, **c** cyclopentane is a ring hydrocarbon.

Different types of formulae

We can represent organic molecules using a variety of different formulae. Using butane, C_4H_{10} and butene, C_4H_8 as examples:

- The **molecular formula** shows the number of each type of atom present in one molecule of the compound:

  butane C_4H_{10} butene C_4H_8

- The **condensed formula** shows the atoms bonded to each carbon atom in a molecule as well as the position of any double or triple bonds:

$$CH_3CH_2CH_2CH_3 \qquad CH_3CH=CHCH_3$$
butane $\qquad\qquad\qquad$ butene

- The **displayed formula** shows all atoms and all bonds present in the molecule.

$$H-\overset{\displaystyle H}{\underset{\displaystyle H}{\overset{|}{\underset{|}{C}}}}-\overset{\displaystyle H}{\underset{\displaystyle H}{\overset{|}{\underset{|}{C}}}}-\overset{\displaystyle H}{\underset{\displaystyle H}{\overset{|}{\underset{|}{C}}}}-\overset{\displaystyle H}{\underset{\displaystyle H}{\overset{|}{\underset{|}{C}}}}-H$$
butane

$$H-\overset{\displaystyle H}{\underset{\displaystyle H}{\overset{|}{\underset{|}{C}}}}-\overset{\displaystyle H}{\overset{|}{C}}=\overset{\displaystyle H}{\overset{|}{C}}-\overset{\displaystyle H}{\underset{\displaystyle H}{\overset{|}{\underset{|}{C}}}}-H$$
butene

The formulae above are only two-dimensional. Ball-and-stick models or space-filling models help to show us the three-dimensional structure of organic molecules (Figure 12.1.3).

Functional groups

Organic compounds are classified according to the **functional group** they contain. A functional group is an atom, a group of atoms or two carbon atoms with a double or triple bond between them that is characteristic of a class of organic compounds. Examples of functional groups in organic compounds are: C=C in alkenes, —OH in alcohols and —COOH in alkanoic acids. Different classes of organic compounds have different functional groups. The chemical properties of organic compounds depend on the properties of the functional group or groups that they contain.

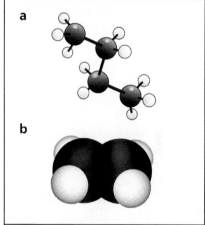

Figure 12.1.3 **a** Ball-and-stick model of butane, **b** space-filling model of ethene

KEY POINTS

1. Saturated organic compounds contain only carbon–carbon single bonds.

2. Unsaturated organic compounds contain one or more double or triple bonds.

3. Organic compounds can exists as unbranched chains, branched chains or rings.

4. A molecular formula shows the number of each type of atom in a molecule.

5. A condensed formula for an organic compound shows the atoms bonded to each carbon atom in a molecule as well as the position of any double or triple bonds.

6. A displayed formula shows all the atoms and bonds in a molecule.

7. A functional group is an atom or group of atoms that is characteristic of a class of organic compounds.

Homologous series: formulae and nomenclature

At the end of this topic you should be able to:

- describe the characteristics of a homologous series
- write the general and molecular formulae for alkanes, alkenes, alcohols and alkanoic acids
- deduce the homologous series given the fully displayed and condensed formulae of compounds
- write fully displayed structures and names of unbranched alkanes, alkenes, alcohols and alkanoic acids.

EXAM TIPS

- An alternative name for alcohols is alkanols. An alternative name for alkanoic acids is carboxylic acids.
- The stems for unbranched alkanes with 7 to 10 carbon atoms are: 7 = hept-, 8 = oct-, 9 = non-, 10 = dec-.
- When drawing the structures of alkenes, remember that carbon forms four bonds around itself. It is a common error to draw too many hydrogen atoms attached to the C atoms joined by a double bond.

Homologous series

A **homologous series** is a group of compounds that all contain the same functional group. The members of the same homologous series:

- can be represented by a **general formula**. For example, each member of the alkane homologous series has the general formula C_nH_{2n+2} where n is the number of carbon atoms.
- have the same functional group
- differ from the members immediately before or after by a CH_2 group
- have similar chemical properties (because they have the same functional group)
- show a gradual change in physical properties as the number of carbon atoms in the compounds increases.

Table 12.2.1 shows some examples of the homologous series you will study.

Note that the functional group for alkanes, alkenes and alkanoic acids must be attached to an alkyl group such as $-CH_3$, $-C_2H_5$, etc. (see 12.3) or a hydrogen atom. The $-OH$ group of an alcohol can only be attached to an alkyl group.

Table 12.2.1 Homologous series

Homologous series	Functional group	General formula	Example
alkane	$-\overset{\displaystyle H}{\underset{\displaystyle H}{C}}-H$	C_nH_{2n+2}	ethane CH_3CH_3
alkene	$\text{\textbackslash}C=C\text{/}$	C_nH_{2n}	ethene $CH_2=CH_2$
alcohol	$-O-H$	$C_nH_{2n+1}OH$	ethanol CH_3CH_2OH
alkanoic acid	$-C\overset{\displaystyle O}{\underset{\displaystyle O-H}{}}$	$C_nH_{2n+1}COOH$	CH_3COOH ethanoic acid

Naming straight chain organic compounds

When naming organic compounds:

- The first part of the name (the stem) depends on the number of carbon atoms present in the longest chain of carbon atoms (see also 12.3), e.g. meth- for one carbon atom, eth- for two carbon atoms and prop- for three carbon atoms.
- The second part of the name (the suffix) usually depends on the functional group:

-ane for alkanes -ene for alkenes

-ol for alcohols -oic acid for alkanoic acids

Alkanes are saturated hydrocarbons which can exist as unbranched chains or branched chains.

Table 12.2.2 Names and structures of the first six alkanes

Stem	**Number of carbon atoms**	**Name and molecular formula**	**Displayed formula**
meth-	1	methane, CH_4	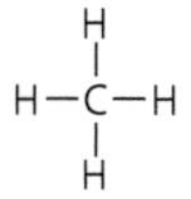
eth-	2	ethane, C_2H_6	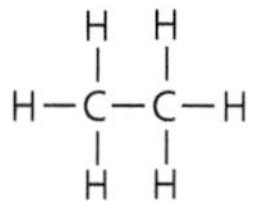
prop-	3	propane, C_3H_8	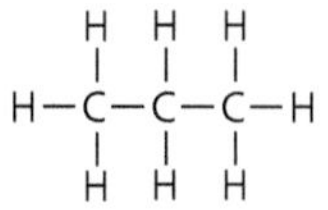
but-	4	butane, C_4H_{10}	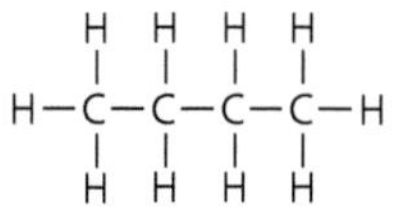
pent-	5	pentane, C_5H_{12}	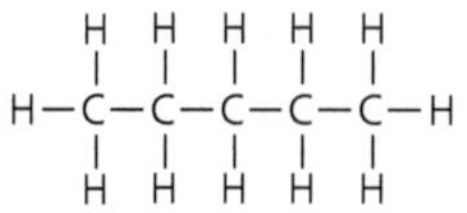
hex-	6	hexane, C_6H_{14}	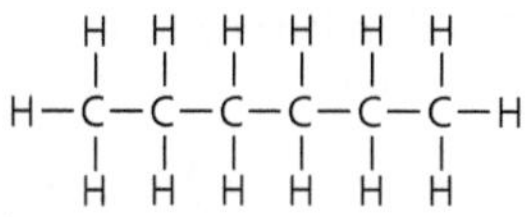

Figure 12.2.1 shows examples of condensed and displayed formulae of some **alkenes**, **alcohols** and **alkanoic acids**.

KEY POINTS

1. Members of the same homologous series have the same functional group and general formula and have similar chemical properties.
2. Successive members in the same homologous series differ from the next by a CH_2 group and show a gradual change in physical properties.
3. Organic compounds are named using a stem showing the number of carbon atoms in the longest unbranched chain.
4. The stem names in organic compounds (the number of carbon atoms are shown in brackets) are meth- (1), eth- (2), prop- (3), but- (4), pent- (5), hex- (6).

DID YOU KNOW?

Over 4 million organic compounds are known. In the past 10 years alone, over 500 000 new organic compounds have been made.

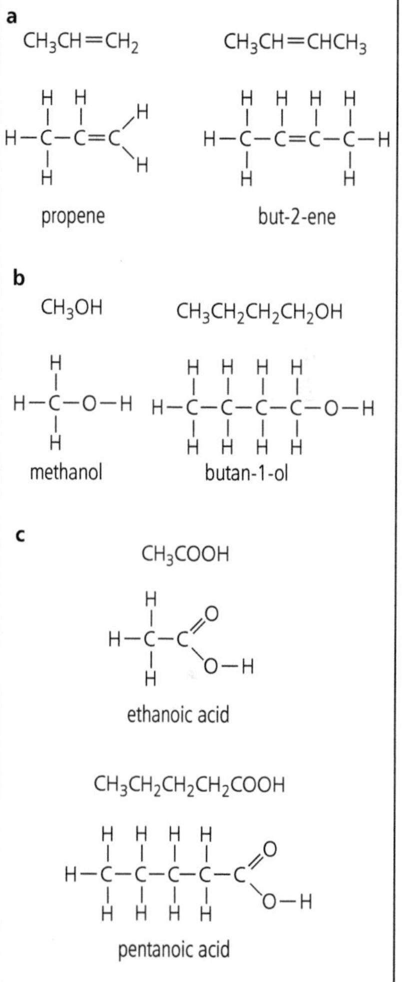
a
CH3CH=CH2
CH3CH=CHCH3
propene
but-2-ene
b
CH3OH
CH3CH2CH2CH2OH
methanol
butan-1-ol
c
CH3COOH
ethanoic acid
CH3CH2CH2CH2COOH
pentanoic acid

Figure 12.2.1 Names and structures of some **a** alkenes, **b** alcohols, **c** alkanoic acids

Isomers and their nomenclature

At the end of this topic you should be able to:

- write fully displayed structures and names of alkenes and branched alkanes
- define structural isomerism
- write the fully displayed structures of isomers given their molecular formulae.

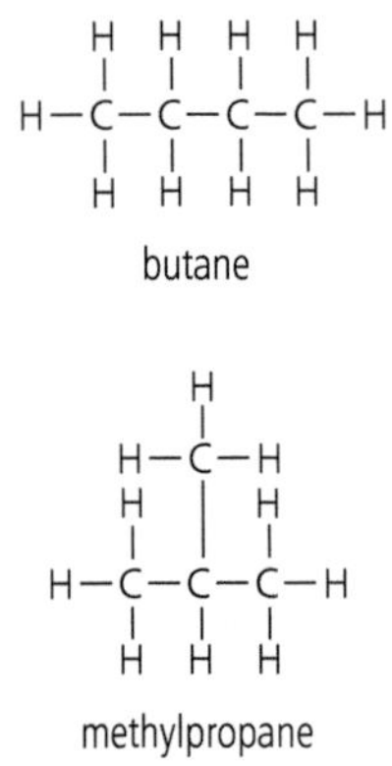

Isomers

Compounds with the same molecular formula but different structural formulae are called **structural isomers**. Two types of structural isomerism are:

- **Chain isomerism**: The structure of the carbon skeleton differs. For example, butane has the same molecular formula as methylpropane, C_4H_{10}, but butane has an unbranched chain whereas methylpropane has a branched chain (Figure 12.3.1).
- **Position isomerism**: The position of the functional group differs. For example, the position of the double bond in pent-1-ene is different from the position in pent-2-ene (Figure 12.3.2(a)).

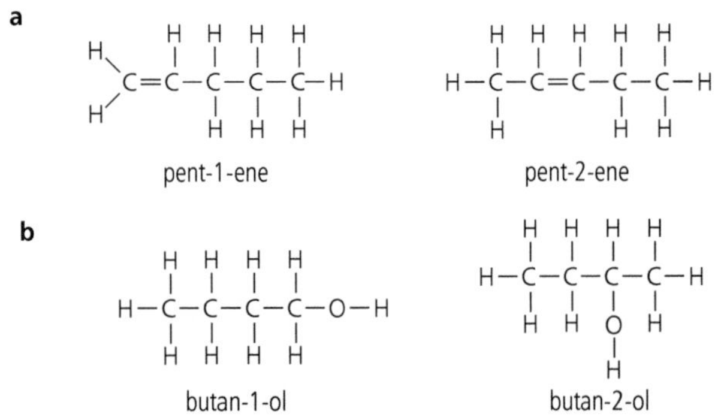

Figure 12.3.1

a

pent-1-ene

pent-2-ene

b

butan-1-ol

butan-2-ol

Figure 12.3.2 Position isomerism: **a** two position isomers of pentene, **b** two position isomers of butanol

Naming branched chain isomers

The chains that come off the side of the longest carbon chain in a branched chain compound are called **alkyl groups**.

- Alkyl groups have the general formula C_nH_{2n+1}
- We name alkyl groups by adding the suffix -yl to the stem name, e.g.

  $-CH_3$ is methyl, $-C_2H_5$ is ethyl, $-C_3H_7$ is propyl, $-C_4H_9$ is butyl.

The procedure for naming a branched chain alkane is:

- Find the longest chain of carbon atoms and name the compound after the number of carbon atoms in this chain. In the example in Figure 12.3.3 the longest chain contains six carbon atoms, so the compound is named after hexane.
- Look for the side chain(s) and name it/them. In this example the side chain is methyl-. So the compound is a methylhexane.
- Look at the position of the alkyl side chain. Number from one end of the longest carbon chain so that the side chain is given the lowest number possible. In Figures 12.3.3 and 12.3.4 the methyl group comes off from the third carbon atom.

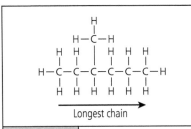

Longest chain

Figure 12.3.3

- Name the compound by including the position of the alkyl group as a number followed by a hyphen. In this case the compound is 3-methylhexane.

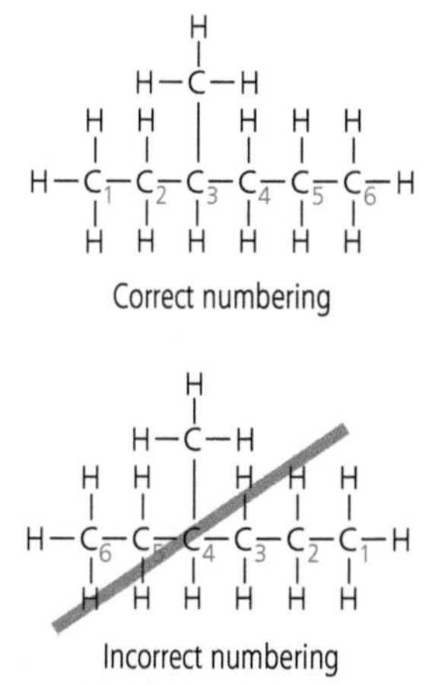

More examples

Figure 12.3.5 shows some more examples of organic compounds for naming.

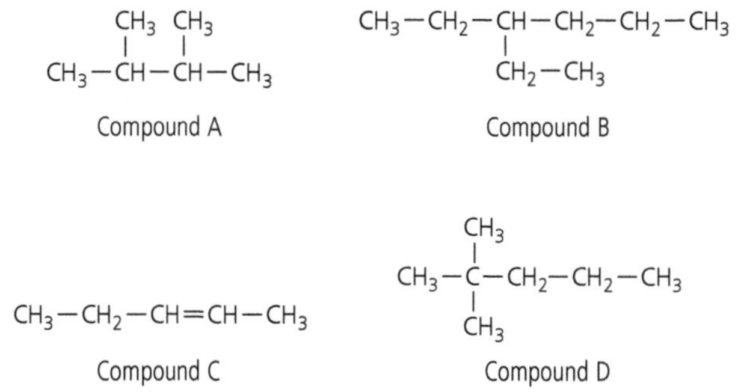

Compound A

Compound B

Compound C

Compound D

Figure 12.3.5

Compound A is 2,3-dimethylbutane. The longest chain has four carbon atoms (butane). Two methyl groups come off at carbon atoms 2 and 3. Note the comma between the 2 and the 3.

Compound B is 3-ethylhexane. The longest chain has six carbon atoms (hexane). An ethyl group comes off from the third carbon atom counting from the left.

Compound C is pent-2-ene. The chain has five carbon atoms and a double bond (pentene). The lowest number that can be given to one of the double-bonded carbon atoms is arrived at when you count from the right. So the name is pent-2-ene and not pent-3-ene. When naming alkenes, the position of the double bond is shown by writing the number between the stem and the suffix.

Compound D is 2,2-dimethylpentane. When there is more than one alkyl group, each is numbered even when it comes off at the same carbon atom.

How many different displayed formulae?

The molecular formula of pentane is C_5H_{12}. By arranging the carbon skeleton in as many different ways as possible, we can draw all the different isomers with the molecular formula C_5H_{12} (Figure 12.3.6).

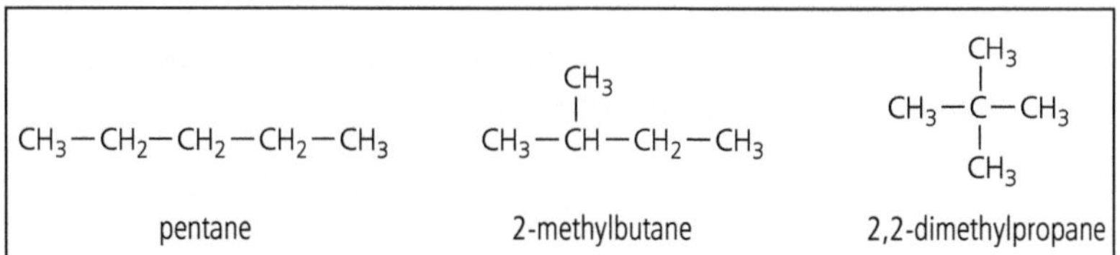

pentane

2-methylbutane

2,2-dimethylpropane

Figure 12.3.6 The compound with the molecular formula C_5H_{12} has three isomers.

Correct numbering

Incorrect numbering

Figure 12.3.4

EXAM TIP

When drawing the structure of branched hydrocarbons, make sure that the longest chain of carbon atoms is drawn horizontally.

KEY POINTS

1 Structural isomers have the same molecular formula but different displayed formulae.

2 In chain isomerism, the structure of the carbon skeleton is different.

3 In position isomerism, the position of the functional group is different.

4 Alkyl groups have the general formula C_nH_{2n+1}

5 Isomers are named taking into consideration the number of carbon atoms in the longest chain and the position and nature of the alkyl side chains.

12.4

Sources of hydrocarbons

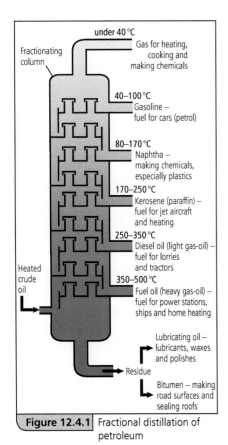

Figure 12.4.1 Fractional distillation of petroleum

Natural gas and petroleum

Petroleum (crude oil) and natural gas are natural sources of hydrocarbons that are found trapped between impervious (non-porous) layers of rock below the Earth's surface. **Natural gas** is mainly methane. It also contains a smaller amount of ethane, propane and butane. **Petroleum** is a thick liquid mixture of unbranched, branched and ring hydrocarbons in which some natural gas is also dissolved.

Fractional distillation of petroleum

Petroleum refining involves removal of impurities, then separation of the hydrocarbon mixture into smaller groups of hydrocarbons called **fractions**. Each fraction consists of a mixture of hydrocarbons having a limited range of molar masses and number of carbon atoms. Fractional distillation is carried out using a fractionating column (Figure 12.4.1).

- The petroleum is heated to 400 °C.
- There is a gradient of temperature in the column, which is hotter at the bottom than at the top.
- Hydrocarbons with very high molar mass do not vaporise and are tapped off at the bottom of the column. Those with lower molar masses undergo fractional distillation (see 2.5).
- As distillation proceeds, the more volatile hydrocarbons in the petroleum, which have a lower molar mass and lower boiling point, move further up the column.
- Less volatile hydrocarbons, with a higher molar mass and higher boiling point, do not move as far up the column.
- As the hydrocarbon vapours move up the column, the ones with lower boiling points move further ahead of those with higher boiling points.
- At particular points in the column, the vapour containing hydrocarbons with a particular range of molar masses and boiling points condenses. These liquid mixtures of hydrocarbons (fractions) are removed from the column.
- The petroleum gases which contain hydrocarbons with 1–4 carbon atoms do not condense at the temperatures within the column. These are removed at the top of the column.

Table 12.4.1 shows some uses of different fractions obtained by the fractional distillation of petroleum.

Table 12.4.1 Uses of petroleum fractions

Fraction	Number of carbon atoms in fraction	Use of fraction
Refinery gas	1–4	Gas for heating and cooking, manufacture of petrochemicals
Gasoline (petrol) and naphtha	4–10	Gasoline for car fuel Naphtha for making chemicals
Kerosene	10–16	Fuel for jet aircraft and heating
Diesel oil	16–20	Fuel for cars, lorries and buses
Fuel oil	20–25	Fuel for power stations, ships and home heating
Lubricating oil	more than 25	Lubricants, waxes and polishes
Bitumen	more than 30	Road surfacing and roofing

Cracking

Some fractions from the distillation of petroleum are more useful than others. We use more gasoline (petrol) than can be supplied by the fractional distillation of petroleum. We use a process called **cracking** to convert fractions containing larger hydrocarbon molecules, which are less useful, into smaller, more useful hydrocarbons. Kerosene and diesel oil are often cracked to make:

• more gasoline (petrol)

• more alkenes, which are useful materials for making other chemicals such as polymers (see 14.2)

• hydrogen.

Cracking is the thermal decomposition of longer-chained alkanes to make shorter-chained alkanes and alkenes.

Thermal cracking

In **thermal cracking**, fractions containing larger alkanes are heated at a high pressure at temperatures above 700 °C. A mixture of smaller alkanes and alkenes is formed. For example:

$$C_8H_{18}(g) \longrightarrow C_5H_{12}(g) + C_3H_6(g)$$
octane   pentane   propene

$$C_{12}H_{26}(g) \longrightarrow C_8H_{18}(g) + C_4H_8(g)$$
dodecane   octane   butene

Thermal cracking produces a relatively high proportion of alkenes.

Catalytic cracking

In **catalytic cracking** the gaseous kerosene or diesel oil fractions are passed through a mixture of silicon(IV) oxide and aluminium oxide at 400–500 °C. The oxide mixture acts as a catalyst. Catalytic cracking produces a relatively high proportion of hydrocarbons for use in gasoline (petrol).

KEY POINTS

1 Natural gas is mainly methane with small amounts of ethane, propane and butane.

2 Petroleum is a natural source of hydrocarbons containing from 1 to over 30 carbon atoms in their molecules.

3 The fractional distillation of petroleum (crude oil) produces fractions with particular uses.

4 A fraction is a mixture of hydrocarbons having a limited range of molar masses and number of carbon atoms.

5 Cracking is the thermal decomposition of larger hydrocarbon molecules to form smaller hydrocarbon molecules and alkenes.

6 Thermal cracking uses high temperature and high pressure.

7 Catalytic cracking uses a temperature of 400–500 °C and a catalyst.

Alkanes

Alkanes: an introduction

Alkanes are saturated hydrocarbons with the general formula C_nH_{2n+2}. The structures of the first four unbranched alkanes are shown in Figure 13.1.1.

methane (CH_4)   ethane (C_2H_6)   propane (C_3H_8)   butane (C_4H_{10})

| **Figure 13.1.1** |

The alkanes are colourless compounds showing a gradual change in physical properties as the number of carbon atoms in the unbranched chain increases. For example, the boiling points increase in a regular way as the number of carbon atoms in the unbranched chain increases (Figure 13.1.2). The first four members of the homologous series are gases at r.t.p. Alkanes with unbranched chains of 5–17 carbon atoms are liquids at r.t.p. Alkanes with unbranched chains of more than 17 carbon atoms are solids at r.t.p.

Combustion of alkanes

In the presence of excess oxygen or air (which contains 21% oxygen), alkanes burn with a clear blue flame, which does not appear sooty (smoky). In the presence of excess air, we say that the alkane undergoes **complete combustion**. The products are carbon dioxide and water. These are oxidation–reduction reactions, in which the carbon and hydrogen are oxidised and the oxygen is reduced. Examples are:

$$CH_4(g) + 2O_2(g) \longrightarrow CO_2(g) + 2H_2O(l)$$

$$2C_4H_{10}(g) + 13O_2(g) \longrightarrow 8CO_2(g) + 10H_2O(l)$$

If oxygen (or air) is not in excess, alkanes undergo **incomplete combustion**. The products of incomplete combustion are carbon monoxide and water. Some carbon may also remain unreacted.

$$2C_3H_8(g) + 7O_2(g) \longrightarrow 6CO(g) + 8H_2O(l)$$

The flame produced from incomplete combustion can be yellow and sooty because of the unreacted carbon particles present.

Reaction of alkanes with halogens

Alkanes do not react with halogens in the dark. If we mix a gaseous halogen with an alkane in the presence of sunlight or ultraviolet (uv) light a reaction takes place. When chlorine reacts with methane, a chlorine atom replaces a hydrogen atom in the methane. This is called **halogenation**.

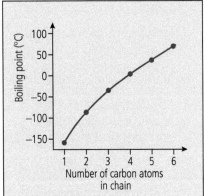

Figure 13.1.2 The boiling points of the unbranched alkanes vary in a regular way.

The chemical structure diagram at the top shows:

$$H-\overset{\displaystyle H}{\underset{\displaystyle H}{C}}-H \;+\; Cl-Cl \;\xrightarrow{\text{uv light}}\; H-\overset{\displaystyle H}{\underset{\displaystyle H}{C}}-Cl \;+\; HCl$$

methane   chloromethane

A reaction such as this, in which one atom or group of atoms replaces another, is called a **substitution reaction**.

In the presence of excess chlorine, the hydrogen atoms are substituted one by one until there are none left.

$$CH_3Cl(g) + Cl_2(g) \xrightarrow{\text{uv light}} CH_2Cl_2(l) + HCl(g)$$
dichloromethane

$$CH_2Cl_2(l) + Cl_2(g) \xrightarrow{\text{uv light}} CHCl_3(l) + HCl(g)$$
trichloromethane

$$CHCl_3(l) + Cl_2(g) \xrightarrow{\text{uv light}} CCl_4(l) + HCl(g)$$
tetrachloromethane

Apart from combustion, the reactions of alkanes are generally substitution reactions.

Uses of alkanes

Alkanes are good fuels because they burn cleanly and release a lot of energy on combustion. Gaseous alkanes such as methane, propane and butane are used as fuels in bottled gas. LPG (liquefied petroleum gas) is used as a fuel in cars. Mixtures of liquid alkanes are used for a variety of fuels (see 12.4).

Liquid alkanes are used as solvents for a variety of organic substances, e.g. in marking pens.

Biogas production

When manure or household waste is left for a time in the absence of air, the organic material it contains begins to decompose (break down). Bacteria and fungi that respire in the absence of air are responsible for this decomposition. They produce gases such as methane, carbon dioxide and hydrogen sulfide. The gaseous mixture, which is largely methane, can be used as a fuel called **biogas**. Some farmers use the biogas from animal and plant waste for heating or to produce electricity.

Figure 13.1.3 Biogas digesters turn animal and plant waste into methane gas.

Alkenes

At the end of this topic you should be able to:

• describe the reactions of alkenes in terms of burning, reaction with halogens, reaction with acidified potassium manganate(VII) and hydrogen

• describe the reactions of alkenes as mainly addition reactions

• describe tests to distinguish between alkanes and alkenes

• relate the properties of alkenes to their uses as starting materials for synthesis including the synthesis of polymers.

EXAM TIP

You should not use the sootiness of the flame as a positive test to distinguish saturated from unsaturated compounds. It only gives a rough guide. You should use the test using bromine water or potassium manganate(VII). See opposite for details.

Structure of alkenes

Alkenes are unsaturated hydrocarbons with the general formula C_nH_{2n}. The structures of some alkenes are shown in Figure 13.2.1.

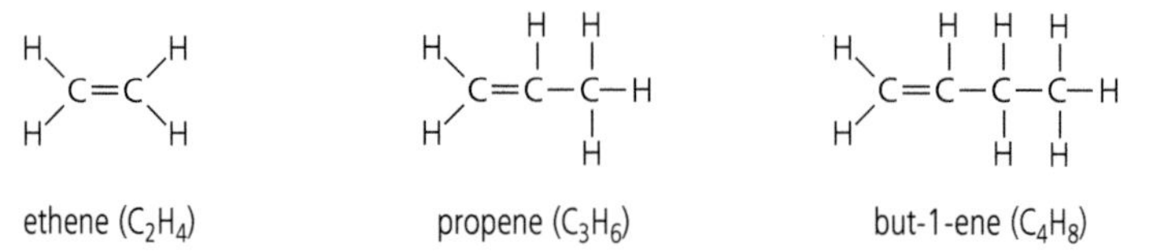

ethene (C_2H_4)   propene (C_3H_6)   but-1-ene (C_4H_8)

Figure 13.2.1

Combustion of alkenes

The complete combustion of an alkene in oxygen produces carbon dioxide and water. The reaction produces a large amount of energy. For example:

$$C_4H_8(g) + 6O_2(g) \longrightarrow 4CO_2(g) + 4H_2O(l)$$

Alkenes have a higher ratio of carbon to hydrogen than alkanes. When they burn in air, in addition to carbon dioxide and water, carbon monoxide and unreacted carbon particles are also formed. The carbon particles make the flame yellow and sooty (blackish). We can use the colour of the flame as a rough guide for distinguishing between alkanes and alkenes. When burnt in air:

• alkanes burn with a clean blue flame
• alkenes burn with a yellow sooty flame.

Addition reactions of alkenes

Most of the reactions of alkenes are **addition reactions**. In an addition reaction, a single product is formed from two (or more) reactant molecules and no other product is made.

Reaction with halogens

Alkenes react with halogens to form dihaloalkanes. The halogen adds across the double bond and no other product is formed. For example, bromine reacts with ethene to form 1,2-dibromoethane:

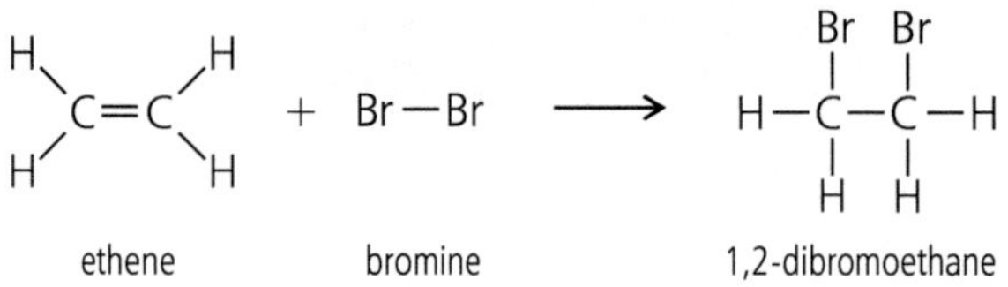

ethene   bromine   1,2-dibromoethane

Bromine is red-brown in colour but 1,2-dibromoethane is colourless. So when we add a drop of bromine to excess alkene, the bromine gets decolourised. This reaction is the basis of the bromine water test for distinguishing between alkanes and alkenes. It is therefore also used to distinguish between C—C bonds in saturated compounds and C=C bonds in unsaturated compounds.

Liquid bromine is too hazardous for use in schools. So we use bromine water instead. This is a solution of bromine in water. Bromine water is red-brown when concentrated and orange when dilute.

- When bromine water is added to an alkane in the dark no reaction occurs. The bromine water remains red-brown (or orange).
- When bromine water is added to an alkene in the dark there is a reaction. The bromine water is decolourised (goes colourless).

Reaction with hydrogen

The addition of hydrogen to an alkene is an example of a **hydrogenation** reaction. Alkanes are formed. Hydrogen gas is passed through the alkene at 150 °C, in the presence of a nickel catalyst. For example:

$$CH_3CH=CH_2 + H_2 \xrightarrow{\text{Ni, 150 °C}} CH_3CH_2CH_3$$
propene   propane

Hydrogenation reactions are used to change vegetable oils into margarine.

Hydration of alkenes

The addition of steam to alkenes is also an addition reaction. It is used in the industrial preparation of alcohols (see 13.3).

Oxidation of alkenes with potassium manganate(VII)

A purple solution of cold acidified potassium manganate(VII) is decolourised by alkenes. This is an oxidation–reduction reaction in which potassium manganate(VII) is the oxidising agent. It can be used as a test to distinguish alkenes from alkanes.

- Alkanes are unaffected by cold dilute acidified potassium manganate(VII).
- Alkenes decolourise a solution of cold acidified potassium manganate. The [O] in the equation represents the oxygen arising from the potassium manganate(VII).

$$CH_2=CH_2 + [O] + H_2O \longrightarrow HO–CH_2–CH_2–OH$$
ethene   ethane-1,2-diol

Uses of alkenes

Alkenes are important chemicals in chemical synthesis. They are used to make:

- alcohols, especially ethanol (see 13.3)
- plastics, e.g. poly(ethene) from ethene, poly(propene) from propene and poly(chloroethene) (PVC) from chloroethene, $CH_2=CHCl$.

Alcohols

At the end of this topic you should be able to:

• relate the properties of alcohols to their functional group in terms of solubility in water and volatility

• describe the hydration of alkenes to produce alcohols

• describe the reactions of ethanol in terms of reaction with sodium, dehydration and oxidation

• describe the principles of the breathalyser test for ethanol.

DID YOU KNOW?

Many organic reactions take place in the absence of water. Because of this, it is general practice not to put state symbols in equations involving organic reactions, especially when an organic reactant is also a solvent.

EXAM TIP

It is important that you know the conditions (temperature, pressure and name of catalyst) for the organic reactions that you learn. These are generally written above the arrow in the equation.

Structure of alcohols

Alcohols contain the —OH functional group (hydroxyl group) and have the general formula $C_nH_{2n+1}OH$. Figure 13.3.1 shows the structures of three alcohols.

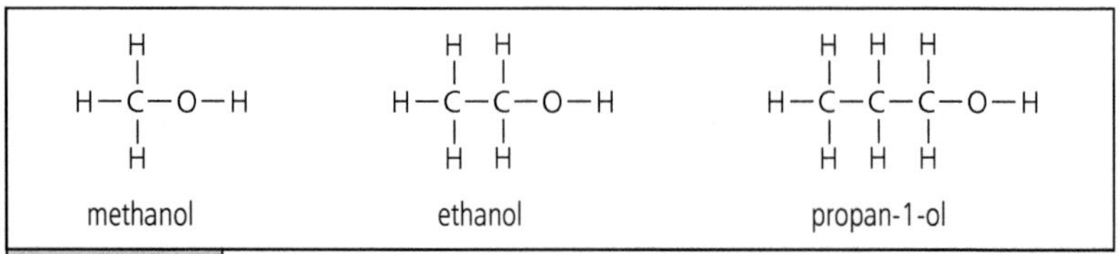

methanol   ethanol   propan-1-ol

Figure 13.3.1

Some physical properties of alcohols

• Alcohols evaporate much less easily than the corresponding alkanes with the same number of carbon atoms. We say they are less **volatile**. Volatility is related to the boiling point of a compound – the lower the volatility, the higher the boiling point. Alcohols evaporate less easily than the corresponding alkanes because the presence of the —OH group causes them to be polar (see 5.6). There is a stronger force of attraction between alcohol molecules than those in the corresponding alkane. So alcohols are liquids or solids at r.t.p.

• Alkanes are insoluble in water. Alcohols are more soluble than the corresponding alkanes with the same number of carbon atoms. This is because the polar —OH group is present in alcohols. There is a much stronger force of attraction between the alcohol and water molecules than between the corresponding alkane and water molecules. The alcohols get less soluble in water as the length of their carbon chain increases. Methanol and ethanol are very soluble in water.

Manufacture of alcohols by hydration

Alcohols are manufactured by the reaction of steam with a gaseous alkene. This is an addition reaction. The reaction is also called a **hydration reaction** because it involves the addition of water (Figure 13.3.2). The conditions for the reaction are:

• a catalyst of concentrated phosphoric acid

• a temperature of 330 °C

• a pressure of 60–70 atmospheres.

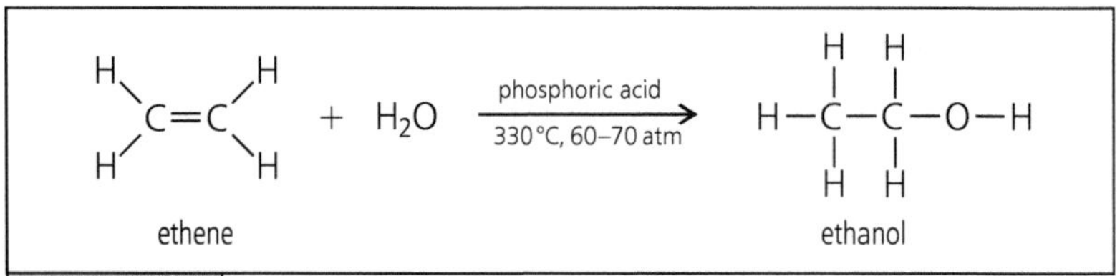

ethene   phosphoric acid / 330 °C, 60–70 atm   ethanol

Figure 13.3.2 The addition reaction between ethene and steam

Reaction of alcohols

Combustion

Many alcohols burn in excess air with a clean blue flame. Carbon dioxide and water are formed. The equation below represents the combustion of ethanol.

$$CH_3CH_2OH + 3O_2 \longrightarrow 2CO_2 + 3H_2O$$

Reaction with sodium

Ethanol reacts with sodium to form sodium ethoxide and hydrogen. The reaction is similar to that between sodium and water.

$$2CH_3CH_2OH + 2Na \longrightarrow 2CH_3CH_2ONa + H_2$$
$$\text{ethanol} \qquad\qquad \text{sodium ethoxide}$$

Dehydration

When ethanol is mixed with concentrated sulfuric acid and heated to 170 °C, ethene is formed. This reaction is called a **dehydration reaction** because water is removed.

$$CH_3CH_2OH \xrightarrow{\text{conc. } H_2SO_4,\ 170\,°C} CH_2{=}CH_2 + H_2O$$
$$\text{ethanol} \qquad\qquad\qquad \text{ethene}$$

The concentrated sulfuric acid acts as a dehydrating agent.

Oxidation

Alcohols are oxidised to alkanoic acids by heating with the oxidising agent potassium manganate(VII). An alternative oxidising agent is potassium dichromate(VI). In both cases a few drops of concentrated sulfuric acid are needed for the best conditions for oxidation. The heating is done under reflux. This involves heating the reactants in the apparatus shown in Figure 13.3.3. Having the condenser in the upright position prevents the volatile alcohol from escaping.

The oxidation of ethanol to ethanoic acid using potassium dichromate(VI), $K_2Cr_2O_7$, can be represented by the equation:

$$CH_3CH_2OH + 2[O] \xrightarrow{H^+/\ K_2Cr_2O_7} CH_3COOH + H_2O$$

In this reaction, the orange dichromate(VI) ions are converted to green Cr^{3+} ions by the reducing agent, ethanol.

The breathalyser test

Acidified potassium dichromate(VI) was used in early breathalysers to test the alcohol content of a driver's breath. The driver blows into a bag containing acidified potassium dichromate(VI), which is orange in colour. If the driver's breath contains ethanol vapour, the potassium dichromate will start to turn green as Cr^{3+} ions are formed. The degree to which the potassium dichromate turns green can be used to estimate the approximate concentration of alcohol in the breath. Modern breathalysers use electronic methods for detecting ethanol concentration.

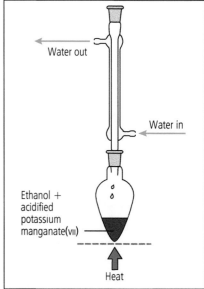

Figure 13.3.3 Reflux apparatus for preparing ethanoic acid from ethanol

KEY POINTS

1 Alcohols are less volatile and more soluble in water than alkanes with the same number of carbon atoms.

2 Ethanol is manufactured by the hydration of ethene using a catalyst of phosphoric acid.

3 Alcohols undergo complete combustion to carbon dioxide and water.

4 Ethanol reacts with sodium to form sodium ethoxide and hydrogen.

5 Ethanol is dehydrated by heating with concentrated sulfuric acid.

6 Ethanol is oxidised to ethanoic acid by refluxing with acidified potassium manganate(VII).

7 Early breathalysers worked by observing the colour change when acidified potassium dichromate is reduced by ethanol vapour.

Fermentation

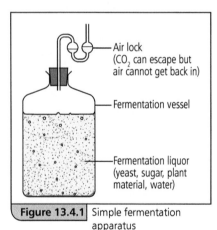

Figure 13.4.1 Simple fermentation apparatus

Air lock (CO₂ can escape but air cannot get back in)

Fermentation vessel

Fermentation liquor (yeast, sugar, plant material, water)

The fermentation of carbohydrates

Bacteria and yeasts produce enzymes which catalyse **fermentation** reactions in organic materials, especially in plant materials. Fermentation is the breakdown of organic materials by microorganisms with effervescence (bubbles) and the release of heat energy. Most vegetable material can be fermented but the most commonly used materials are carbohydrates such as glucose, sucrose and starch. Fermentation is used to make alcoholic drinks. The main alcohol in these drinks is ethanol. The overall reaction for the fermentation of glucose is:

$$C_6H_{12}O_6 \xrightarrow{\text{enzymes in yeast}} 2C_2H_5OH + 2CO_2$$
glucose ethanol carbon dioxide

The conditions needed for fermentation are the following:

- Temperatures of between about 15 °C and 35 °C. Too low a temperature will slow down the rate of the enzyme-catalysed reactions too much. Too high a temperature will denature the enzymes (see 10.4).
- Absence of oxygen. The yeasts that are responsible for alcoholic fermentation are anaerobic. This means that they respire in the absence of oxygen. If oxygen is allowed into the mixture, bacteria may grow and spoil the alcoholic fermentation by producing acids that have a bad taste.
- Reaction mixture with a pH value near pH 7. Too acidic or alkaline pH values would slow down the rate of reaction of the enzymes.
- Presence of water. Yeast is a living organism, so water is needed for it to survive and grow.

Figure 13.4.1 shows the apparatus that can be used to ferment small quantities of plant material.

Winemaking

The yeasts that cause alcoholic fermentation are naturally present on the surface of many plants. Wine is made from grapes by:

- crushing the grapes (which contain natural yeast on their surface). If the yeast content of the grapes is low, particular strains of yeast are added.
- putting the crushed grapes into a vat (wooden or stainless steel) and allowing fermentation to take place using the natural sugars in the grape.
- drawing off the juice from the grape pulp.
- fermenting the juice in wooden or stainless steel vats so that excess sugar is removed. When the wine is ready, it is bottled.

The manufacture of rum

There is a limit to the concentration of alcohol that can be produced by fermentation. When the alcohol content rises above 15% by volume, it kills the yeast. Spirits such as rum are made by distilling the fermentation mixture when the alcohol reaches a suitable concentration. Rum is made by fermenting molasses, a product of sugar refining (see 2.6). The process is carried out as follows:

- The molasses is diluted with water so that the sugar content is about 15% and yeast is added to the mixture.
- The yeast ferments the molasses to ethanol and carbon dioxide. A variety of other reactions also occur, which give particular flavours to the rum.
- After 48 hours of fermentation, the fermentation liquid is distilled. This can either take place in a pot still or in a column still.

  - In a pot still, heat is applied directly and the alcohol and aroma compounds giving the characteristic flavours evaporate and are then condensed. This is an example of simple distillation.
  - In a column still, the column is filled with materials that give a large surface area for condensation. The rising vapour, which is higher in ethanol content than the fermentation mixture, condenses in the higher levels of the column which are cooler. The vapours are higher in alcoholic content the higher up the still they reach. This is an example of fractional distillation. The distillate from this fractional distillation contains 96% ethanol. This is diluted with water and put in oak barrels to age.

- Ageing in oak gives particular flavours to the rum and makes it taste smoother.
- After between 1 year and 20 years, depending on the quality of rum required, liquid from different barrels can be blended to make particular brands of rum.

Ethanol from fermentation

Making ethanol for industrial use by fermentation has some advantages and disadvantages compared with making ethanol by hydration of ethene.

- Fermentation requires distillation and the ethanol produced by distillation still contains some water. The ethanol produced by hydration is relatively pure.
- For fermentation, the rate of reaction is slow. For hydration, the rate of reaction is fast.
- Fermentation needs a lot of very large tanks and can only be made in batches. Hydration enables ethanol to be made continuously.
- Fermentation is a simple method and uses renewable resources. Hydration is relatively complex, and the high temperature, high pressure and catalyst are expensive. Hydration uses non-renewable resources (petroleum fractions).

Figure 13.4.2 Rum is aged in oak casks.

KEY POINTS

1 Fermentation of glucose produces carbon dioxide and ethanol as products.

2 The conditions for fermentation are yeast, temperature between 15 °C and 35 °C and absence of air.

3 Wine is made by fermentation of grapes.

4 Rum is made by fermentation of molasses.

5 The fermented liquor from rum is distilled by simple distillation or fractional distillation to increase the ethanol content.

6 Making ethanol for industrial use by fermentation has some advantages and some disadvantages compared with making it by hydration.

Alkanoic acids

At the end of this topic you should be able to:

- describe the physical properties of alkanoic acids in terms of volatility and solubility
- describe the reactions of alkanoic acids with metals, metal oxides, metal hydroxides and carbonates.

EXAM TIP

When writing formulae for alkanoic acids, remember to count the carbon atom in the —COOH group. For example, $CH_3CH_2CH_2COOH$ is butanoic acid and not propanoic acid.

Structure of alkanoic acids

Alkanoic acids (**carboxylic acids**) contain the —COOH functional group (carboxylic acid group) and have the general formula $C_nH_{2n+1}COOH$. The structures of three alkanoic acids are shown in Figure 13.5.1.

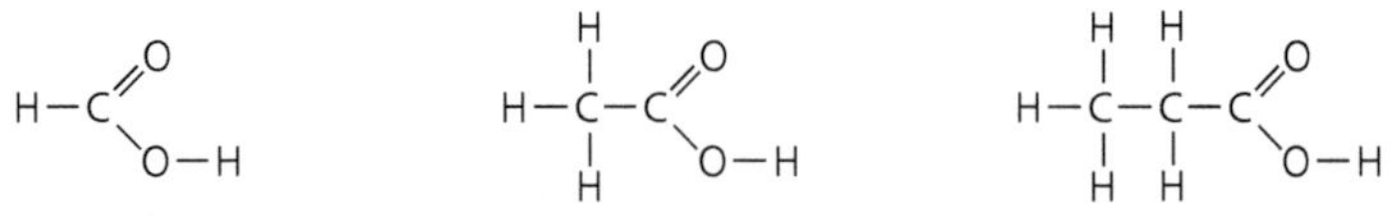

methanoic acid (HCOOH) ethanoic acid (CH_3COOH) propanoic acid (C_2H_5COOH)

Figure 13.5.1

Some physical properties of alkanoic acids

- Alkanoic acids are less volatile than the corresponding alkanes with the same number of carbon atoms. The presence of the —COOH group causes them to be polar (see 5.6). There is a stronger force of attraction between alkanoic acid molecules than those in the corresponding alkane. So alkanoic acids are liquids or solids at r.t.p.
- Alkanoic acids are more soluble than the corresponding alkanes with the same number of carbon atoms. This is because of the presence of the polar —COOH group. There is a much stronger force of attraction between the alkanoic acid and water molecules than between the corresponding alkane and water molecules. The alkanoic acids get less soluble in water as the length of their carbon chain increases. Methanoic acid and ethanoic acid are very soluble in water.

Reactions of alkanoic acids

Reaction with metals

Aqueous solutions of alkanoic acids react with metals to form a salt and hydrogen gas. For example:

$$2HCOOH(aq) + 2Na(s) \longrightarrow 2HCOONa(aq) + H_2(g)$$
methanoic acid   sodium methanoate

$$2CH_3COOH(aq) + Mg(s) \longrightarrow (CH_3COO)_2Mg(aq) + H_2(g)$$
ethanoic acid   magnesium ethanoate

The alkanoic acids are weak acids (see 7.2). The compounds formed are called alkanoates. They are salts of alkanoic acids and are ionic compounds.

Reaction with metal oxides

Aqueous solutions of alkanoic acids react with many metal oxides. A salt and water are formed. This is a simple acid–base reaction. For example:

$$MgO(s) + 2C_3H_7COOH(aq) \longrightarrow (C_3H_7COO)_2Mg(aq) + H_2O(l)$$

butanoic acid   magnesium butanoate

Reaction with hydroxides

Aqueous solutions of alkanoic acids react with metal hydroxides. A salt and water are formed. This is a neutralisation reaction. For example:

$$NaOH(aq) + CH_3COOH(aq) \longrightarrow CH_3COONa(aq) + H_2O(l)$$

ethanoic acid   sodium ethanoate

The weak alkali ammonia reacts in a similar way:

$$NH_3(aq) + CH_3COOH(aq) \longrightarrow CH_3COONH_4(aq)$$

ammonia   ammonium ethanoate

Reaction with carbonates

Aqueous solutions of alkanoic acids react with carbonates. A salt, water and carbon dioxide are formed. For example:

$$Na_2CO_3(s) + 2CH_3COOH(aq) \longrightarrow 2CH_3COONa(aq) + H_2O(l) + CO_2(g)$$

ethanoic acid   sodium ethanoate

Reaction with alcohols

In the presence of an acid catalyst, alkanoic acids react with alcohols on heating to produce compounds called **esters**. Water is also formed. For example:

$$CH_3COOH + C_2H_5OH \underset{}{\overset{H^+}{\rightleftharpoons}} CH_3COOC_2H_5 + H_2O$$

ethanoic acid ethanol   ethyl ethanoate

For more details about this reaction see 13.6.

Figure 13.5.2 The sting of fire ants contains methanoic acid.

KEY POINTS

1. Alkanoic acids contain the —COOH functional group.

2. Alkanoic acids are less volatile and more soluble in water than the corresponding alkanes with the same number of carbon atoms.

3. Alkanoic acids react with reactive metals to form metal salts and hydrogen.

4. Alkanoic acids react with some metal oxides to form metal salts and water.

5. Alkanoic acids are neutralised by alkalis to form a salt and water.

6. Alkanoic acids react with carbonates to form a salt, water and carbon dioxide.

7. Alkanoic acids react with alcohols in the presence of an acid catalyst to form esters.

EXAM TIPS

- The reactions of alkanoic acids are very similar to those of mineral acids. When writing the formulae of the salts formed, remember that the RCOO part should be put in brackets if the metal forms an ion with a 2+ charge.
- You should be aware that many chemistry textbooks call alkanoic acids carboxylic acids.

Esters

At the end of this topic you should be able to:

• describe the functional group present in esters

• describe the formation of esters from alcohols and alkanoic acids

• describe the hydrolysis of esters.

Esters are used in flavourings and perfumes. For example, ethyl methanoate is used in raspberry flavourings and 3-methylbutyl ethanoate is used in pear flavourings.

Figure 13.6.3 The smell of many fruits is due to particular types of esters.

The structure of esters

The functional group in esters is:

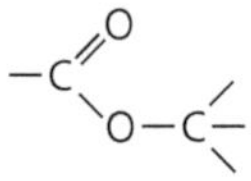

The groups required to complete each bond shown in the diagram above can be either hydrogen or an alkyl group. Some examples of esters are shown in Figure 13.6.1.

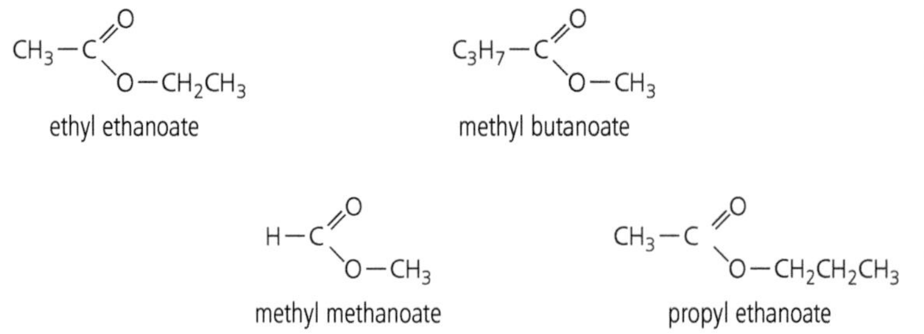

$$CH_3-C \overset{O}{\underset{O-CH_2CH_3}{}}$$
ethyl ethanoate

$$C_3H_7-C \overset{O}{\underset{O-CH_3}{}}$$
methyl butanoate

$$H-C \overset{O}{\underset{O-CH_3}{}}$$
methyl methanoate

$$CH_3-C \overset{O}{\underset{O-CH_2CH_2CH_3}{}}$$
propyl ethanoate

Figure 13.6.1

Esters are named after the acid from which they are made. So the '-oate' part of the name comes last and the name of the alcohol prefix comes first. For example:

• $C_3H_7COOC_2H_5$ is ethyl butanoate

• $HCOOC_3H_7$ is propyl methanoate.

Formation of esters

Esters are synthesised by warming an alcohol with an alkanoic acid. This is called **esterification**. An acid catalyst, usually concentrated sulfuric acid is used. After warming, the reaction mixture is poured into a dilute solution of sodium carbonate, which reacts with any excess acid (Figure 13.6.2). The typical sweet smell of the ester is then made obvious.

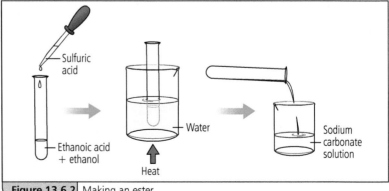

Figure 13.6.2 Making an ester

Using the reaction of ethanoic acid with ethanol as an example:

$$CH_3COOH + C_2H_5OH \underset{}{\overset{H^+, \text{ heat}}{\rightleftharpoons}} CH_3COOC_2H_5 + H_2O$$

ethanoic acid   ethanol   ethyl ethanoate

When the ethanoic acid reacts with the alcohol, water is removed. This type of reaction is an example of a **condensation reaction**. In a condensation reaction, two molecules join together with the elimination (removal) of a small molecule.

$$CH_3C\overset{\displaystyle O}{\underset{\boxed{O-H}}{\diagup}} + \boxed{H}-O-C_2H_5 \rightleftharpoons CH_3C\overset{\displaystyle O}{\underset{O-C_2H_5}{\diagup}} + \boxed{H-O-H}$$

Hydrolysis of esters

Hydrolysis is the breakdown of a compound by water. Hydrolysis is speeded up by reacting the compound with either an acid or an alkali (see Figure 13.6.4).

Acid hydrolysis

- The ester is heated under reflux with a strong acid, e.g. sulfuric acid.
- The reaction is reversible. So the ester is not completely hydrolysed.
- An alkanoic acid and an alcohol are formed. For example:

$$CH_3COOCH_3 + H_2O \underset{}{\overset{H^+, \text{ reflux}}{\rightleftharpoons}} CH_3COOH + CH_3OH$$

methyl ethanoate   ethanoic acid   methanol

Alkaline hydrolysis

- The ester is heated under reflux with a strong base, e.g. aqueous sodium hydroxide.
- The reaction is not reversible. So the ester is completely hydrolysed.
- An alcohol and the salt of an alkanoic acid are formed. For example:

$$CH_3COOCH_3 + NaOH \overset{\text{reflux}}{\longrightarrow} CH_3COONa + CH_3OH$$

methyl ethanoate   sodium ethanoate   methanol

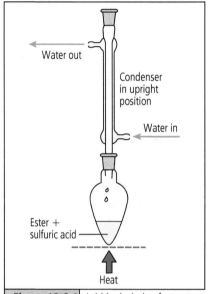

Figure 13.6.4 Acid hydrolysis of an ester

KEY POINTS

1 The functional group present in esters is

$$-C\overset{\displaystyle O}{\underset{O-C}{\diagup}}$$

2 Esters are formed by a condensation reaction between an alcohol and an alkanoic acid by heating with a sulfuric acid catalyst.

3 A condensation reaction is a reaction in which two molecules join together with the elimination (removal) of a small molecule.

4 Hydrolysis is the breakdown of a compound using water.

5 Acid hydrolysis of an ester produces an alkanoic acid and an alcohol. The reaction does not go to completion.

6 Alkaline hydrolysis of an ester produces an alcohol and the salt of an alkanoic acid.

14 Large organic molecules

14.1 Soaps

$$C_{15}H_{31}COOCH_2$$
$$C_{15}H_{31}COOCH$$
$$C_{15}H_{31}COOCH_2$$

Figure 14.1.2 This fat has three ester links.

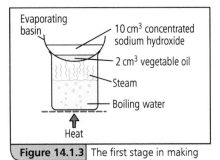

Figure 14.1.3 The first stage in making soap

Natural esters

Both animal fats and plant oils have ester links in them. Fats can be made from the esterification of glycerol (which contains —OH groups) with long-chain alkanoic acids, e.g. $C_{15}H_{31}COOH$. Figure 14.1.1 shows the formula for both glycerol and a long-chain alkanoic acid. The zig-zag line represents the carbon chain (alkyl group) of the alkanoic acid.

```
a                          b
CH₂—OH
|
CH—OH         ⌇⌇⌇⌇⌇⌇—COOH
|                         ‖
CH₂—OH                    O
```

Figure 14.1.1 **a** The formula of glycerol, **b** the simplified formula for a long-chain alkanoic acid

Figure 14.1.2 shows the formula for a fat.

Making soap

Soaps are sodium or potassium salts of long-chain carboxylic acids. Fats and oils can be hydrolysed by sodium hydroxide to form soaps. This process is called **saponification**. The method used in the school laboratory is:

1 Heat a fat or oil with concentrated sodium hydroxide in steam (from a steam bath) for 15 minutes (see Figure 14.1.3).

2 Add concentrated sodium chloride solution to the mixture.

3 Stir and heat for a further 5 minutes.

4 Let the mixture cool. The soap forms on the surface of the mixture.

5 Skim off the soap from the surface of the mixture.

Figure 14.1.4 shows the equation for the saponification of the fat, glyceryl stearate by sodium hydroxide.

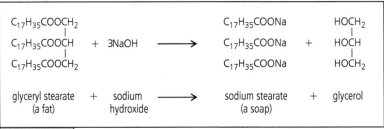

Figure 14.1.4 Soaps are formed by the hydrolysis of fats (or oils).

Soapless detergents

A **detergent** is a substance that removes stains and dirt from materials. **Soapless detergents** differ from soaps in the nature of the group at the 'head end' of the molecule (see Figure 14.1.5).

a

$COO^- Na^+$

b

Hydrocarbon 'tail'   Ionic 'head'

Figure 14.1.5 **a** A soapy detergent (soap), **b** a soapless detergent, which has a sulfonate 'head end'

Water softening

Soft water contains hardly any dissolved calcium or magnesium salts. Detergents form lather (foam) when they are shaken with soft water. In some places the water is 'hard' because it contains dissolved calcium and magnesium salts (see 17.2). **Hard water** does not lather well with soap. It forms a scum of insoluble calcium or magnesium salts.

$$2C_{17}H_{35}COONa(aq) + Ca^{2+}(aq) \longrightarrow (C_{17}H_{35}COO)_2Ca(s) + 2Na^+(aq)$$

soap   calcium ions   soap scum
                in hard water

Soapless detergents make a better lather in hard water than soaps because the calcium or magnesium salts formed are soluble. So they do not form a scum.

The environmental impact of detergents

Most detergents are harmful to the environment.

- Many detergents, both soapy and soapless, cannot be decomposed in the environment. They are non-biodegradable. Soapless detergents produce foam and soaps produce scum. Both foam and scum reduce the amount of oxygen dissolving in water and so lead to the death of aquatic organisms.
- Detergents destroy the oily layer on the surface of fish, which protects them from bacteria and parasites. So more fish get diseases and die.
- Low concentrations of detergent kill fish eggs and decrease their ability to breed.
- Phosphates are added to soapless detergents to improve their cleaning action. Phosphates can cause eutrophication (see 16.4).
- The foam produced by detergents can reduce the effective treatment of sewage in sewage treatment works.

KEY POINTS

1 Soaps are sodium or potassium salts of long-chain alkanoic acids.

2 Soap is prepared by the hydrolysis of fats or oils with concentrated sodium hydroxide solution.

3 The hydrolysis of fats or oils to make a soap is called saponification.

4 When shaken with soft water, detergents cause lather to form.

5 Hard water contains dissolved calcium and magnesium salts.

6 Soaps form a scum when shaken with hard water but soapless detergents do not.

7 Detergents can cause the death of fish by reducing the amount of oxygen in the water and by destroying the oily layer on the surface of fish.

Polymers

At the end of this topic you should be able to:

- define the term polymer
- distinguish between addition and condensation polymers
- describe the polymerisation reactions involved in the formation of polyalkenes
- state a use of a named polyalkene.

DID YOU KNOW?

Poly(ethene) was discovered by chance by a German chemist, Hans von Pechmann, in 1898. He was heating a chemical called diazomethane and noticed that a white, waxy substance was formed in addition to other products. It was suggested that the waxy substance contained long hydrocarbon chains. It was called polymethylene. It was not until 1933, however, that an industrial method for the production of poly(ethene) was discovered, again by chance!

EXAM TIP

When writing the formula for an addition polymer don't forget that the double bond changes to a single bond and remember to draw in the 'continuation bonds'.

Macromolecules

Macromolecules are very large molecules made up of repeating units. Carbon in the form of diamond is a macromolecule made up of repeating units of carbon atoms arranged in tetrahedra (see 5.5). Plastics, proteins and starch are also macromolecules.

Polymers and polymerisation

Polymers are macromolecules made up by linking at least 50 small molecules called **monomers**. Figure 14.2.1 shows the formation of the polymer poly(ethene) from its monomers.

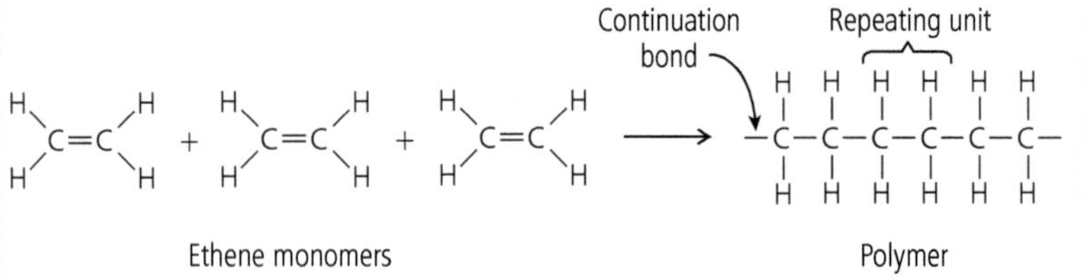

Figure 14.2.1 Ethene monomers bond together to form the polymer poly(ethene).

- The repeating units in polymers are connected by covalent bonds.
- The monomers are the small molecules that combine together to form the polymer, either with or without the elimination of a small molecule.
- The conversion of monomers to polymers is called **polymerisation**.

There are two types of polymerisation:

Addition polymerisation occurs when monomers containing a $C=C$ double bond combine to form the polymer and no other compound is formed.

Condensation polymerisation occurs when monomers are linked to form the polymer and a small molecule is eliminated (see 14.3).

Addition polymers

For addition polymerisation to occur, one of the bonds in the $C=C$ double bond of each alkene monomer breaks and forms a bond with an adjacent monomer. The polymer formed has only single bonds. When the monomers are alkenes, the polymer is called a **poly(alkene)**. Poly(alkenes) can be thought of as very long-chain alkanes. Other polymers are based on alkene monomers where one or more hydrogen atoms are substituted by groups such as $-Cl$, $-CN$ or $-OH$.

The conditions required to make most addition polymers are high pressure, heat and a catalyst.

The name of an addition polymer is based on the name of the monomer from which it is formed. Some examples are given in Table 14.2.1.

Table 14.2.1 Some addition polymers

Name of monomer	Chemical name of polymer	Common name of polymer
ethene	poly(ethene)	polythene
propene	poly(propene)	polypropene
chloroethene	poly(chloroethene)	polyvinyl chloride (PVC)
tetrafluoroethene	poly(tetrafluoroethene)	Teflon®
phenylethene	poly(phenylethene)	polystyrene

Writing equations for addition polymerisation

When the monomer contains alkyl groups or other functional groups such as —Cl or —OH, we can represent the equation in a relatively simple way. Figure 14.2.2 represents the polymerisation of propene monomers, $CH_3CH=CH_2$, to form poly(propene).

In writing this equation we:

- draw the monomer on the left with the side chains drawn vertically
- put a letter n in front of the formula of the monomer to show that there is a large number of monomer molecules
- draw the structure of the polymer after the arrow by drawing the monomer with a single bond instead of a double bond
- put 'continuation bonds' at both ends of the molecule
- put square brackets through the continuation bonds
- put a letter n at the bottom right-hand corner to show that the unit repeats itself many times.

Figure 14.2.3 represents the equation for the polymerisation of chloroethene to form poly(chloroethene).

Some uses of addition polymers

- Poly(ethene): plastic bottles, plastic bags, clingfilm wrap (plastic wrap)
- Poly(propene): crates for bottles, ropes, carpets
- Poly(chloroethene), PVC: pipe fittings, water pipes, gutters, electrical cable insulation
- Poly(tetrafluoroethene): non-stick pans
- Poly(phenylethene): plastic toys, expanded foam

Figure 14.2.4 Many articles can be made from polymers.

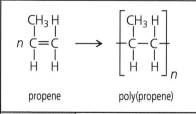

Figure 14.2.2 Propene monomers bond together to form the polymer poly(propene).

Figure 14.2.3 Forming poly(chloroethene)

Condensation polymers

Condensation polymerisation

In condensation polymerisation, monomer molecules are linked together and a small molecule is eliminated. Examples of the small molecules eliminated are water, hydrogen chloride and ammonia. An example of a condensation reaction is shown in Figure 14.3.1, where an amide linkage is formed by the reaction of an alkanoic acid with an amine.

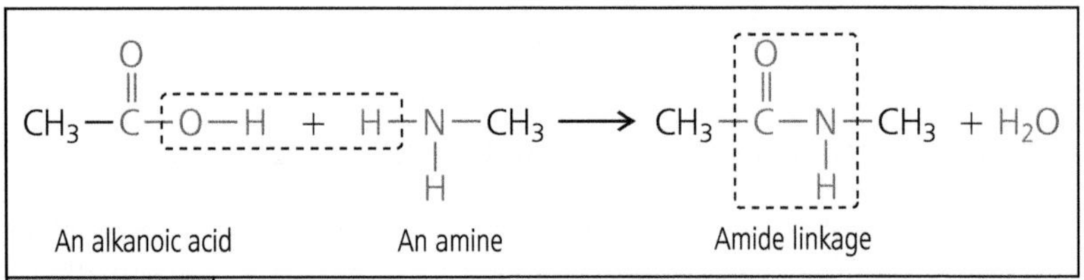

Figure 14.3.1 When an amide linkage is formed, water is eliminated.

Condensation polymerisation may involve two different monomers. In order to form a condensation polymer from two different monomers, each monomer must have at least two functional groups. Three types of linkages in condensation polymers are shown in Figure 14.3.2.

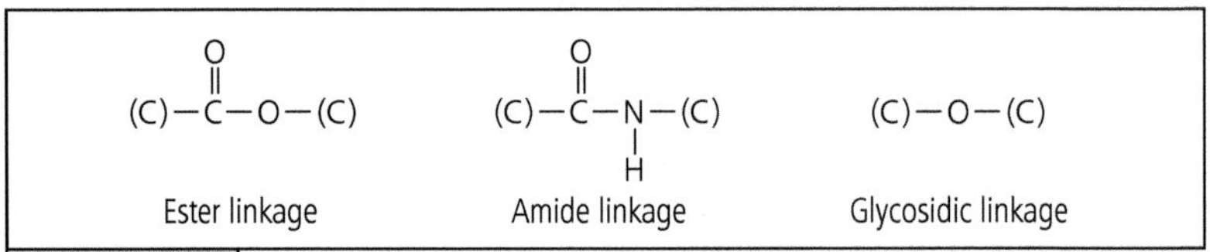

Figure 14.3.2

Polyamides

Nylon is a **polyamide**. The monomers for polyamides are dialkanoic acids and diamines. We can represent the structures of these compounds as in Figure 14.3.3.

In these diagrams the coloured blocks represent the rest of the molecule.

When these molecules react, each —COOH group reacts with an —NH$_2$ group to form an amide linkage and a molecule of water is eliminated (Figure 14.3.4).

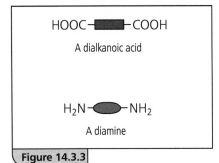

HOOC—■—COOH

A dialkanoic acid

H$_2$N—⬭—NH$_2$

A diamine

Figure 14.3.3

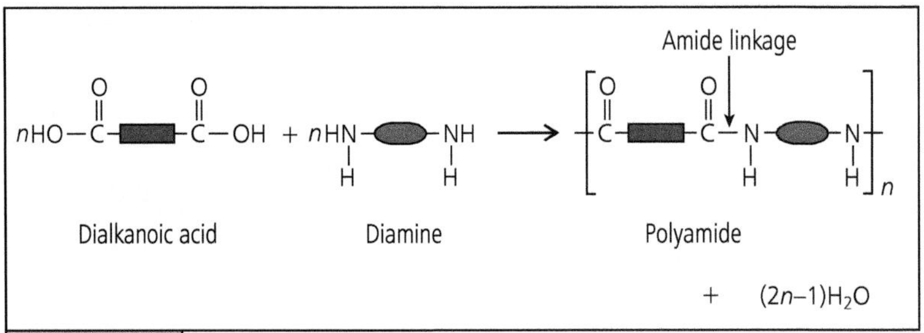

Figure 14.3.4 Formation of a polyamide

Polyesters

Terylene is a **polyester**. The monomers for polyesters are dialkanoic acids and diols. When these molecules react, each —COOH group reacts with an —OH group to form an ester linkage, and a molecule of water is eliminated (Figure 14.3.5).

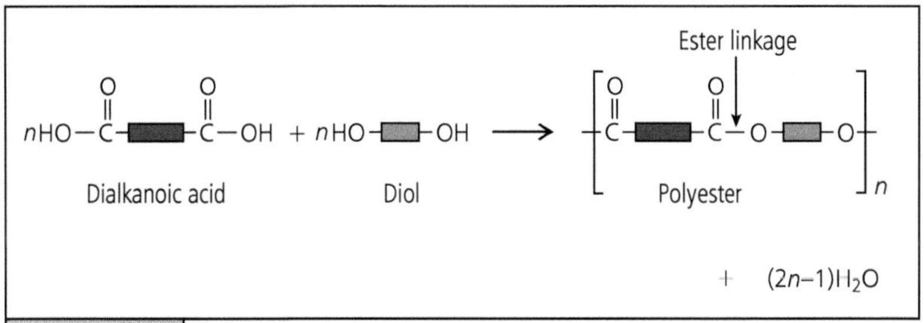

Figure 14.3.5 Formation of a polyester

Polysaccharides

Glucose is a simple sugar (monosaccharide). Starch is a polymer of glucose. So starch is a **polysaccharide**. Starch is a natural plant product. When glucose molecules react together in the presence of enzymes, particular —OH groups react and form a glycosidic linkage. A molecule of water is eliminated (Figure 14.3.7).

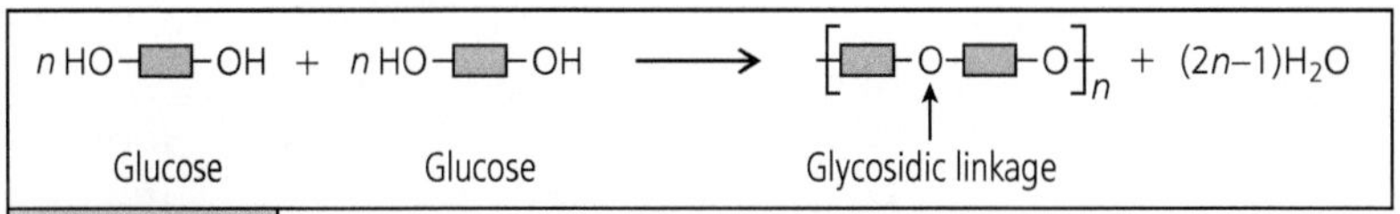

Figure 14.3.7

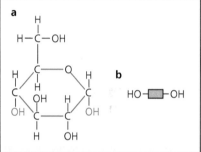

Figure 14.3.6 **a** A glucose molecule, **b** simplified structure of glucose

Cellulose is a polysaccharide present in the cell walls of plants. The glycosidic linkage is slightly different to that in starch. Cellulose is used in making paper, cellophane and rayon.

Some uses of condensation polymers

- Polyamides: Nylon is used to make seatbelts, fishing lines, clothing, carpets and ropes.
- Polyesters: Terylene is used for fabrics such as bedsheets, clothing and towels. Other polyesters are used to make plastic bottles and carpets.
- Polysaccharides: Starch is used in glues, in papermaking and for stiffening clothes.

KEY POINTS

1 In condensation polymerisation, monomer molecules are linked together and a small molecule is eliminated.

2 The linkage in polyamides is the amide linkage, —CONH—.

3 The linkage in polyesters is the ester linkage, —COO—.

4 The linkage in polysaccharides is the glycosidic linkage, —O—.

5 Polyamides, polyesters and polysaccharides have particular uses, e.g. nylon is used to make ropes and clothes.

DID YOU KNOW?

Not all nylon is made by condensation reactions. A ring compound called caprolactam, which contains an N—H group as well as a C=O group, is heated in an atmosphere of nitrogen, and the ring breaks at the amide group. The chains which are formed join to make nylon. No other molecule is formed.

DID YOU KNOW?

When glucose molecules polymerise, the linkage is called a glycosidic linkage. The prefix glyc- means sweet. Both glucose and glycerol are sweet. There are many words relating to sugars that begin with the prefix glyc-, e.g. glycosides are particular types of carbohydrates that form ring compounds.

DID YOU KNOW?

Starch can exist as single chains or as branched chains. Specific enzymes catalyse the reaction causing branches to form.

Section B Practice exam questions

SECTION B: Multiple-choice questions

1 From the four compounds shown, identify which pair of compounds belongs to the same homologous series.

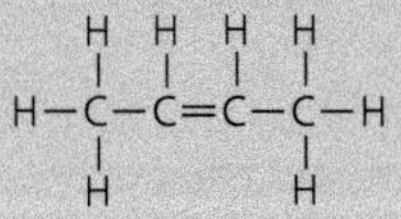

I

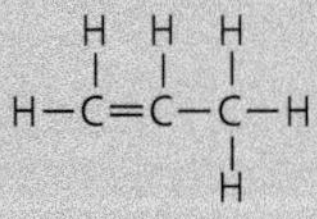

II

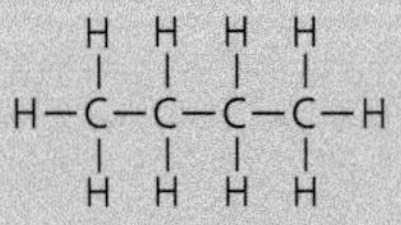

III

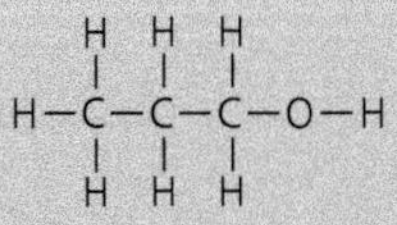

IV

a **I** and **II**

b **I** and **III**

c **II** and **IV**

d **III** and **IV**

2 Which of the following equations correctly shows the complete combustion of butane?

a $C_4H_8 + 5O_2 \longrightarrow 3CO_2 + 4H_2O$

b $C_4H_8 + 6O_2 \longrightarrow 4CO_2 + 4H_2O$

c $C_4H_{10} + 9O_2 \longrightarrow 4CO_2 + 5H_2O$

d $C_4H_{10} + 6\frac{1}{2}O_2 \longrightarrow 4CO_2 + 5H_2O$

3 Which of the following is the product when propene reacts with chlorine in the dark?

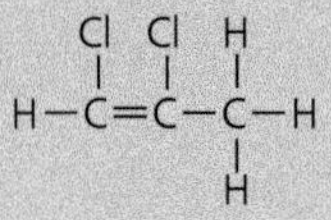

a

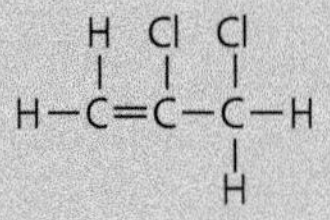

b

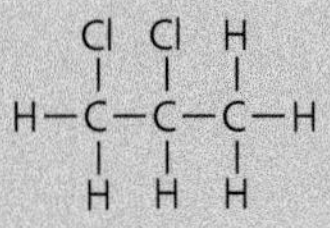

c

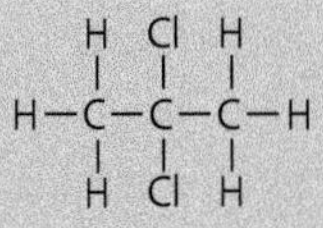

d

4 When sodium metal reacts with ethanol, a gas is produced. Which of the following observations would be made when this gas is tested as indicated?

a The gas produces a milky white precipitate with limewater.

b The gas makes a 'popping' sound with a lighted splint.

c The gas rekindles a glowing splint.

d The gas turns damp blue litmus paper red.

5 Which of the following is the correct balanced equation for the reaction of ethanoic acid with magnesium hydroxide?

a $Mg(OH)_2 + 2CH_3COOH \longrightarrow Mg(CH_3COO)_2 + 2H_2O$

b $MgOH + CH_3COOH \longrightarrow Mg(CH_3COO) + H_2O$

c $Mg(OH)_2 + CH_3COOH \longrightarrow Mg(CH_3COO)_2 + H_2O$

d $Mg(OH)_2 + 2CH_3COOH \longrightarrow Mg(CH_3COO)_2 + 4H_2O$

6 Propene is converted to polypropene by which of the following types of reaction?

a Dehydrogenation

b Hydrogenation

c Addition polymerisation

d Condensation polymerisation

7 Which of the following molecules is an alkanoic acid?

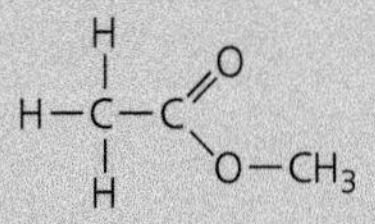

a

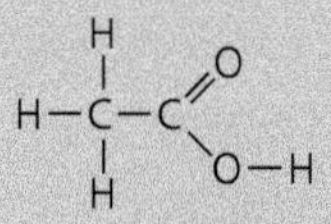

b

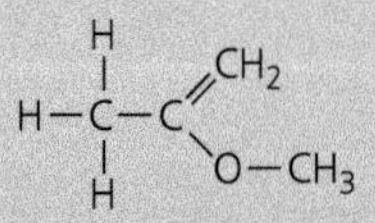

c

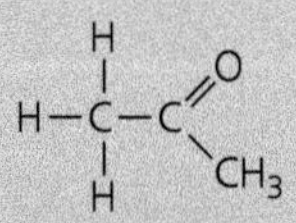

d

8 a Compounds A (C_4H_{10}) and B (C_5H_{12}) are hydrocarbons.

  i Draw possible, **fully displayed** structures of compounds A and B. *(2)*

  ii State the names that match the structures that you have drawn. *(2)*

  iii State the name of the homologous series to which compound A belongs. *(1)*

 b Anaerobic fermentation is used in the production of wines.

  i Define anaerobic fermentation. *(2)*

  ii Write a balanced chemical equation for the reaction occurring during fermentation. *(2)*

  iii State **one** reason why high temperatures are **not** suitable for anaerobic fermentation? *(1)*

 c Esters can undergo hydrolysis in aqueous sodium hydroxide solution.

  i State **one** other method of hydrolysing esters. *(1)*

  ii Draw the fully displayed structures of the products of the alkaline hydrolysis reaction of ethyl ethanoate. *(2)*

ethyl ethanoate

 d i Define polymerisation. *(1)*

  ii The figure below represents a monomer. What type of polymerisation reaction would the monomer shown below undergo? *(1)*

monomer

  iii State the type of polymer that would be formed. *(1)*

9 Petroleum contains many different hydrocarbons, which are separated by fractional distillation.

 a On what physical property of the hydrocarbons does fractional distillation depend? *(1)*

 b Explain how fractional distillation separates hydrocarbons into different fractions. *(4)*

 c Give a use of:

  i the naphtha fraction

  ii bitumen fraction *(2)*

 d Some longer-chain alkanes are cracked to produce shorter-chain alkanes and alkenes.

  i Why do oil companies carry out cracking? *(2)*

  ii What conditions are needed for catalytic cracking? *(2)*

  iii Write an equation for the cracking of dodecane, $C_{12}H_{26}$, to form hexane and one other compound containing three carbon atoms. *(2)*

10 Alcohols are a homologous series of compounds which are more volatile and more soluble in water than the alkanes with the same number of carbon atoms.

 a What is the meaning of the term *volatile*? *(1)*

 b Explain why ethanol is less volatile than ethane. *(3)*

 c Explain why ethanol is more soluble in water than ethane. *(4)*

 d Ethanol is manufactured by the hydration of ethene.

  i What conditions are needed for this hydration? *(3)*

  ii Give two advantages of manufacturing ethanol by hydration over manufacturing it by fermentation. *(2)*

 e i Write an equation for the reaction of sodium with propanol. *(1)*

  ii Explain why the organic product of the reaction in part **i** is soluble in water. *(1)*

  iii Write an equation for the reaction of butanol with ethanoic acid and name the organic product *(2)*

15.1 Properties of metals

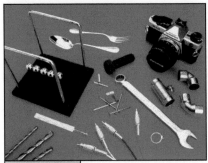

Figure 15.1.1 A wide variety of objects are made from metals.

EXAM TIP

When answering questions about the physical properties of metals in general, make sure that you select the properties that are common to all of them. It is incorrect to suggest that sodium has a high melting point and is hard.

Physical properties of metals

Most metals have the following physical properties:

• They are good conductors of electricity.
• They are good conductors of heat.
• They are malleable: they can be beaten into different shapes.
• They are ductile: they can be drawn into wires.
• They are **lustrous**: they have a shiny surface when freshly cut.

In addition, the transition metals have the following physical properties:

• They have a high density: they have a high mass per cm³ of metal.
• They are **sonorous**: they ring when hit with a hard object.
• They have high melting points and boiling points.
• They are hard.

Table 15.1.1 shows the physical properties of some metals.

Table 15.1.1 Physical properties of some metals

Metal	Melting point (°C)	Density (g cm⁻³)	Relative tensile strength	Hardness
Sodium	98	0.97	<1	Very soft (can be cut with a knife)
Magnesium	649	1.74	4	Fairly hard
Aluminium	660	2.70	7	Fairly hard
Iron	1535	7.86	21	Hard
Copper	1083	8.92	13	Hard
Zinc	420	7.14	11	Fairly hard

The list below gives further information about the physical properties of some metals.

• The physical properties of calcium are similar to those of magnesium.
• All Group I metals are soft and have a very low density.
• Tin and lead are fairly soft metals. They are harder than sodium but softer than magnesium and calcium.
• Mercury is a liquid at r.t.p.
• Most metals are silvery in colour when freshly cut. Copper is pinkish-brown in colour.

Chemical properties of metals

Action of oxygen

Most metals react with oxygen or air to form oxides, e.g.

$$2Mg(s) + O_2(g) \longrightarrow 2MgO(s)$$
magnesium   magnesium oxide

$$4Al(s) + 3O_2(g) \longrightarrow 2Al_2O_3(s)$$
aluminium   aluminium oxide

Metals low in the electrochemical series, e.g. gold, do not react (see 15.3).

Action of water

Metals high in the electrochemical series react with cold water. A metal hydroxide and hydrogen are formed, e.g.

$$2Na(s) + 2H_2O(l) \longrightarrow 2NaOH(aq) + H_2(g)$$
sodium   sodium hydroxide

$$Ca(s) + 2H_2O(l) \longrightarrow Ca(OH)_2(aq) + H_2(g)$$
calcium   calcium hydroxide

Reactive meals slightly lower in the electrochemical series, e.g. magnesium or iron, react very slowly or not at all with water. They may react with hot water or steam to form a metal oxide and hydrogen.

$$Mg(s) + H_2O(l) \longrightarrow MgO(s) + H_2(g)$$
magnesium   warm   magnesium
          water   oxide

$$3Fe(s) + 4H_2O(g) \longrightarrow Fe_3O_4(s) + 4H_2(g)$$
iron   steam   iron(II,III) oxide

Metals lower than hydrogen in the electrochemical series do not react with water.

Action of dilute acids

Metals above hydrogen in the electrochemical series react with dilute hydrochloric acid to form the metal chloride (a salt) and hydrogen. They also react with dilute sulfuric acid to form the metal sulfate (a salt) and hydrogen. Examples are:

$$Zn(s) + 2HCl(aq) \longrightarrow ZnCl_2(aq) + H_2(g)$$
zinc   hydrochloric   zinc   hydrogen
     acid   chloride

$$Mg(s) + H_2SO_4(aq) \longrightarrow MgSO_4(aq) + H_2(g)$$
magnesium   sulfuric   magnesium   hydrogen
        acid   sulfate

Note:

- The reaction of sodium and calcium with dilute acids can be explosive, so is never carried out in a school laboratory.
- Metals such as copper, silver and gold, which are lower in the electrochemical series than hydrogen, do not react with dilute hydrochloric or sulfuric acid.

Reactions of some metal compounds

At the end of this topic you should be able to:

- describe the reaction of metallic oxides with dilute hydrochloric and sulfuric acid
- describe the reactions of metallic hydroxides with dilute hydrochloric acid and sulfuric acid
- describe the action of heat on metal nitrates, carbonates, hydroxides and oxides.

Reaction of metal oxides with acids

Metal oxides react with dilute hydrochloric acid or dilute sulfuric acid to form a salt and water. Some of the reactions may be slow. They can be speeded up by heating.

With dilute hydrochloric acid a metal chloride and water are formed. For example:

$$ZnO(s) + 2HCl(aq) \longrightarrow ZnCl_2(aq) + H_2O(l)$$
zinc oxide   zinc chloride

With dilute sulfuric acid a metal sulfate and water are formed. For example:

$$Al_2O_3(s) + 3H_2SO_4(aq) \longrightarrow Al_2(SO_4)_3(aq) + 3H_2O(l)$$
aluminium oxide   aluminium sulfate

Reaction of metal hydroxides with acids

Many metal hydroxides react with dilute hydrochloric acid or dilute sulfuric acid to form the corresponding salt and water. These are examples of neutralisation reactions (see 7.6).

With dilute hydrochloric acid a metal chloride and water are formed. For example:

$$Ca(OH)_2(s) + 2HCl(aq) \longrightarrow CaCl_2(aq) + 2H_2O(l)$$
calcium hydroxide   calcium chloride

With dilute sulfuric acid a metal sulfate and water are formed. For example:

$$2NaOH(aq) + H_2SO_4(aq) \longrightarrow Na_2SO_4(aq) + 2H_2O(l)$$
sodium hydroxide   sodium sulfate

Reaction of metal carbonates with acids

Metal carbonates react with dilute hydrochloric acid or dilute sulfuric acid to form the corresponding salt, carbon dioxide and water (see 7.3). For example:

$$ZnCO_3(s) + H_2SO_4(aq) \longrightarrow ZnSO_4(aq) + CO_2(g) + H_2O(l)$$
zinc carbonate   zinc sulfate

The action of heat on some metal compounds

Some metal nitrates, carbonates, hydroxides and oxides break down on heating. We call this type of reaction **thermal decomposition**.

The correct chemical name for sodium nitrate, $NaNO_3$, is sodium nitrate(v). The correct chemical name for sodium nitrite, $NaNO_2$, is sodium nitrate(III). We do not always use the correct chemical names, however, because these compounds are so well known by their old names. Nitrogen dioxide, the poisonous brown gas given off when nitrates other than Group I nitrates are heated, is properly called nitrogen(IV) oxide.

Thermal decomposition of nitrates

All nitrates decompose when heated. There are some differences in the decomposition products, depending on the reactivity of the metal in the metal nitrate.

- The nitrates of Group I metals apart from lithium nitrate decompose to form the metal nitrite and oxygen, For example:

$$2NaNO_3(s) \xrightarrow{heat} 2NaNO_2(s) + O_2(g)$$

    sodium nitrate   sodium nitrite   oxygen

- The nitrates of most other metals decompose to form the metal oxide, nitrogen dioxide (nitrogen(IV) oxide) and oxygen:

$$2Cu(NO_3)_2 \xrightarrow{heat} 2CuO(s) + 4NO_2(g) + O_2(g)$$

    copper(II)   copper(II)   nitrogen   oxygen
    nitrate   oxide   dioxide

- The nitrates of very unreactive metals decompose to form the metal, nitrogen dioxide and oxygen.

$$2AgNO_3 \xrightarrow{heat} 2Ag(s) + 2NO_2(g) + O_2(g)$$

    silver(I) nitrate   silver   nitrogen   oxygen
                                    dioxide

Thermal decomposition of carbonates

Many carbonates decompose when heated to form the metal oxide and carbon dioxide. For example:

$$CaCO_3(s) \xrightarrow{heat} CaO(s) + CO_2(g)$$

    calcium   calcium   carbon
    carbonate   oxide   dioxide

Group I carbonates apart from lithium carbonate, e.g. sodium carbonate, Na_2CO_3, do not decompose on heating.

Thermal decomposition of metal hydroxides and oxides

Most metal hydroxides decompose on heating. A metal oxide and water are formed. For example:

$$Zn(OH)_2(s) \xrightarrow{heat} ZnO(s) + H_2O(g)$$

    zinc hydroxide   zinc oxide

Group II hydroxides decompose in a similar way. Most Group I metal hydroxides do not decompose. Lithium hydroxide is an exception. It decomposes to lithium oxide and water.

Most oxides do not decompose when heated. A few oxides of unreactive metals do decompose. An example is the decomposition of silver(I) oxide:

$$2Ag_2O(s) \xrightarrow{heat} 4Ag(s) + O_2(g)$$

KEY POINTS

1 Metal oxides and metal hydroxides react with dilute hydrochloric acid or dilute sulfuric acid to form the corresponding metal salt and water.

2 Metal carbonates react with acids to form a salt, carbon dioxide and water.

3 Thermal decomposition is the breaking down of a compound by heating.

4 Group I nitrates decompose to form a nitrite and oxygen whereas most other nitrates decompose to from an oxide, nitrogen dioxide and oxygen.

5 Most metal hydroxides decompose on heating to form an oxide and water.

6 Metal carbonates, apart from Group I carbonates, decompose to form an oxide and carbon dioxide.

Metals and the electrochemical series

At the end of this topic you should be able to:

• describe the reactivity of metals based on displacement reactions, reaction with oxygen, and the relative ease of decomposition of their nitrates, carbonates, hydroxides and oxides

• deduce the order of reactivity of metals based on experimental results or data supplied.

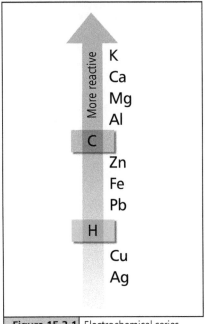

Figure 15.3.1 Electrochemical series including carbon and hydrogen

The electrochemical series revisited

In 9.3 we saw that metals can be placed in order of reactivity by reacting metals with different metal salts. The electrochemical series shows the order of reactivity of metals, with the most reactive at the top. As we go up the electrochemical series the metals lose electrons more readily and become stronger reducing agents. Figure 15.3.1 shows the relative reactivity of the metals. It also includes the relative ease with which carbon and hydrogen act as reducing agents by losing electrons when reacting with metal oxides (see 15.4).

Reactivity based on displacement reactions

• Zinc will reduce the Cu^{2+} ions in copper(II) sulfate:

$$Zn(s) + Cu^{2+}(aq) \longrightarrow Zn^{2+}(aq) + Cu(s)$$

So zinc is above copper in the electrochemical series.

• Magnesium will reduce the Zn^{2+} ions in zinc sulfate:

$$Mg(s) + Zn^{2+}(aq) \longrightarrow Mg^{2+}(aq) + Zn(s)$$

So magnesium is above zinc in the electrochemical series.

• Silver will not react with the Cu^{2+} ions in copper(II) sulfate.

So silver is below copper in the electrochemical series.

By carrying out a series of displacement reactions like this, we can put the elements in the order of their reactivity: magnesium (most reactive) > zinc > copper > silver.

Reaction with oxygen

Table 15.3.1 shows some observations made when different metals react with oxygen.

Table 15.3.1 Reaction of some metals with oxygen

Metal	Reactivity with oxygen
Aluminium	A thin ribbon burns rapidly
Copper	Does not burn but its surface turns black
Iron	Burns only when it is in powder form or as iron wool
Gold	Does not react
Magnesium	A thin ribbon burns very rapidly

From these results, we can put these metals in the following order of reactivity:

most reactive ——— magnesium aluminium iron copper gold ——→ least reactive

Ease of thermal decomposition

The more reactive a metal, the more difficult it is to decompose its nitrate, carbonate or hydroxide on heating. Table 15.3.2 shows the lowest temperatures at which some Group II carbonates decompose significantly.

Table 15.3.2 Decomposition temperatures of some carbonates

Carbonate	Barium carbonate	Calcium carbonate	Magnesium carbonate	Strontium carbonate
Decomposition temperature (°C)	1360	900	540	1280

From the data, you can see that the order of ease of decomposition is:

magnesium (easiest to decompose) $\longrightarrow$ calcium $\longrightarrow$ strontium $\longrightarrow$ barium.

So the order of the metal reactivity is:

barium (most reactive) $\longrightarrow$ strontium > calcium $\longrightarrow$ magnesium (least reactive)

Some observations on the amount of nitrogen dioxide (brown gas) produced when different nitrates undergo thermal decomposition is shown in Table 15.3.3.

Table 15.3.3 Effect of heating on some nitrates

Nitrate	Effect of heating
Barium nitrate	Hardly any brown gas is produced, even on strong heating.
Copper(II) nitrate	Large amounts of brown gas are produced on gentle heating.
Magnesium nitrate	Some brown gas is produced on strong heating.

From this information, you can see that the order of reactivity of the metals is:

barium (most reactive) $\longrightarrow$ magnesium $\longrightarrow$ copper (least reactive)

Similar information can be obtained from the ease of thermal decomposition of hydroxides. A high temperature is needed to decompose barium hydroxide (barium is very reactive) but a relatively lower temperature is needed to decompose zinc hydroxide (zinc is less reactive). The hydroxides of the Group I metals (apart from lithium) do not decompose. This is because the Group I metals are very reactive.

Reaction with acids

Only metals above hydrogen in the electrochemical series react with acids to produce hydrogen gas. By observing the reaction of different metals with $1\,mol\,dm^{-3}$ hydrochloric acid, we can deduce the order of reactivity of the metals (Table 15.3.4):

calcium (most reactive) $\longrightarrow$ magnesium $\longrightarrow$ zinc $\longrightarrow$ copper (least reactive)

Table 15.3.4 Reaction of some metals with hydrochloric acid

Metal	Reactivity with hydrochloric acid
Calcium	Bubbles produced very rapidly
Copper	No reaction
Magnesium	Bubbles produced steadily
Zinc	Bubbles produced slowly

KEY POINTS

1 The order of reactivity of metals can be deduced by reference to the displacement reactions of metals.

2 The reactivity of some metals can be deduced from the rate of reaction of the metals with oxygen or acids.

3 The reactivity of some metals can be deduced from the ease of decomposition of their nitrates, carbonates or hydroxides.

4 The greater the ease of decomposition of metal nitrates, carbonates or hydroxides, the lower is the reactivity of the metal.

At the end of this topic you should be able to:

- relate the principles underlying the extraction of a metal to its position in the electrochemical series
- describe the extraction of iron
- describe the extraction of aluminium.

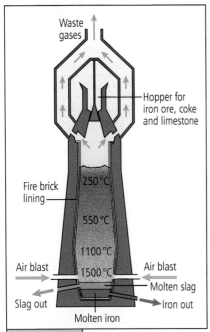

| Figure 15.4.1 | A blast furnace for extracting iron from iron ore |

Waste gases

Hopper for iron ore, coke and limestone

Fire brick lining

250 °C

550 °C

1100 °C

Air blast — 1500 °C — Air blast

Molten slag

Slag out — Iron out

Molten iron

| Figure 15.4.2 | Metal ores are extracted in huge quantities. |

The extraction of metals

We can carry out the reduction of iron(III) oxide to iron by heating with carbon since carbon releases electrons better than iron. If we look at Figure 15.3.1 (in 15.3), we can see that zinc, iron, lead, copper and silver could be extracted from their oxides using carbon since they are lower than carbon in the electrochemical series. For example:

$$PbO(s) + C(s) \longrightarrow Pb(s) + CO(g)$$

In the laboratory, unreactive metals such as copper can be extracted from their oxides using hydrogen. Copper is below hydrogen in the electrochemical series. So copper(II) oxide can be reduced by passing hydrogen over heated copper oxide:

$$CuO(s) + H_2(g) \longrightarrow Cu(s) + H_2O(g)$$

Metals above carbon in the electrochemical series are usually extracted by electrolysis because they are better at releasing electrons than is carbon. So aluminium and magnesium, among other metals are extracted using electrolysis.

The extraction of iron

The raw materials for making iron are iron ore, coke (carbon), limestone (calcium carbonate) and air. The commonest ore of iron is haematite, which is largely iron(III) oxide, Fe_2O_3. The iron is extracted in a blast furnace (Figure 15.4.1). The main reducing agent is carbon monoxide, which is formed by reactions within the furnace.

The reactions producing iron are:

- Coke burns in a hot blast of air to form carbon dioxide.
- Carbon dioxide reacts with coke to form carbon monoxide:

$$CO_2(g) + C(s) \longrightarrow 2CO(g)$$

- Carbon monoxide reduces iron(III) oxide to iron:

$$Fe_2O_3(s) + 3CO(g) \longrightarrow 2Fe(l) + 3CO_2(g)$$

The iron flows to the bottom of the furnace and is removed periodically.

Iron ore contains silicon(IV) oxide as an impurity. Limestone is added to the furnace to remove this impurity. The reactions involved are:

- Limestone (calcium carbonate) decomposes on heating to form calcium oxide:

$$CaCO_3(s) \longrightarrow CaO(s) + CO_2(g)$$

- Calcium oxide reacts with the silicon(IV) oxide to form calcium silicate (slag).

$$CaO(s) + SiO_2(l) \longrightarrow CaSiO_3(l)$$

The liquid slag is less dense than iron. It flows to the bottom of the furnace and forms a layer above the iron. The slag is run off periodically.

The extraction of aluminium

Aluminium is extracted by electrolysis using carbon (graphite) electrodes (Figure 15.4.3). The electrolysis is carried out in long, narrow cells with many electrodes.

Aluminium oxide is purified from its ore (bauxite). Aluminium oxide has a very high melting point (2040 °C). It is difficult and expensive to keep the aluminium oxide molten at this temperature. But it needs to be molten for electrolysis to occur. So the mineral cryolite, Na_3AlF_6, is added. When molten, the cryolite dissolves the aluminium oxide and lowers the melting point of the electrolyte to about 900 °C.

The reactions at the electrodes are:

- Cathode: $Al^{3+} + 3e^- \longrightarrow Al$

  Aluminium ions are reduced to aluminium. The molten aluminium sinks to the bottom of the cell and is tapped off at the bottom of the cell or siphoned off.

- Anode: $2O^{2-} \longrightarrow O_2 + 4e^-$

  Oxide ions are oxidised to oxygen gas. As the hot oxygen gas bubbles off, it reacts with the graphite anodes to form carbon dioxide. The graphite anodes 'burn away' and eventually have to be replaced.

The overall reaction for this electrolysis is:

$$2Al_2O_3 \longrightarrow 4Al + 3O_2$$

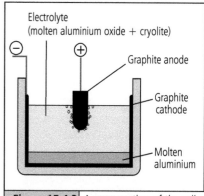

Electrolyte (molten aluminium oxide + cryolite)

Graphite anode

Graphite cathode

Molten aluminium

Figure 15.4.3 A cross-section of the cell used in the extraction of aluminium

EXAM TIP

You do not have to remember details of the purification of bauxite or technical details of the blast furnace or the electrolysis cell for producing aluminium. You should concentrate on the processes and the equations.

KEY POINTS

1. Metals below carbon in the electrochemical series are generally extracted by heating with carbon.

2. Metals above carbon in the reactivity series are generally extracted by electrolysis.

3. In the blast furnace, iron(III) oxide is reduced by carbon monoxide formed within the furnace.

4. The limestone added to the blast furnace decomposes on heating to form calcium oxide, which reacts with silicon(IV) oxide impurities to form slag.

5. Aluminium is extracted by the electrolysis of molten aluminium oxide in cryolite using graphite electrodes.

6. Molten cryolite dissolves the aluminium oxide and lowers the melting point of the electrolyte.

DID YOU KNOW?

Some chemists have been researching the possibility of reducing iron(III) oxide to iron using hydrogen even though iron is above hydrogen in the electrochemical series. At very high temperatures, the relative positions of iron and hydrogen in the electrochemical series change so that the reaction becomes possible.

Uses of metals and alloys

At the end of this topic you should be able to:

- explain why metal alloys are often used in place of metals
- relate the properties of aluminium, iron and lead and their alloys to their uses.

Alloys

An **alloy** is a mixture, within a metallic lattice, of two or more metals or a mixture of one or more metals with a non-metal. The atoms in a pure metal have a regular arrangement. When a metal is alloyed with a second metal, the arrangement of the lattice becomes less regular. The atoms of the second metal disrupt the regular arrangement because they are smaller or larger (Figure 15.5.1).

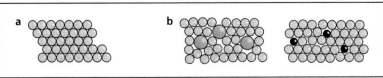

Figure 15.5.1 **a** A pure metal has a regular arrangement of atoms. **b** In alloys the regular arrangement is disrupted.

Alloying metals has particular advantages in terms of metallic properties. For example, alloys are often stronger and harder than the metals from which they are made. The presence of the larger or smaller atoms of one of the metals disrupts the regular metallic structure. This reduces the ability of the layers to slide over each other when a force is applied (Figure 15.5.2).

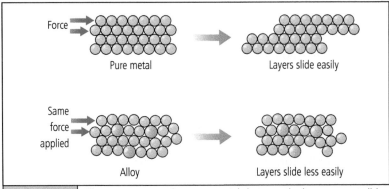

Figure 15.5.2 Alloys are stronger than pure metals because the layers cannot slide as easily.

EXAM TIP

An alloy is not just a mixture of metal crystals. The atoms of one metal form part of the crystal lattice of another metal. Unlike most mixtures, it is quite difficult to separate the different metals in an alloy by physical means, although we can get the pure metals back again by chemical means.

Modifying properties

Aluminium and aluminium alloys

Pure aluminium is ductile. It has a low density and is resistant to corrosion because it has an oxide film on its surface. So it is used for making window frames, food containers and cans, especially for foods and drinks that are acidic.

- Duralumin alloy (Al with small amounts of copper, manganese, magnesium and silicon) is used for making aircraft bodies. The alloy is much stronger than pure aluminium but still has a low density.

DID YOU KNOW?

Some modern alloys have 'memory' properties. Springs made from a type of 'smart alloy' can open out when the temperature is 90°C but go back to their original form when the temperature drops.

- Aluminium alloys containing 10% magnesium are used for building ships because they have improved resistance to corrosion by seawater.
- Alloys of aluminium with silicon (up to 12%) and nickel are used to make the cylinder heads for car engines because they do not expand very much when heated.

Steel alloys

Pure iron is too weak to be useful. The iron from the blast furnace is too brittle to be used for constructing bridges and buildings because it contains too much carbon. Steel is an alloy of iron with carbon or with carbon and other metals. There are several types:

- Mild steel (about 0.25% carbon) is soft and malleable. So it is used for making wires and in general engineering, e.g. car bodies and buildings where shaping is required. It is also used to make cans for foods and drinks, where it is covered with tin to prevent it from rusting.
- High carbon steel (between 0.5% and 1.4% carbon) is harder but more brittle. It is used to make tools such as hammers and chisels.
- Low alloy steels contain between 1% and 5% of other metals such as chromium, manganese, nickel and titanium. They are hard and strong and have low ductility and malleability. Nickel steels are used for bridges and bicycle chains, where strength is required. Tungsten steel is used for high-speed tools because it does not change shape at high temperatures.
- Stainless steels may contain up to 20% chromium and up to 10% nickel. They are strong and resist corrosion. So they are used for the construction of industrial chemical vessels, surgical instruments and cutlery.

Lead and lead alloys

Lead is a very soft metal. It was formerly used for making water pipes because it is very malleable. It is relatively unreactive, so it is also used to line the reaction vessels in some chemical plants. The main use of lead nowadays is in car batteries.

Solders are alloys of lead and tin. The melting point of solders is lower than that of either pure lead or pure tin. Solders have the following uses:

- Joining metals. Solder is easily melted and has a good adhesive power (it sticks metals together strongly). Solder containing 95% tin and 5% lead is used for joining components of electrical apparatus.
- For joining pipes together a solder containing 66% lead, 32% tin and 2% antimony is used.
- Articles made from pieces of tin are joined by using a solder containing 60% lead and 40% tin.

Other alloys

- Brass (copper and zinc) is stronger than copper but is relatively malleable. So it is used for musical instruments and ornaments.
- Bronze (copper and tin) is harder than either copper or tin alone. So it is used for moving parts of machines, statues and bells.

EXAM TIP

You do not have to remember the percentages of particular metals in different alloys. Concentrate on relating the uses of the alloys to their properties and how the alloy improves the properties of the metal.

KEY POINTS

1 An alloy is a mixture, within a metallic lattice, of two or more metals or a mixture of one or more metals with a non-metal.

2 Alloys are used instead of pure metals because they have improved properties such as increased hardness, increased strength or increased resistance to corrosion.

3 Alloys of aluminium have increased strength and increased resistance to corrosion.

4 Alloys of iron (steels) have increased strength, hardness and resistance to corrosion.

5 Low alloy steels are used where strength is required. High alloy steels are used where both strength and resistance to corrosion are required.

6 Solders are alloys of lead and tin which are used for joining metals.

Metals and the environment

At the end of this topic you should be able to:

• describe the conditions needed for the corrosion of metals with reference to iron and aluminium

• explain the importance of metals and their compounds to living systems and the environment

• discuss the harmful effects of metals and their compounds to living systems and the environment.

EXAM TIP

It is important that you distinguish between corrosion and rusting. Rusting is a reaction involving oxygen and water and the formation of hydrated iron(III) oxide. Corrosion of iron increases as acidity increases but rusting of iron is most rapid under alkaline conditions.

DID YOU KNOW?

As well as Fe^{2+}, other metal ions essential for life include copper(II) ions which are needed for efficient respiration and manganese(II) ions which are attached to some enzymes in the body, which prevent unwanted oxidations.

Corrosion

Corrosion is the gradual dissolving away of a metal inwards from its surface. Reactive metals such as magnesium and iron corrode if the conditions in which they are placed are acidic. For reactive metals, the greater the acidity of the environment in which the metal is placed, the faster is the rate of corrosion. In general, the more reactive the metal, the faster is the rate of corrosion. Although aluminium is a reactive metal, it is relatively resistant to corrosion. This is because a freshly formed surface of aluminium reacts with oxygen to form a thin oxide layer. This oxide layer does not easily flake off and is chemically unreactive. Alkalis also corrode some metals.

Rusting

Rusting is a special form of corrosion that only applies to iron and iron alloys. Rusting only occurs when both water and oxygen (from the air) are present. The oxygen and air react with the iron to form hydrated iron(III) oxide (rust):

$$2Fe(s) + 1\tfrac{1}{2}O_2(g) + xH_2O(l) \longrightarrow Fe_2O_3.xH_2O(s)$$

Rust flakes off the surface of iron very easily. When it flakes off, a fresh iron surface is exposed to allow further rusting. Figure 15.6.1 shows an experiment to study the conditions for rusting.

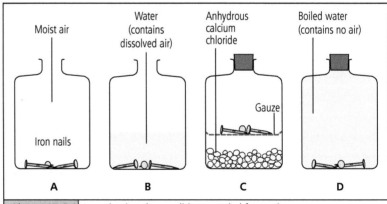

Figure 15.6.1 Investigating the conditions needed for rusting

In bottles A and B, the iron rusts because both water and oxygen from the air are present. In bottle C the iron does not rust because the anhydrous calcium chloride removes the water vapour from the air. In bottle D the iron does not rust because boiling the water removes all the air. Rusting is dependent on the pH of the air or water in which the iron is placed. Rusting is greater if the pH of the environment is alkaline.

The importance of metals to life

- Chlorophyll is an essential substance for plants to make glucose by photosynthesis. The chlorophyll molecule traps the energy from the Sun. Complex energy transfers then convert the energy via oxidation–reduction reactions to form glucose. At the centre of the chlorophyll molecule is a magnesium ion. Without this magnesium ion, chlorophyll will not absorb sunlight very well.

- Iron(II) ions are important in the correct functioning of haemoglobin in red blood cells. Haemoglobin is a protein that carries oxygen around the body. A molecule called haem is attached to the protein. At the centre of the haem molecule is an Fe^{2+} ion bonded to four nitrogen atoms. Oxygen bonds to the Fe^{2+} ion. The haemoglobin carries oxygen around the body to the tissues where it is needed for respiration.

- Zinc ions are bonded to an enzyme (carbonic anhydrase) present in red blood cells. The enzyme catalyses the removal of carbon dioxide from the blood. It makes the reaction about a million times faster than it would be without the enzyme. The zinc ions play a critical part in the way the reaction works.

Toxic metals

Many metals and metal compounds harm living things if they escape from factories or are dumped by humans. For example:

- Compounds of lead were formerly added to petrol to improve the combustion of the fuel. Very few fuels now contain lead compounds. The exhaust gases from vehicles using this fuel contain lead and lead compounds. Lead compounds are still used in some paints in some parts of the world. Lead is also used in some car batteries. If these paints or batteries are not disposed of correctly, lead may get into groundwater or air. Lead compounds are poisonous. They harm the nervous system, including the brain, especially in young children.

- Arsenic compounds are poisonous. They can get into groundwater from mining waste and from disposal of some electrical components.

- The starter batteries of many cars contain cadmium and nickel electrodes. If disposed of incorrectly, poisonous cadmium can get into the groundwater.

- Mercury can be spilled from broken thermometers in hospitals and laboratories. Mercury and its compounds are particularly poisonous to fish and it can accumulate in the food chain and eventually poison humans (Figure 15.6.2).

Disposal of metals incorrectly may cause problems:

- Metals may react with water and/or air and corrode to form soluble compounds that are poisonous. These diffuse into the soil and eventually enter rivers.

- Rust from iron may form unsightly pools of waste that reduce plant growth.

- Waste from aluminium extraction may react with water and form flammable gases.

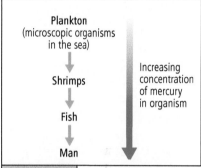

Figure 15.6.2 The concentration of mercury increases along a food chain.

16 Non-metals

16.1

Properties of some non-metals

Figure 16.1.1 Some non-metallic elements: sulfur, bromine, phosphorus, carbon and iodine

EXAM TIP

If you are asked to describe the difference between metals and non-metals, it is best to select differences in electrical and thermal conductivity, malleability (as opposed to brittleness) and density at r.t.p. There are fewer exceptions to the general rules if you choose these.

Physical properties of non-metals

Many non-metals are gases at r.t.p. but others are solids and bromine is a liquid. The physical properties of non-metals are largely the opposite to those of metals.

Most non-metals:

- do not conduct electricity. An exception is carbon in the form of graphite.
- do not conduct heat. An exception is carbon in the form of graphite.
- are brittle when in the solid form. So they break apart easily when hit. The exceptions are non-metals with giant structures.
- have low melting points and boiling points in comparison with most metals. Many are gases at r.t.p.
- have a dull surface when in the solid form. Crystalline forms of non-metals, however, may appear shiny, e.g. carbon as diamond.
- have a much lower density at r.t.p. in comparison with most metals.
- are soft and so are easily scratched with a knife. An exception is carbon in the form of diamond.

Table 16.1.1 compares some physical properties of selected non-metals.

Table 16.1.1 Physical properties of some non-metals

Element	Melting point (°C)	Melting point (°C)	Density at r.t.p. (g cm⁻³)	Appearance
Hydrogen	−259	−253	0.000083	Colourless gas
Carbon (diamond)	+3550	+4827	3.51	Colourless solid
Nitrogen	−210	−196	0.00116	Colourless gas
Oxygen	−218	−183	0.00133	Colourless gas
Sulfur	+119	+445	1.96	Yellow solid
Chlorine	−101	−35	0.00296	Green gas

Chemical properties of non-metals

Reaction with oxygen

Many non-metals burn in excess oxygen or in air (which is 21% oxygen) to form oxides. For example:

$$2H_2(g) + O_2(g) \longrightarrow 2H_2O(l)$$
$$S(s) + O_2(g) \longrightarrow SO_2(g)$$
$$C(s) + O_2(g) \longrightarrow CO_2(g)$$

Nitrogen does not combine with oxygen at r.t.p. although it will react at high temperatures and in the presence of an electric spark. Chlorine does not react with oxygen.

Reaction with metals

Some non-metals react with metals high in the electrochemical series when heated. For example:

- Sodium burns in chlorine to form sodium chloride:

$$2Na(s) + Cl_2(g) \longrightarrow 2NaCl(s)$$

Other halogens react in a similar way.

- Magnesium burns in oxygen to form magnesium oxide:

$$2Mg(s) + O_2(g) \longrightarrow 2MgO(s)$$

- When heated, iron combines with molten sulfur to form iron(II) sulfide:

$$Fe(s) + S(l) \longrightarrow FeS(s)$$

- When heated, reactive metals such as sodium and aluminium react with hydrogen to form metal hydrides:

$$2Na(s) + H_2(g) \longrightarrow 2NaH(s)$$

Oxidising and reducing properties

- Hydrogen is a good reducing agent. At high temperatures, hydrogen reduces metal oxides below zinc in the electrochemical series to the metal. For example:

$$PbO(s) + H_2(g) \longrightarrow Pb(s) + H_2O(g)$$

Under suitable conditions (high temperature, pressure and a catalyst) hydrogen reduces nitrogen to ammonia:

$$N_2(g) + 3H_2(g) \rightleftharpoons 2NH_3(g)$$

- Carbon is also a good reducing agent. At high temperatures, it reduces metal oxides below aluminium in the reactivity series to the metal. For example:

$$ZnO(s) + C(s) \longrightarrow Zn(s) + CO(g)$$

- Oxygen is a good oxidising agent, oxidising most metals to metal oxides and some non-metals to non-metal oxides. For example:

$$2Mg(s) + O_2(g) \longrightarrow 2MgO(s)$$

$$4P(s) + 5O_2(g) \longrightarrow P_4O_{10}(s)$$

- Chlorine is a good oxidising agent, either as a gas or as an aqueous solution. For example, it oxidises:

  – hydrogen to hydrogen chloride:

$$H_2(g) + Cl_2(g) \longrightarrow 2HCl(g)$$

  – ammonia to nitrogen:

$$2NH_3(g) + 3Cl_2(g) \longrightarrow N_2(g) + 6HCl(g)$$

  – aqueous bromides to aqueous bromine:

$$2KBr(aq) + Cl_2(aq) \longrightarrow 2KCl(aq) + Br_2(aq)$$

The preparation of gases

Preparation of gases: an introduction

When we prepare a gas in the laboratory, we need to consider:

• whether the gas is soluble or insoluble in water.

• how to collect the gas. This depends on the density of the gas: whether it is denser or less dense than air (see Figure 16.2.1).

• how to dry the gas to free it from water vapour. In selecting a drying agent, we need also to consider whether the gas itself reacts with the drying agent.

Preparation of carbon dioxide

Carbon dioxide is prepared by dropping dilute hydrochloric acid onto marble chips (calcium carbonate) (Figure 16.2.2).

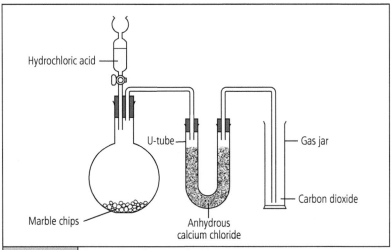

Figure 16.2.2 Preparation of carbon dioxide

In this preparation:

• Carbon dioxide denser than air. So it is collected in the gas jar by upward displacement of air.

• Carbon dioxide is soluble in water, so it is preferable not to collect it over water.

• The carbon dioxide coming from the reaction flask will have some water vapour in it. This arises from the water in the dilute hydrochloric acid. The carbon dioxide can be passed over anhydrous calcium chloride in a U-tube to dry it. (Calcium oxide, another drying agent, cannot be used because moist carbon dioxide is acidic and reacts with the basic calcium oxide.)

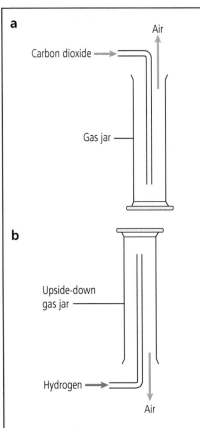

Figure 16.2.1 **a** Carbon dioxide is denser than air, so is collected by **upward displacement** of air. **b** Hydrogen is less dense than air, so is collected by **downward displacement** of air.

Preparation of oxygen

Concentrated hydrogen peroxide is dropped slowly from a dropping funnel into a flask containing manganese(IV) oxide catalyst.

$$2H_2O_2(aq) \longrightarrow O_2(g) + 2H_2O(l)$$

In this preparation:

- The oxygen is collected in the gas jar by downward displacement of water (Figure 16.2.3).
- Oxygen is only slightly soluble in water, so most of the oxygen produced will be collected in the gas jar.
- The oxygen in the gas jar will contain some water vapour because it is collected over water. If the oxygen is required dry, it can be passed over anhydrous calcium chloride in a U-tube.

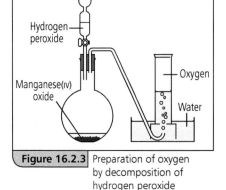

Figure 16.2.3 Preparation of oxygen by decomposition of hydrogen peroxide

Preparation of ammonia

Ammonia is an alkaline gas that is very soluble in water. Ammonia can be prepared by warming any alkali with any ammonium salt. A paste of calcium hydroxide and ammonium chloride is heated gently (Figure 16.2.4).

$$2NH_4Cl(aq) + Ca(OH)_2(aq) \longrightarrow 2NH_3(g) + CaCl_2(aq) + 2H_2O(l)$$

In this preparation:

- Ammonia is less dense than air. So it is collected in the gas jar by downward displacement of air.
- Ammonia is soluble in water, so it is preferable not to prepare it using an aqueous solution of an alkali.
- The ammonia is passed over calcium oxide to dry it. Calcium chloride cannot be used because ammonia reacts with it. It cannot be dried with concentrated sulfuric acid because the acid reacts with ammonia (neutralisation reaction).

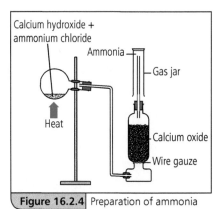

Figure 16.2.4 Preparation of ammonia

KEY POINTS

1 Gases that are denser than air are collected by upward displacement of air. Gases that are less dense than air are collected by downward displacement of air.

2 Calcium chloride or concentrated sulfuric acid can be used for drying oxygen or carbon dioxide because they do not react with these gases.

3 Calcium oxide is used for drying ammonia because it does not react with ammonia.

Uses of non-metals and their compounds

At the end of this topic you should be able to:

- describe the uses of gases based on their properties
- list the uses of some non-metals.

Figure 16.3.1 Oxygen is used in the oxyacetylene torch to join or cut metals.

EXAM TIP

You do not have to know lots of uses for each non-metal. Two uses will generally be sufficient. Concentrate on those uses mentioned in the syllabus.

Uses of some gases

Carbon dioxide

- Some fire extinguishers contain carbon dioxide gas under pressure or produce carbon dioxide when sprayed on the fire (see 7.4). Carbon dioxide is denser than air and 'blankets' the fire, preventing oxygen from reaching it. Carbon dioxide extinguishers are especially useful for dealing with fires involving flammable liquids and electrical equipment.
- The 'fizz' in fizzy drinks is made by pumping carbon dioxide into the drink under pressure.

Oxygen

- We need a constant supply of oxygen for respiration, which takes place in all the cells of our body. Oxygen is used in hospitals to improve the respiration of patients with poor blood flow, blood poisoning and heart disease.
- Oxygen is used in welding (joining) metals. In an oxyacetylene welding torch, acetylene (ethyne, C_2H_2) burns in oxygen. A very hot flame is produced, which is capable of melting most metals.
- A major use of oxygen is in steel production. A blast of oxygen is blown through the molten iron. The oxygen oxidises many of the impurities in the iron and the impurities are then removed.

Uses of some non-metals and their compounds

Carbon

- Carbon in the form of diamond is used in jewellery because of its lustre.
- Diamond is used in drill tips for high-speed drills because of its hardness.
- Graphite is used in pencil 'leads' and as electrodes.
- Carbon fibres are used to strengthen some types of plastic, especially those where extra strength is required, e.g. parts of pumps.

Sulfur

- The major use of sulfur is for the industrial production of sulfuric acid.
- Sulfur is used in the manufacture of tyres to make the rubber harder. This is called **vulcanisation**.
- Sulfur powder is used as a fungicide on plant materials.

Phosphorus

- The main use of phosphorus is in the production of phosphate fertilisers.
- Phosphorus sulfide is used to make the heads of 'strike anywhere' matches. A violet allotrope of phosphorus is used to make the strip on the box of safety matches.
- A small amount of phosphorus is used to make the alloy, phosphor-bronze.

Chlorine

- Chlorine is used to make sodium hypochlorite, which is present in many bleaches.
- The active ingredients of some insecticides are chlorine-containing compounds.
- Chlorine is used to sterilise swimming pools and in water treatment.
- A major use of chlorine is to make the monomer for the plastic, PVC.
- Some dry cleaning and industrial solvents and refrigerants contain compounds of chlorine. Many of these are being withdrawn because they are harmful to the ozone layer (see 16.4).

Nitrogen

- The major use of nitrogen is to make fertilisers. Fertilisers are spread on the soil by farmers to increase the yield of their crops. Fertilisers provide some of the essential elements needed for plant growth: nitrogen (N), phosphorus (P) and potassium (K). So these fertilisers are called NPK fertilisers. When nitrogen from the air combines with hydrogen at 450 °C and 200 atmospheres pressure, in the presence of a catalyst, ammonia, NH_3, is formed. The ammonia is then reacted with nitric acid and phosphates are added to make NPK fertilisers (Figure 16.3.2).
- Nitrogen is used as an inert atmosphere to prevent substances being oxidised, and as a coolant.

Silicon

- Silicon in highly purified form is used for making silicon chips for computers.
- Sand contains silicon(IV) oxide. Glass is made by heating sand with lime (calcium oxide) and sodium carbonate.
- Glass fibres are silicates (compounds of silicon and oxygen). Glass fibres can be used to strengthen plastics (fibreglass). Fibreglass has a low density and is strong. So it is used to make pipes, storage tanks, roofing and boat hulls.
- Silicates containing traces of transition element atoms are used for jewellery, e.g. emeralds.
- Clay contains a variety of silicate minerals. When clay is baked, ceramics are formed. Examples of ceramics are earthenware pottery, stoneware and porcelain.

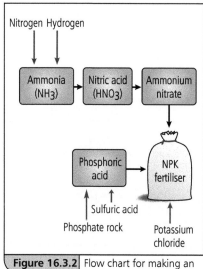

Figure 16.3.2 Flow chart for making an NPK fertiliser

KEY POINTS

1. Carbon dioxide is used in fire extinguishers.
2. Oxygen is used in hospitals and for welding.
3. Carbon in the form of diamond is used for jewellery. Carbon in the form of graphite is used in pencil 'leads' and as electrodes.
4. Sulfur is used in the manufacture of tyres.
5. Phosphorus is used on matchboxes and is present in NPK fertilisers.
6. Chlorine is used to make bleaches and in water treatment.
7. Nitrogen is used to make fertilisers.
8. Silicates are used for strengthening plastics, in ceramics and glass. Silicates containing transition element atoms are used in jewellery.

At the end of this topic you should be able to:

- describe the harmful effects of non-metals and their compounds on living systems and the environment
- describe the problems raised by the disposal of solid waste, particularly plastics.

EXAM TIP

When you revise, make sure that you cross-reference other sections of the syllabus. For example, you can find information about carbon monoxide in 13.1 and 15.6.

DID YOU KNOW?

Herbicides and pesticides can accumulate in fatty tissues of animals. They get more and more concentrated up the food chain. They can adversely affect the reproduction of marine mammals and birds.

Pollution

Pollution occurs when contaminating materials are introduced into the natural environment (earth, air or water). Pollutants generally have an unfavourable effect on the environment.

The effect of specific pollutants

Sulfur dioxide

- Fuels such as coal, petroleum and natural gas contain sulfur.
- When burnt, sulfur is oxidised to sulfur dioxide. Reactions in the atmosphere convert some of the sulfur dioxide to sulfur trioxide.
- The sulfur dioxide and sulfur trioxide react with water in the air to form acids.
- The acid falls to the ground dissolved in the rainwater. This is called **acid rain**.
- Rain is described as acid rain if it has a pH lower than 5.6.
- Acid rain causes death of trees and some aquatic organisms, decrease in soil fertility, erosion of buildings made of carbonate rocks (limestone, marble) and corrosion of metal structures such as bridges.

Hydrogen sulfide

- Hydrogen sulfide, H_2S, is formed from the breakdown of organic matter under anaerobic conditions, e.g. in swamps and in biogas digesters (see 13.1). It is also formed during petroleum refining and industrial coke ovens.
- Hydrogen sulfide is poisonous to humans and animals.

Oxides of nitrogen

- Nitrogen oxides (NO and NO_2) are formed by the combination of nitrogen and oxygen at high temperatures in petrol and diesel engines.
- Nitrogen(II) oxide, NO, can be further oxidised in the atmosphere to NO_2. The NO_2 can dissolve in rain to form acid rain.
- In the presence of hydrocarbons from car exhausts, ozone and sunlight, nitrogen oxides react to form **photochemical smog** which contains many harmful chemicals.
- Nitrogen dioxide can harm the lungs and irritate the nose, throat and eyes. The other compounds present in photochemical smog are even more harmful irritants and can cause asthma.

Carbon dioxide and methane

- Energy is emitted from the surface of the Earth as infrared radiation. Much of this infrared radiation is trapped by gases in the atmosphere.

- Carbon dioxide is formed when fuels are burnt. Methane is formed as a result of bacterial action in swamps, rice paddy fields and the digestive systems of animals.
- Carbon dioxide and methane are **greenhouse gases**. They are good absorbers of infrared radiation. The absorption of infrared radiation by greenhouse gases leads to the heating of the atmosphere. This is called **global warming**.
- An increase in the concentration of carbon dioxide and methane in the atmosphere due to increased industrialisation and more intensive agriculture results in more infrared radiation being absorbed by the atmosphere.
- The atmosphere heats up more than usual. Global warming is increased.
- The effects of increased global warming include melting of the polar ice caps, causing a rise in sea levels, more violent and unpredictable weather, formation of more deserts and increasing the temperature of the oceans, leading to the death of corals.

Chlorofluorocarbons (CFCs) and the ozone layer

- High in the atmosphere is a layer of ozone which reduces the amount of ultraviolet radiation reaching the Earth.
- The **CFCs** formerly used as refrigerants and in aerosol sprays, catalyse the breakdown of ozone into oxygen.
- The breakdown of ozone results in the formation of holes in the ozone layer. So more ultraviolet radiation reaches the Earth's surface.
- This results in increased risk of getting skin cancer, eye cataracts and reduced resistance to some diseases.

Nitrates and phosphates

Nitrates and phosphates cause **eutrophication**. The processes leading to eutrophication are:

- Nitrates and phosphates from fertilisers spread on fields may dissolve in groundwater and get into lakes and rivers.
- Nitrates and phosphates cause excessive growth of algae so that they cover the surface of the water.
- Water plants, including algae, die because of lack of sunlight. Aerobic bacteria feed on the plant remains. The bacteria multiply.
- The aerobic bacteria use up the oxygen in the water, so aquatic animals die.

Solid waste

The main sources of pollution from non-metals is from glass, paper and plastics.

- Broken glass can cause injury to animals. It can also cause fires by acting as a lens, focusing the Sun's rays on flammable material.
- Printing inks from paper dumped in the ground may contain toxic elements such as arsenic and cadmium. Bleaches and chlorine compounds from paper are also harmful.

KEY POINTS

1 Sulfur dioxide arising from burning fossil fuels causes acid rain.

2 Nitrogen oxides from car exhausts cause acid rain and photochemical smog.

3 Carbon monoxide and hydrogen sulfide are toxic gases.

4 Carbon dioxide absorbs infrared radiation. It is a greenhouse gas.

5 Increase in the concentration of carbon dioxide in the atmosphere increases global warming.

6 CFCs catalyse the breakdown of ozone, leading to increased incidence of skin cancer and cataracts.

7 Eutrophication is caused by excessive amounts of nitrates and phosphates in lakes and rivers.

8 Plastic waste may cause harm to animals by getting trapped in their lungs or gullet.

17 Water

17.1 Properties of water

LEARNING OUTCOMES

At the end of this topic you should be able to:

- relate the unique properties of water to its functions in living systems
- describe how the density of water changes with temperature
- explain the high specific heat capacity and low volatility of water
- describe the solvent properties of water.

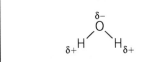

Figure 17.1.1 Water is a polar molecule.

DID YOU KNOW?

The relatively strong intermolecular forces between the δ^+ hydrogen atoms and the δ^- oxygen atom in water are called hydrogen bonds. The strength of a hydrogen bond is about a third that of some covalent bonds, e.g. F—F. Liquid water below 4°C still has a considerable amount of 'ice-like' structure in it.

The water molecule

Water is a small molecule. It is a **polar molecule**. Polar molecules have a partial positive charge on one end of their molecule and a partial negative charge on the other. These partial charges are shown by the symbols δ^+ and δ^- (Figure 17.1.1). Solvents that are not charged (or where the centre of partial charges δ^+ and δ^- is the same) are called **non-polar**. The intermolecular forces between polar molecules are stronger than the intermolecular forces between non-polar molecules of a similar size.

The density of water at different temperatures

For most liquids, the density increases as the temperature decreases. The density continues to increase as the liquid freezes. The solid has a higher density than the corresponding liquid because the molecules are more closely packed. Water is unusual: at 4°C its density starts to decrease and when it freezes at 0°C, there is a sudden decrease in density (Figure 17.1.2(a)). So ice floats in water.

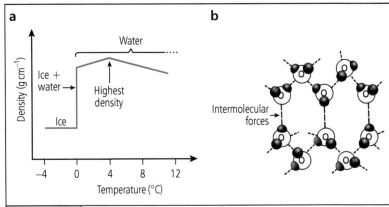

Figure 17.1.2 **a** The density of water at different temperatures, **b** the structure of ice

Ice is less dense than water because it has a relatively open cage-like structure (Figure 17.1.2(b)) that allows the molecules to be further apart than in the liquid. When ice melts, this structure begins to collapse.

In freezing weather, the fact that ice is less dense than water is important for the survival of fish and other aquatic organisms. The denser water remains below the ice so that the aquatic organisms still have access to food from the river or lake bed.

Other properties of water

Water has a higher specific heat capacity and boiling point than most other molecules of comparable molar mass. For example, the boiling point of water ($M_r = 18$) is $+100\,°C$ whereas the boiling point of methane ($M_r = 16$) is $-164\,°C$. Water is not as volatile as many organic solvents because of its relatively high boiling point. These properties can be explained by the presence of the relatively strong intermolecular forces between the polar water molecules compared with the weaker intermolecular forces between non-polar molecules of similar molar mass.

Water as a solvent

Water is a good solvent in everyday life as well as in industry. The polar nature of water allows it to dissolve both ionic compounds as well as polar covalent molecules. Figure 17.1.4 shows the process of dissolving.

Figure 17.1.3 This insect can skate on the surface of the water because water has a high surface tension due to its relative strong intermolecular forces.

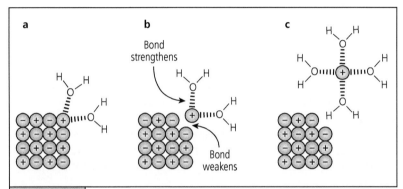

Figure 17.1.4 **a** Water molecules bond to the ions. **b** The forces between the ions weaken. **c** Water molecules surround the ions to keep them in solution.

Water is essential to life because many of the chemical reactions in living things take place in aqueous solution. Many of the compounds in our bodies contain polar groups such as $-OH$, $-COOH$ and $-NH_2$ or ions derived from these, e.g. COO^-. Water is essential so that these compounds can dissolve and react. Dissolved ions play an important part in nerve conduction. The layer of water around ions plays an important part in allowing some ions to pass through cell membranes while preventing others from passing. In addition, water plays a part in hydrolysis reactions in the body.

DID YOU KNOW?

The specific heat capacity of a substance is the amount of heat energy required to raise the temperature of 1 g of a substance by $1\,°C$. The specific heat capacity of water is relatively high ($4.17\,J\,g^{-1}\,°C^{-1}$) whereas for non-polar solvents such as tetrachloromethane CCl_4, it is low ($0.84\,J\,g^{-1}\,°C^{-1}$).

Living things cannot survive extremes of temperature. The high specific thermal capacity of the water present in all living organisms helps them to survive because it takes a relatively large amount of energy to change the temperature of water.

KEY POINTS

1 Water is a polar molecule.

2 Ice is less dense than water.

3 Water has its maximum density at $4\,°C$.

4 Water has a higher specific heat capacity and boiling point and a lower volatility than most other molecules of comparable molar mass.

5 Water is a good solvent for ionic and polar covalent compounds.

6 The solvent properties of water are essential to life.

EXAM TIP

Make sure that you know the importance of water in supporting life as well as its unusual physical properties.

Leaching, hard water and water treatment

17.2

At the end of this topic you should be able to:

- describe the consequences of the solvent properties of water in terms of leaching and hardness of water
- describe the differences between soft water and permanent and temporary hardness of water
- describe the methods used in the treatment of water for domestic purposes
- describe water softening.

Leaching

Dissolved substances can get into lakes and rivers by moving through the soil. Soil particles are usually surrounded by a thin layer of water. In most soils, water is constantly moving through the soil and useful nutrients as well as pollutants get washed out of the soil. This is called **leaching**. Leaching plays an important part in removing soil minerals and in transferring pollutants from the soil into lakes and rivers. It can also play a part in making water hard.

Hard and soft water

When rainwater containing dissolved carbon dioxide moves through rocks such as limestone, it reacts with the calcium or magnesium carbonate. Calcium and magnesium hydrogencarbonates are formed in solution in water. The Ca^{2+} and Mg^{2+} ions cause water to be hard. Hard water forms a scum of insoluble calcium or magnesium salts with soap (see 14.1). Hard water also forms limescale (calcium carbonate) inside kettles and water pipes. Soft water contains hardly any dissolved calcium or magnesium ions and does not form a scum with soap.

Water softening

You can remove calcium and magnesium ions from hard water by:

- adding sodium carbonate (washing soda). A precipitate of calcium carbonate (or magnesium carbonate) is formed, so removing the Ca^{2+} and Mg^{2+} ions from solution.

$$Ca^{2+}(aq) + CO_3^{2-}(aq) \longrightarrow CaCO_3(s)$$

- distillation. This removes all impurities, but it is expensive because a lot of energy is used.
- using an **ion-exchange** resin. The resin has sodium ions bound to its surface. When water containing calcium or magnesium ions is run through an ion-exchange column, the calcium (or magnesium) ions replace the sodium ions on the surface of the resin (Figure 17.2.2). When each calcium ion binds to the resin, two sodium ions are released into the water. The sodium ions do not make the water hard.

Figure 17.2.1 The evaporation of hard water has created these features in Harrison's Cave, Barbados.

Temporary and permanent hardness

Temporary hardness is caused by dissolved calcium and magnesium hydrogencarbonates. It can be removed by boiling, because the hydrogencarbonates decompose and the Ca^{2+} and Mg^{2+} ions precipitate out of solution.

$$Ca(HCO_3)_2(aq) \longrightarrow CaCO_3(s) + CO_2(g) + H_2O(l)$$

Precipitation of calcium carbonate from temporary hard water builds up as a 'fur' inside kettles and hot water pipes.

Permanent hardness cannot be removed by boiling. It is caused by calcium sulfate and magnesium sulfate. These soluble salts do not decompose when heated. So the hardness has to be removed using sodium carbonate, by distillation or by using an ion-exchange resin.

Water treatment

Water can be purified at home by:

- Boiling for 15 minutes to kill most microorganisms.
- Using a fine filter to trap larger particles and larger microorganisms. Bacteria and smaller microorganisms are not, however, removed.
- Chlorination. A chlorine-containing bleach or water purification tablets are added to the water, stirred, then left for 30 minutes. The chlorine kills all microorganisms.

Large-scale purification of water involves several steps:

1 Impure water from rivers, lakes and underground wells passes through screens to remove large objects, e.g. twigs, animal remains.

2 The water is stored in reservoirs and suspended matter, e.g. soil particles, is allowed to settle. Aluminium sulfate or iron(III) sulfate is added to help the smaller particles suspended in the water to settle.

3 The water passes through a sand and gravel filter. This removes any tiny suspended particles that were not removed in the reservoirs.

4 Carbon may be added to remove foul smells from the water.

5 **Chlorination**: Chlorine is added to kill harmful microorganisms such as bacteria.

6 The pH of the water is adjusted and then run off for homes and factories.

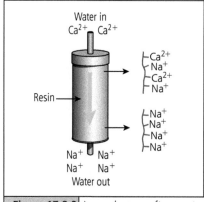

Figure 17.2.2 Ion exchange softens water because the calcium ions stay on the column after replacing the sodium ions.

KEY POINTS

1 Leaching removes soluble compounds from the soil so that they drain into lakes and rivers.

2 Water containing dissolved carbon dioxide reacts with carbonate rocks to form hard water.

3 Hard water contains aqueous calcium and magnesium ions. Soft water does not contain these ions.

4 Hard water can be made soft by using washing soda, by distillation or by using an ion-exchange column.

5 Permanent hardness is caused by dissolved calcium and magnesium sulfates.

6 Temporary hardness is caused by dissolved calcium hydrogencarbonate.

7 Temporary hardness can be removed by boiling. Permanent hardness cannot be removed by boiling.

EXAM TIP

You do not have to know all the details about the large-scale purification of water that you see in some textbooks. You should concentrate on the reasons for settlement, filtration and chlorination.

18 Green chemistry

18.1 The principles of green chemistry

What is green chemistry?

Pollution of the air, water and land around us is becoming more and more of a problem with increasing world population and industrialisation. In 15.6 and 16.4 we explored some of these problems. **Green chemistry** deals with how to prevent harming the environment in the first place. It does this by improving chemical processes and manufacturing techniques for making materials such as plastics, clothing and glass. It also improves the way that metals are extracted from their ores and the way that bulk chemicals, such as sulfuric acid, are made. Most products are made through a series of chemical reactions (chemical **synthesis**). Each reaction in this series may require one or more reactants as well as a catalyst (Figure 18.1.1).

The main problems arising from the chemical industry are:

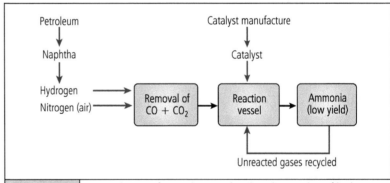

Figure 18.1.1 Ammonia manufacture is more than just the reaction of hydrogen and nitrogen.

- the use and production of hazardous substances
- inefficient energy use, e.g. high temperatures and pressures
- low **percentage yield** and low **atom economy**.

$$\text{percentage yield} = \frac{\text{amount of required product obtained}}{\text{maximum amount of product expected}} \times 100$$

$$\text{atom economy} = \frac{\text{molar mass of required product}}{\text{molar masses of all the products}} \times 100$$

In order to reduce some of these problems, scientists have developed the idea of green chemistry (also called **sustainable chemistry**).

Green chemistry is defined as: a set of principles that reduces or eliminates the use and generation of hazardous substances in the manufacture and use of chemical products.

The twelve principles of green chemistry

The twelve principles of green chemistry are:

1 Prevention: It is better to reduce waste than to treat it after it has been formed.

2 Atom economy: The methods used for synthesis should use up as many of the materials used in the process as possible and incorporate these into the required product. In other words, the atom economy should be as near 100% as possible.

3 Less hazardous chemical synthesis: The harm of reactants, products and catalysts to the environment and life should be minimised.

4 Safer chemical products: The effectiveness of the products should not be reduced at the same time as decreasing their possible harm.

5 Safer solvents and other agents: Reactions should be devised so that harmful solvents, catalysts and substances used in separation techniques are not used or their use is minimised.

6 Minimum energy requirements: As little energy as possible should be used. The reactions should be carried out at r.t.p. if possible. The heat evolved in exothermic reactions should be used for another job and not released to the environment, e.g. as hot water.

7 Use of renewable raw materials: Raw materials and **feedstocks** should be renewable instead of depleting natural resources. A feedstock is a material taken from nature (or a substance that has undergone some slight processing) that is used as the starting material for a chemical process, e.g. air, iron ore, the naphtha fraction from petroleum distillation.

8 Reduce use of additional chemicals or additional steps: When a substance is synthesised in several steps, particular chemicals (blocking groups) are used to stop reactive groups reacting in unwanted ways. The blocking groups are removed later.

9 Use of catalysts: The use of catalysts reduces energy costs because the reaction takes place at a lower temperature. The more specific the catalyst for a particular reaction is, the less is the likelihood of getting additional unwanted products.

10 Nature of breakdown of products: Products should be designed so that they break down in the environment to form harmless substances. The breakdown products should not stay in the environment for a long time.

11 Monitoring to prevent pollution: Each step in a chemical synthesis should be monitored for the presence of pollutants and methods should be developed to control the formation of these pollutants or their release into the environment.

12 Minimise chemical accidents: The hazards presented by reactants and products should be taken into account. Conditions chosen should minimise these.

Examples of green chemistry

EXAM TIP

You do not need to make an in-depth study of green chemistry or give details of particular examples. You do, however, need to understand how to apply the principles of green chemistry to examples that have been provided, e.g. some solvents are harmful, so search for alternative harmless ones.

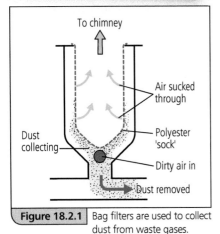

Figure 18.2.1 Bag filters are used to collect dust from waste gases.

Example 1: Maleic anhydride

Maleic anhydride is used in the manufacture of polyester resins and paints. It was formerly manufactured by heating benzene, C_6H_6, with oxygen in the presence of a catalyst:

$$C_6H_6 + 4\tfrac{1}{2}O_2 \longrightarrow C_4H_2O_3 + 2CO_2 + 2H_2O$$
benzene   maleic anhydride

It is now manufactured from butane:

$$C_4H_{10} + 3\tfrac{1}{2}O_2 \longrightarrow C_4H_2O_3 + 4H_2O$$
butane   maleic anhydride

The process using butane is 'greener' because:

• The atom economy in terms of carbon is better. There is no loss of carbon.

• No carbon dioxide is produced. So the reaction does not increase global warming.

Example 2: Treating emissions

Coal and oil-fired power stations and other industries burning fossil fuels have to take steps to control the release of harmful gases into the air.

• **Flue gas desulfurisation** is used to remove sulfur dioxide arising from burning fossil fuels containing sulfur. The gases containing sulfur dioxide are passed through powdered calcium oxide, which is kept in constant movement. The sulfur dioxide reacts to form harmless calcium sulfite, $CaSO_3$:

$$SO_2(g) + CaO(s) \longrightarrow CaSO_3(s)$$

The calcium sulfite can be used to make sulfuric acid.

• **Filters** are used to remove dust and particles from chemical plants and power stations. Air is drawn through the filters and dust collects on the outside (see Figure 18.2.1).

• **Catalytic converters** are used to reduce the emission of harmful gases such as carbon monoxide and nitrogen oxides from petrol engines. The exhaust gases from the car engine are passed over a platinum or rhodium catalyst. Harmful nitrogen oxides are converted to harmless nitrogen. Toxic carbon monoxide is converted to harmless carbon dioxide.

$$2NO(g) + 2CO(g) \longrightarrow N_2(g) + 2CO_2(g)$$

Example 3: Making polyesters

A chemical called propene-1,3-diol is used to make polyesters for carpets and clothing. The chemical is made from propene. Propene is a product arising from cracking the naphtha fraction of petroleum.

Propene-1,3-diol can now be made by using genetically modified bacteria. The genetically modified bacterium *Escherichia coli* (*E. coli*) can be grown on mashed-up corn.

The process using bacteria is 'greener' because:

- The process does not depend directly on non-renewable resources such as petroleum. Renewable corn is used as a feedstock.
- Less carbon dioxide is produced. So there is less effect on the environment.
- The energy costs are lower because on average lower temperatures are used.
- The process uses an efficient catalyst: enzymes in the bacteria.

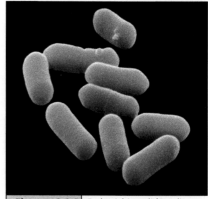

Figure 18.2.2 *Escherichia coli* (*E.coli* bacteria). Genetically modified strains of this bacterium can be used to make propene in a 'green' way.

Example 4: Fuels from algae

Chemists are currently investigating new ways of using algae (simple plants) to make **biofuels**. Methane and hydrocarbons containing 6–12 carbon atoms per molecule can be produced from particular strains of algae. Other strains can produce butanol. The algae are grown in water in glass vessels or reservoirs in the presence of light and suitable nutrients. Carbon dioxide is bubbled through the mixture. Although relatively small amounts of hydrocarbons are produced compared with petroleum fractionation, the process is 'greener' because:

- The process does not depend directly on non-renewable resources such as petroleum.
- Carbon dioxide is absorbed for photosynthesis, so the process is almost 'carbon neutral'.
- The energy costs are lower because the process occurs at r.t.p.
- The process uses an efficient catalyst: enzymes in the algae.

Example 5: Using an improved catalyst

We can attach an alkyl group to benzene, C_6H_6, by reacting it with an alkene in the presence of an aluminium chloride catalyst.

$$C_6H_6 + CH_3CH{=}CH_2 \longrightarrow C_6H_5CH(CH_3)_2$$

Water is added to the reaction to stop more alkyl groups being added (quenching). The water reacts with the catalyst, forming hydrogen chloride gas.

When the catalyst is modified by combining it with silica, the process is 'greener' because:

- The yield is higher.
- No corrosive fumes of hydrogen chloride are produced.
- The catalyst can be filtered and reused.

KEY POINTS

1 Genetically modified bacteria can be used to produce compounds useful for chemical synthesis.

2 Algae can be used to produce fuels.

3 Flue gas desulfurisation, filters and catalytic converters are used to reduce the emission of harmful compounds into the atmosphere.

4 Improvements in catalysts can lead to greater yields, and a reduction in harmful emissions.

Identification of cations

DID YOU KNOW?

Some transition element cations give a characteristic colour to their aqueous solutions, e.g. copper(II) ions in aqueous solution are often blue, solutions containing iron(II) ions are often light green, solutions containing iron(III) ions are often yellow.

Figure 19.1.1 Transition metal ions can be identified from the colour of their hydroxides.

Tests for cations using sodium hydroxide

Many metal cations can be identified by observing the colour of the precipitate formed by the addition of dilute sodium hydroxide to an aqueous solution of the substance under test. If the sodium hydroxide is not in excess, a metal hydroxide is formed. In excess sodium hydroxide, some of the precipitates may dissolve.

- If a white precipitate forms, which is insoluble in excess sodium hydroxide, a Group II cation such as Ca^{2+}, may be present.

$$Ca^{2+}(aq) + 2OH^-(aq) \longrightarrow Ca(OH)_2(s)$$

- If a white precipitate is formed that dissolves when excess sodium hydroxide is added to give a colourless solution, Al^{3+}, Pb^{2+} or Zn^{2+} ions may be present. This is due to the formation of soluble aluminates, plumbates or zincates.

sodium hydroxide not in excess:

$$Al^{3+}(aq) + 3OH^-(aq) \longrightarrow Al(OH)_3(s)$$

in excess sodium hydroxide:

$$\underset{\text{aluminium hydroxide}}{Al(OH)_3(s)} + OH^-(aq) \longrightarrow \underset{\text{aluminate ion}}{Al(OH)_4^-(aq)}$$

The equations for lead(II) hydroxide and zinc hydroxide dissolving in excess sodium hydroxide are:

$$\underset{\text{lead(II) hydroxide}}{Pb(OH)_2(s)} + 2OH^-(aq) \longrightarrow \underset{\text{plumbate(II) ion}}{Pb(OH)_4^{2-}(aq)}$$

$$\underset{\text{zinc hydroxide}}{Zn(OH)_2(s)} + 2OH^-(aq) \longrightarrow \underset{\text{zincate ion}}{Zn(OH)_4^{2-}(aq)}$$

- If a coloured precipitate is formed, the colour may be used to identify the cation (Figure 19.1.1). A metal hydroxide is formed that is insoluble in excess sodium hydroxide.

$$\underset{\text{iron(II) ions}}{Fe^{2+}(aq)} + 2OH^-(aq) \longrightarrow \underset{\substack{\text{iron(II) hydroxide}\\\text{grey-green gelatinous precipitate}}}{Fe(OH)_2(s)}$$

$$\underset{\text{iron(III) ions}}{Fe^{3+}(aq)} + 3OH^-(aq) \longrightarrow \underset{\substack{\text{iron(III) hydroxide}\\\text{red-brown gelatinous precipitate}}}{Fe(OH)_3(s)}$$

$$\underset{\text{copper(II) ions}}{Cu^{2+}(aq)} + 2OH^-(aq) \longrightarrow \underset{\substack{\text{copper(II) hydroxide}\\\text{pale blue precipitate}}}{Cu(OH)_2(s)}$$

Tests for cations using aqueous ammonia

Aqueous ammonia contains hydroxide ions (see 7.2). The observations and ionic equations for most of the reactions are the same as the reactions and ionic equations using sodium hydroxide. There are some exceptions:

- Zn^{2+} ions can be distinguished from Al^{3+} ions and Pb^{2+} ions by the use of aqueous ammonia. Zinc hydroxide dissolves in excess aqueous ammonia to form a colourless solution. Aluminium hydroxide and lead hydroxide do not dissolve.

$NH_3(aq)$ not in excess:

$$Zn^{2+}(aq) + 2OH^-(aq) \longrightarrow Zn(OH)_2(s)$$

$NH_3(aq)$ in excess:

$$Zn(OH)_2(s) + 4NH_3(aq) \longrightarrow Zn[(NH_3)_4]^{2+}(aq) + 2OH^-(aq)$$
$$\text{colourless solution}$$

- Copper hydroxide dissolves in excess aqueous ammonia to form a deep blue solution.

$NH_3(aq)$ not in excess:

$$Cu^{2+}(aq) + 2OH^-(aq) \longrightarrow Cu(OH)_2(s)$$

$NH_3(aq)$ in excess:

$$Cu(OH)_2(s) + 4NH_3(aq) \longrightarrow Cu[(NH_3)_4]^{2+}(aq) + 2OH^-(aq)$$
$$\text{deep blue solution}$$

A confirmatory test for lead(II) ions

Aqueous solutions containing lead and aluminium ions both give white precipitates with sodium hydroxide or ammonia. Both precipitates are soluble in excess alkali. A confirmatory test for lead(II) ions is to add some aqueous potassium iodide. A yellow precipitate of lead(II) iodide is formed:

$$Pb^{2+}(aq) + 2I^-(aq) \longrightarrow PbI_2(s)$$

Aluminium ions do not give a precipitate on addition of aqueous potassium iodide.

Testing for ammonium ions

When a compound containing ammonium ions, NH_4^+, is heated gently with aqueous sodium hydroxide, ammonia is given off. Ammonia turns red litmus blue (see Figure 19.1.2).

$$NH_4^+(aq) + OH^-(aq) \longrightarrow NH_3(g) + H_2O(l)$$

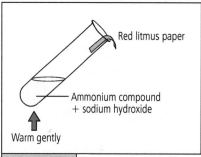

Red litmus paper

Ammonium compound + sodium hydroxide

Warm gently

Figure 19.1.2 Red litmus turns blue when a solution containing NH_4^+ ions is warmed with aqueous sodium hydroxide.

KEY POINTS

1 Solutions containing Ca^{2+}, Pb^{2+}, Zn^{2+} or Al^{3+} ions give white precipitates on addition of sodium hydroxide or aqueous ammonia when the sodium hydroxide or ammonia is not in excess.

2 Solutions containing Cu^{2+}, Fe^{2+} or Fe^{3+} ions give coloured precipitates on addition of sodium hydroxide or aqueous ammonia.

3 Precipitates of aluminium, lead or zinc hydroxides dissolve in excess sodium hydroxide.

4 Precipitates of zinc hydroxide or copper hydroxide dissolve in excess aqueous ammonia.

5 In aqueous solution, lead(II) ions react with aqueous potassium iodide to from a yellow precipitate.

6 Ammonia is released when an aqueous solution of ammonium ions is heated with aqueous sodium hydroxide.

Identification of anions

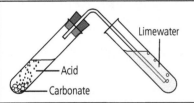

Figure 19.2.1 A carbonate is present if on addition of an acid, the gas released turns limewater milky.

DID YOU KNOW?

A more reliable test for a nitrate is to add aqueous sodium hydroxide and aluminium powder to the suspected nitrate. On warming, ammonia is released if a nitrate is present.

Figure 19.2.2 Precipitates of AgCl (left), AgBr and AgI (right)

Identifying carbonates

• All carbonates reacts with acids to produce carbon dioxide, e.g.
$$CO_3^{2-}(s) + 2H^+(aq) \longrightarrow CO_2(g) + H_2O(l)$$
The carbon dioxide released turns limewater milky (Figure 19.2.1).

• Many carbonates decompose to form carbon dioxide when strongly heated, e.g.
$$SrCO_3(s) \longrightarrow SrO(s) + CO_2(g)$$

• Soluble carbonates form a white precipitate on addition of barium nitrate or barium chloride.
$$CO_3^{2-}(aq) + Ba^{2+}(aq) \longrightarrow BaCO_3(s)$$
The precipitate dissolves in dilute acid, releasing carbon dioxide.

Identifying sulfates

• The solution to be tested is first acidified with nitric acid to remove any carbonates. Aqueous barium chloride or barium nitrate is then added. If a sulfate is present, a white precipitate of barium sulfate is observed.
$$Ba^{2+}(aq) + SO_4^{2-}(aq) \longrightarrow BaSO_4(s)$$
The precipitate does not dissolve on addition of dilute acid.

Identifying sulfites

• Sulfites contain the ion SO_3^{2-}. When an aqueous sulfite is heated with a dilute acid, sulfur dioxide, SO_2, is released.
$$SO_3^{2-}(aq) + 2H^+(aq) \longrightarrow SO_2(g) + H_2O(l)$$
Sulfur dioxide has a choking acidic smell. It turns damp blue litmus paper red. Its presence can be confirmed by bubbling the gas through a solution of potassium manganate(VII). The solution of potassium manganate(VII) turns from purple to colourless if sulfur dioxide is present.

• Aqueous sulfites form a white precipitate with barium nitrate or barium chloride.
$$SO_3^{2-}(aq) + Ba^{2+}(aq) \longrightarrow BaSO_3(s)$$
The precipitate dissolves in dilute acid, releasing sulfur dioxide on heating.

Identifying nitrates

• Many nitrates decompose when the solid nitrate is heated to release nitrogen dioxide.
$$2Cu(NO_3)_2 \longrightarrow 2CuO(s) + 4NO_2(g) + O_2(g)$$

– Nitrogen dioxide can be identified as a brown, choking gas.

– Oxygen relights a glowing splint (see 19.3).

Not all nitrates decompose to form nitrogen dioxide (see 15.2). So the test for oxygen is the most reliable indication of the presence of a nitrate.

Identifying halides

Using aqueous silver nitrate

1 Add dilute nitric acid to an aqueous solution of the suspected halide.

2 Then add aqueous silver nitrate and observe the colour of the precipitate (Figure 19.2.2).

3 Add excess aqueous ammonia and see if the precipitate dissolves.

- Chlorides give a white precipitate of silver chloride:

$$Ag^+(aq) + Cl^-(aq) \longrightarrow AgCl(s)$$

The silver chloride precipitate dissolves readily in a little aqueous ammonia.

- Bromides give a cream-coloured precipitate of silver bromide:

$$Ag^+(aq) + Br^-(aq) \longrightarrow AgBr(s)$$

The silver bromide precipitate dissolves only in excess concentrated aqueous ammonia.

- Iodides give a pale yellow precipitate of silver iodide:

$$Ag^+(aq) + I^-(aq) \longrightarrow AgI(s)$$

The silver iodide precipitate does not dissolve in excess concentrated aqueous ammonia.

Using aqueous lead nitrate

1 Add dilute nitric acid to an aqueous solution of the suspected halide.

2 Then add aqueous lead nitrate and observe the colour of the precipitate.

- Chlorides give a white precipitate of lead(II) chloride:

$$Pb^{2+}(aq) + 2Cl^-(aq) \longrightarrow PbCl_2(s)$$

- Bromides give a pale yellow precipitate of lead bromide:

$$Pb^{2+}(aq) + 2Br^-(aq) \longrightarrow PbBr_2(s)$$

- Iodides give a deep yellow precipitate of lead iodide:

$$Pb^{2+}(aq) + 2I^-(aq) \longrightarrow PbI_2(s)$$

Warming with concentrated sulfuric acid

- Chlorides produce white, acidic fumes of hydrogen chloride.
- Bromides produce orange-brown fumes of bromine vapour.
- Iodides produce a black solid (iodine) and a purple iodine vapour.

EXAM TIP

The effect of heat on carbonates, nitrates and sulfates is a less satisfactory method of identifying these cations than other tests. This is because some carbonates, nitrates and sulfates do not decompose or only decompose at temperatures higher than that of a Bunsen burner flame.

KEY POINTS

1 Carbonates produce carbon dioxide when heated and nitrates produce oxygen. Some nitrates produce nitrogen dioxide when heated.

2 When reacted with dilute acids, carbonates produce carbon dioxide and sulfites produce sulfur dioxide.

3 Aqueous solutions of halide ions react with silver nitrate or lead nitrate to form characteristically coloured precipitates.

4 Barium nitrate or barium chloride gives a white precipitate with aqueous solutions of sulfates, sulfites or carbonates.

5 When warmed with concentrated sulfuric acid, halides produce characteristically coloured products.

Identification of gases

At the end of this topic you should be able to:

- identify gases H_2, O_2, CO_2, NH_3, SO_2, Cl_2, NO_2 and H_2O with reference to colour and smell
- identify H_2, O_2 with reference to a lighted or glowing splint
- identify CO_2, NH_3, SO_2, Cl_2, NO_2 and H_2O by specific chemical reactions
- write equations for the reactions where relevant.

EXAM TIP

A common error is to confuse the tests for hydrogen and oxygen. Remember that a li<u>g</u>hted (splint) has the H for hydrogen and a gl<u>o</u>wing splint has the O for oxygen.

In the presence of water, sulfur dioxide is used as a bleaching agent for fibres such as silk and wool. It reacts with water to form hydrogensulfite ions, which are a reducing agent. The bleaching action is gentle. Chlorine on the other hand is a stronger bleach and works by oxidising stains.

Identifying hydrogen

- Hydrogen is a colourless gas. It has no smell.
- When a lighted splint is put into a test tube of hydrogen, it explodes with a squeaky 'pop'.

Identifying oxygen

- Oxygen is colourless gas. It has no smell.
- When a glowing splint is put into in a test tube of oxygen, the splint relights.

Identifying carbon dioxide

- Carbon dioxide is a colourless gas. It has no smell.
- When carbon dioxide is bubbled through limewater (a solution of calcium hydroxide), the limewater goes milky (Figure 19.3.1(a)). This is due to the formation of a suspension of calcium carbonate:

$$Ca(OH)_2(aq) + CO_2(g) \longrightarrow CaCO_3(s) + H_2O(l)$$

- On continued bubbling of carbon dioxide, the calcium carbonate dissolves to form soluble calcium hydrogencarbonate:

$$CaCO_3(s) + CO_2(g) + H_2O(l) \longrightarrow Ca(HCO_3)_2(aq)$$

- A second way of testing for the presence of small amounts of carbon dioxide is shown in Figure 19.3.1(b).

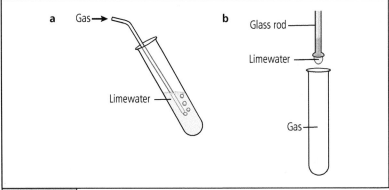

Figure 19.3.1 Two ways of testing for carbon dioxide

Identifying ammonia

- Ammonia is a colourless gas. It has a sharp smell.
- Ammonia turns damp red litmus paper blue. Hydroxide ions are formed when ammonia reacts with the water in the damp litmus paper. The hydroxide ions turn the litmus indicator blue.

$$NH_3(g) + H_2O(l) \rightleftharpoons NH_4^+(aq) + OH^-(aq)$$

- White fumes of ammonium chloride are seen when a drop of concentrated hydrochloric acid on the end of a glass rod is placed near the gas (Figure 19.3.2).

$$NH_3(g) + HCl(g) \rightleftharpoons NH_4Cl(s)$$

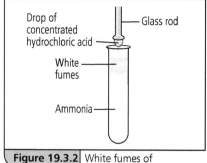

Figure 19.3.2 White fumes of ammonium chloride are formed when the hydrogen chloride, which evaporates from concentrated hydrochloric acid, reacts with ammonia.

Labels in figure: Drop of concentrated hydrochloric acid — Glass rod — White fumes — Ammonia

Identifying hydrogen chloride

- Hydrogen chloride is a colourless gas. It has a pungent, acidic smell.
- Hydrogen chloride can be identified using a drop of concentrated aqueous ammonia on the end of a glass rod. White fumes of ammonium chloride are seen when the drop of ammonia is placed near the hydrogen chloride.

Identifying sulfur dioxide

- Sulfur dioxide is a colourless gas. It has a pungent acidic smell.
- When sulfur dioxide is bubbled through aqueous potassium manganate(VII), the potassium manganate(VII) turns from purple to colourless.
- When sulfur dioxide is bubbled through aqueous potassium dichromate(VI), the potassium dichromate(VI) turns from orange to green.

Identifying nitrogen dioxide

- Nitrogen dioxide is a poisonous red-brown gas. It has a sharp irritating smell.
- Nitrogen dioxide turns damp blue litmus paper red. The nitrogen dioxide reacts with the water in the damp litmus paper to form an acidic solution.

Identifying chlorine

- Chlorine is a poisonous yellow-green gas. It has a sharp, choking bleach-like smell.
- Chlorine turns damp blue litmus paper red and then rapidly bleaches it. The bleaching reaction is often so fast that you may only see the litmus paper being bleached. The chlorine reacts with the water in the damp litmus paper and forms a mixture of hydrochloric and chloric(I) acids. The chloric(I) acid is responsible for the bleaching action.

$$Cl_2(g) + H_2O(l) \longrightarrow HCl(aq) + HClO(aq)$$

Identifying water vapour

- Water vapour is colourless. It has no smell.
- Water vapour turns dry cobalt chloride paper from blue to pink.
- Water vapour turns anhydrous copper(II) sulfate crystals from white to blue.

KEY POINTS

1 Hydrogen is identified using a lighted splint. Oxygen is identified using a glowing splint.

2 Carbon dioxide turns limewater milky.

3 Ammonia turns damp red litmus paper blue.

4 Sulfur dioxide decolourises potassium manganate(VII) and turns potassium dichromate(VI) from orange to green.

5 Hydrogen chloride forms white fumes with ammonia.

6 Nitrogen dioxide is a red-brown gas.

7 Chlorine bleaches damp litmus.

8 Water vapour turns blue cobalt chloride paper pink and anhydrous copper sulfate blue.

Section C Practice exam questions

SECTION C: Multiple-choice questions

1 Which of the statements is generally true about metallic and non-metallic elements of the periodic table?

  a Metallic elements have low melting points.

  b Solid non-metallic elements are shiny looking.

  c Non-metallic elements are poor conductors of electricity.

  d Metallic elements are poor conductors of heat.

2 Metal salts can be prepared from a water insoluble metal carbonate in dilute acid. Which of the following best explains why *excess* solid is mixed with the acid?

  a To produce good crystals

  b To speed up the reaction

  c It is easier to filter the acid than the solid.

  d All the acid is neutralised and the excess solid can be filtered.

3 Which element is used for window frames and other situations exposed to the weather, because it has good anti-corrosion properties?

  a Silver

  b Zinc

  c Aluminium

  d Copper

4 Which of the following is **not** matched correctly?

	Non-metal	Use
a	Hydrogen	Manufacture of ammonia
b	Phosphorus	In matches
c	Chlorine	Ceramics
d	Silicon	Electronic devices

5 Which of the following statements is/are true of green chemistry?

    I It prevents waste.

    II It improves energy efficiency.

    III It uses renewable feedstocks.

  a I only

  b I and II

  c II and III

  d I, II and III

6 Which of the following methods of preparation of hydrogen gas should **not** be attempted in the laboratory?

  a Reacting sodium with dilute hydrochloric acid

  b Reacting magnesium with steam

  c Electrolysis of acidified water

  d Reacting magnesium with dilute hydrochloric acid

7 Which statement is true about the properties of water?

  a The temperature of water rises and falls very quickly.

  b Water is a good solvent because it has a polar nature.

  c Water molecules do not cling to each other.

  d Water changes to steam by condensation.

8 Which of the following statements is **not** true of the use of coke in the extraction of metals?

  a It oxidises the metal oxides to metal.

  b It acts a reducing agent.

  c It is cheap.

  d It supplies heat required for the reaction.

9 a Given part of the metal reactivity series:

sodium   magnesium   zinc   iron   copper   gold

  i Where should hydrogen be placed? Explain. *(2)*

  ii Give a full equation to show iron dissolving in dilute sulfuric acid. *(3)*

  iii Give the *ionic equation* to show iron dissolving in *any* acid. *(3)*

  iv Why is gold found as the pure element? *(1)*

  v Give the reaction between iron(II) sulfate and magnesium. Explain. *(2)*

 b Steel is a mixture of iron and carbon. Bronze is a mixture of copper and tin.

  i Why are steel and bronze called alloys? *(1)*

  Cupronickel can be used to make coins.

  ii What properties should cupronickel have so that it makes good coins? *(3)*

10 a What substances must be in contact with iron before it will rust? *(2)*

 b i What is the chemical structure (name and formula) of rust? *(2)*

  ii Explain why rusting is an example of *oxidation*. *(2)*

 c Car bodies can be doubly protected from rusting with paint and galvanising.

  i Describe and explain the two methods. *(4)*

  ii Will the car body automatically rust if it is deeply scratched? Explain your answer. *(2)*

 d Blocks of magnesium are bolted to a ship's hull.

  i Explain how this reduces steel corrosion. *(2)*

  ii Why must there be no paint between the magnesium and the steel hull? *(1)*

11 Non-metallic oxides are usually acidic or neutral.

 a Give two examples of non-metallic oxides that are acidic. *(2)*

 b Using one non-metallic oxide from part **a**, write an equation to show how it reacts with water. *(3)*

 c Using one non-metallic oxide from part **a**, write an equation to show how it reacts with sodium hydroxide solution. *(3)*

12 The following chart shows reactions of cations with sodium hydroxide.

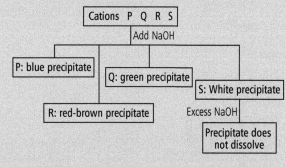

 a Identify cations P, Q, R and S. *(4)*

 b Write an ionic equation for R with NaOH. *(3)*

13 a In the extraction of aluminium:

  i What is the name of the aluminium ore? *(1)*

  ii What is the chemical formula for aluminium oxide? *(1)*

  iii Why is cryolite added to aluminium ore? *(1)*

  iv Write an equation for the anode reaction during the extraction of aluminium by electrolysis *(2)*

  v Why does the anode need to be replaced? *(2)*

 b In the extraction of iron:

  i Which three raw materials are added through the top of the blast furnace? *(3)*

  ii Why is limestone used in the blast furnace? *(1)*

Glossary

A

Acid A proton donor.

Acid anhydride A compound that forms an acid when it reacts with water.

Acid rain Rain which has a pH below 5.6 due to the reaction of rainwater with acidic gases.

Acid salt A salt in which the replaceable hydrogen in the acid has only been partially replaced by one or more metal atoms.

Acid–base indicator A coloured compound or mixture of coloured compounds which changes colour over a specific pH.

Acidic oxide An oxide which reacts with alkalis to form a salt and water.

Activation energy The minimum amount of energy particles must have to react when they collide.

Addition polymerisation Polymerisation of monomers containing a C=C double bond to form a polymer and no other compound is made.

Addition reaction A reaction in which a single product is formed from two or more reactant molecules and no other product is made.

Alcohols Organic compounds with branched or unbranched chains containing the —OH functional group.

Alkali A base which is soluble in water.

Alkanes Saturated hydrocarbons with the general formula C_nH_{2n+2}.

Alkanoic acids Organic compounds with branched or unbranched chains containing the —COOH functional group.

Alkenes Hydrocarbons containing at least one C=C double bond.

Alkyl group The group formed by the removal of a hydrogen atom from an alkane.

Allotropes Different forms of the same element.

Alloy A mixture, within a metallic lattice, of two or more metals or a mixture of one or more metals with a non-metal.

Amphoteric A substance which can act as an acid or a base.

Amphoteric oxide An oxide which reacts with both acids and alkalis.

Anions Negative ions.

Anode The positive electrode.

Anodising The process of increasing the thickness of an unreactive oxide layer on the surface of a metal.

Atom The smallest particle that cannot be broken down by chemical means.

Atom economy

$$\frac{\text{molar mass of required product}}{\text{molar masses of all the products}} \times 100$$

Atomic number The number of protons in the nucleus of an atom.

Avogadro constant The number of atoms in a mole of atoms (6×10^{23} atoms).

Avogadro's law Under the same conditions of temperature and pressure, equal volumes of all gases contain the same number of molecules.

B

Base A proton acceptor.

Basic oxide An oxide which reacts with acids to form a salt and water.

Biofuels Fuels made from the decomposition of biological material.

Biogas A fuel formed by the breakdown of manure or other organic compounds in the absence of air.

Boiling The change of state from liquid to gas that takes place when a liquid boils.

Bond energy The energy needed to break a covalent bond between two particular atoms.

Branched chain hydrocarbons Hydrocarbons with carbon alkyl side groups coming off the main chain.

Brittle Breaks easily when hit.

C

Calorimeter Apparatus for measuring heat energy changes.

Carboxylic acids Another name for alkanoic acids.

Catalyst A substance that speeds up a chemical reaction but remains unchanged at the end of the reaction.

Catalytic converter Part added to vehicle to reduce the emissions of carbon monoxide and nitrogen oxides from exhausts of petrol engines.

Catalytic cracking Cracking using a catalyst at 400–500°C.

Cathode The negative electrode.

Cations Positive ions.

Centrifugation The separation of heavier from lighter particles using the force caused by a spinning action.

CFCs Compounds of carbon, fluorine and chlorine which cause breakdown of ozone into oxygen.

Chain isomerism Isomerism where the structure of the carbon skeleton differs.

Chemical properties Properties that describe how elements and compounds react with other substances.

Chlorination The addition of chlorine in water treatment to kill harmful microorganisms.

Complete combustion The burning of a substance in excess air or oxygen.

Compound A substance made up of two or more different atoms (or ions) joined together by bonds.

Condensation polymerisation Polymerisation occurring when two types of monomer bond together with the elimination of a small molecule.

Condensation reaction A reaction where two molecules join together with the elimination (removal) of a small molecule.

Condensed formula A structural formula showing how the atoms are arranged in a molecule without showing the bonds apart from double or triple bonds.

Condensing The change of state from gas to liquid.

Conductors (electrical) Substances that have a low resistance to the passage of electricity.

Corrosion The gradual dissolving away of a metal inwards from its surface.

Covalent bond A shared pair of electrons.

Cracking The decomposition of larger alkane molecules into a mixture of smaller alkanes and alkenes.

Crystal lattice A regularly repeating arrangement of ions or molecules in three dimensions.

Dehydration reaction A reaction involving the removal of water from a compound.

Delocalised electron Electrons which are not associated with any particular atom.

Detergent A substance that removes stain and dirt from a material.

Diatomic Molecules containing two atoms.

Diffusion The spreading movement of one substance through another due to the random movement of the particles.

Discharge (of ions) The gain or loss of electrons by ions at the electrodes to form atoms or molecules.

Displacement reaction A reaction where one type of atom or ion has replaced another in a compound.

Displayed formula Shows how the atoms and bonds in a compound are arranged.

Dot-and-cross diagram A diagram showing the electronic arrangement of atoms, ions or molecules.

Double bond Two covalent bonds between the same two atoms.

Downward displacement The movement of a gas or liquid downwards due to the pressure of another gas.

Ductile Can be drawn into wires.

Electric charge The product of current in amps × time in seconds.

Electrochemical series The order of reactivity of metals, with the most reactive at the top.

Electrodes Rods which conduct electric current to and from an electrolyte.

Electrolysis The decomposition of a compound by an electric current.

Electrolysis cell A container in which electrolysis is carried out.

Electrolyte A molten ionic compound or a solution containing ions which conducts electricity.

Electrolytic conduction The movement of ions in a liquid or solution when a potential difference is applied.

Electron arrangement A shorthand way of showing the number of electrons in each electron shell of an atom (sometimes called the 'electron configuration').

Electron shells Spherical areas surrounding the nucleus which contain one or more electrons.

Electrons The negatively charged particles outside the nucleus of an atom.

Electroplating Coating of the surface of one metal with a layer of another, usually less reactive, metal.

Element A substance made up of only one type of atom which cannot be broken down into anything simpler by chemical reactions.

Empirical formula Shows the simplest whole number ratio of atoms or ions in a compound.

End point (in acid–base titration) The point where an indicator changes colour in a titration.

Endothermic reaction A reaction which absorbs energy from the surroundings.

Energy profile diagram Diagram showing the heat energy content of the reactants and products on the vertical axis and the reaction pathway on the horizontal axis.

Enthalpy change The heat energy exchanged between a chemical reaction and its surroundings at constant pressure.

Enzymes Biological catalysts.

Ester A compound with the formula R—COO—R' formed by the reaction of an alcohol with an alkanoic acid.

Esterification Making an ester by the reaction of an alcohol with an alkanoic acid.

Eutrophication The processes leading to the death of aquatic organisms as a result of nitrates and phosphates leaching into lakes and rivers.

Evaporation The change of state from liquid to vapour which takes place below the boiling point of a liquid.

Exothermic reaction A reaction which releases energy to the surroundings.

Faraday constant The quantity of electric charge carried by one mole of electrons or one mole of singly charged ions.

Feedstock A material taken from nature or a substance which has undergone slight processing which is used as the starting material for a chemical process.

Fermentation The breakdown of organic materials by microorganisms with effervescence and the release of heat energy.

Filters Equipment used to remove dust and particles from chemical plants and power stations.

Filtrate The solution passing through a filter paper when a mixture of solid and solution are filtered.

Glossary

Flue gas desulfurisation Removal of sulfur dioxide in industry arising from burning fossil fuels containing sulfur.

Formula unit Shows the simplest ratio of ions in an ionic compound.

Fraction A product of petroleum distillation that is a mixture of hydrocarbons having a limited range of molar masses.

Fractional distillation A method used to separate two or more liquids with different boiling points from each other using a distillation column.

Freezing The change of state from liquid to solid.

Functional group A group that is characteristic of a given homologous series.

General formula A formula that can be applied to all members of a given homologous series.

Giant molecular structure A three-dimensional network of covalent bonds.

Global warming The heating of the atmosphere caused by absorption of infrared radiation by greenhouse gases.

Green chemistry A set of principles that reduces or eliminates the use and generation of hazardous substances in the manufacture and use of chemical products.

Greenhouse gases Gases that are good absorbers of infrared radiation and cause global warming.

Groups The vertical columns in the periodic table.

Half equations Equations showing the oxidation and reduction reactions separately.

Halogenation The addition of halogen atoms to a compound or substitution of halogen atoms into a compound.

Halogens The elements in Group VII.

Hard (substance) A substance which is not easily scratched.

Hard water Water that contains dissolved calcium or magnesium salts.

Heat of neutralisation The enthalpy change when one mole of water is formed by the reaction of an acid with an alkali under standard conditions.

Heat of reaction The enthalpy change when the molar amounts of reactants shown in the equation react to give products under standard conditions.

Heat of solution The enthalpy change when one mole of a solute is dissolved in a solvent to form an infinitely dilute solution under standard conditions.

Homologous series A group of compounds with the same general formula and the same functional group.

Hydration reaction A reaction where water is added to form a new product.

Hydrocarbons Compounds containing only carbon and hydrogen atoms.

Hydrogenation A reaction involving the addition of hydrogen to a compound.

Hydrolysis The breaking down of a compound by water.

Incomplete combustion Combustion when air or oxygen is limiting.

Indicator See *Acid–base indicator.*

Insulators Non-conductors.

Ion An atom or group of atoms with either a positive or negative charge.

Ion-exchange (resin) A substance containing bound ions. The ions can be replaced by different ions when a solution containing ions flows through it.

Ionic bond The strong force of attraction between oppositely charged ions.

Ionic equation A symbol equation that shows only those ions which take part in a reaction.

Ionic lattice A crystal lattice of ions.

Ionisation energy The energy needed to remove an electron from an atom or ion.

Isotopes Atoms of an element with the same number of protons but different numbers of neutrons.

Kinetic particle theory The idea that particles are in constant motion.

Law of conservation of mass In a chemical reaction, the mass of the products is equal to the mass of the reactants.

Leaching The washing out of substances (minerals or pollutants) through soil by water.

Limiting reactant The reactant which is not in excess in a reaction.

Lone pairs Pairs of electrons not involved in bonding.

Lustrous Having a shiny surface.

Macromolecules Very large molecules made up of repeating units.

Malleable Can be shaped by hitting.

Mass concentration The number of grams of solute dissolved in a solvent to make $1 \, dm^3$ of a solution.

Mass number The number of protons + the number of neutrons in an atom.

Melting The change of state from solid to liquid.

Metallic bond A bond formed by the attractive forces between the delocalised electrons and the positive ions.

Metallic conduction The movement of mobile electrons through the metal lattice when a potential difference is applied.

Metalloids Elements lying between the metals and non-metals in the periodic table which have some properties of metals and some properties of non-metals.

Mixture This consists of two or more elements or compounds that are not chemically bonded together.

Molar concentration The number of moles of solute dissolved in a solvent to make 1 dm³ of a solution.

Molar gas volume The volume of one mole of gas at r.t.p. or s.t.p.

Molar mass The mass of a substance in moles.

Mole The relative mass (atomic, molecular or formula mass) in grams.

Molecular equation A full symbol equation.

Molecular formula Shows the number of atoms of each particular element in one molecule of a compound.

Molecular structure Structure of simple molecules.

Molecule A particle containing two or more atoms. The atoms can be the same or different.

Monomers The small molecules which react and bond together to form a polymer.

N

Natural gas Fossil fuel extracted from beneath the Earth's surface which is mainly methane.

Neutral oxide An oxide which does not react with acids or alkalis.

Neutralisation reaction The reaction between an acid and a base to form a salt and water.

Neutron The neutral particle in the nucleus of an atom.

Noble gas configuration Atoms having a complete outer shell of electrons.

Non-polar (molecule) Molecules with no partial charge or where the centre of positive and negative charge is the same.

Nucleus A tiny particle in the centre of an atom containing protons and neutrons.

O

Osmosis The overall movement of water molecules through a selectively permeable membrane from where the water is at a higher concentration to where it is at a lower concentration.

Oxidation The gain of oxygen or loss of electrons by a substance.

Oxidation number A number given to each atom or ion in a compound to show the degree of oxidation.

Oxidation–reduction (reactions) Reactions in which oxidation and reduction occur together.

Oxidising agent A substance that accepts electrons and gets reduced.

P

Paper chromatography A method used to separate a mixture of different dissolved substances depending on the solubility of the substances in the solvent and their attraction to paper.

Percentage yield

$$\frac{\text{amount of required product obtained}}{\text{maximum amount of product expected}} \times 100$$

Periodic table Arrangement of elements in order of increasing atomic number so that most groups contain elements with similar properties.

Periodicity The regular occurrence of similar properties of the elements in the periodic table so that elements in a given group have similar properties or a trend in properties.

Periods The horizontal rows in the periodic table.

Permanent hardness Hardness in water which cannot be removed by boiling.

Petroleum A thick liquid mixture of unbranched, branched and ring hydrocarbons extracted from beneath the Earth's surface.

pH scale A scale of numbers from 0 to 14 used to show how acidic or alkaline a solution is.

Photochemical smog Smog caused by the reaction between hydrocarbons from car exhausts, ozone and nitrogen oxides in the presence of sunlight.

Physical properties Properties which do not generally depend on the amount of substance present.

Polar molecule Molecules with a partial positive charge on one end and a partial negative charge on the other.

Pollution Contaminating materials introduced into the natural environment (earth, air or water).

Poly(alkene) Polymer formed when alkene monomers combine.

Polyamide Condensation polymer containing —NH—CO— linkages.

Polyester Condensation polymer containing —COO— linkages.

Polymerisation The conversion of monomers to polymers.

Polymers Macromolecules made up by linking at least 50 monomers.

Polysaccharide Condensation polymer containing —O— linkages.

Position isomerism Isomerism in which the position of the functional group differs.

Precipitate The solid obtained in a precipitation reaction.

Precipitation reaction A reaction in which a solid is obtained when solutions of two soluble compounds are mixed.

Preferential discharge of ions The discharge of only one type of cation or anion during electrolysis.

Protons The positively charged particles in the nucleus of an atom.

R

Radioactive isotopes Isotopes with unstable nuclei, which break down.

Rate of reaction The change in concentration of a reactant or product with time at a stated temperature.

Glossary

Redox (reaction) See *Oxidation–reduction (reactions)*.

Reducing agent A substance which loses electrons and gets oxidised.

Reduction The loss of oxygen or gain of electrons by a substance.

Relative atomic mass The weighted average mass of naturally occurring atoms of an element on a scale where an atom of the carbon-12 isotope has a mass of exactly 12 units.

Relative formula mass The relative mass of one formula unit of a compound on a scale where an atom of the carbon-12 isotope has a mass of exactly 12 units.

Relative masses Masses compared to a standard such as carbon-12.

Relative molecular mass The relative mass of one molecule of a compound on a scale where an atom of the carbon-12 isotope has a mass of exactly 12 units.

Replaceable hydrogen The hydrogen in an acid which can be replaced by a metal or ammonium ion.

Residue The solid remaining on the filter paper when a mixture of solid and solution are filtered.

Ring hydrocarbons Hydrocarbons where the carbon atoms are joined in a ring.

r.t.p. Room temperature and pressure. (20 °C and 1 atmosphere pressure).

Rusting Corrosion of iron and iron alloys caused by the presence of both water and oxygen.

Salt A compound formed when the hydrogen in an acid is replaced by a metal or ammonium ion.

Saponification The hydrolysis of fats or oils to form soaps.

Saturated compounds Organic compounds with only single bonds.

Screening Another word for shielding (see *Shielding*).

Sedimentation The settling of a solid, usually in a liquid.

Separating funnel Piece of apparatus used to separate immiscible liquids which have different densities.

Shielding The effect of inner electron shells reducing the amount of nuclear charge felt by the outer electrons.

Simple distillation The separation of a liquid from a solid which involves the processes of boiling and condensation using a condenser.

Soapless detergents Detergents that have sulfonates or groups other than COO^- groups at the 'head end' of the molecule.

Soaps Sodium or potassium salts of long-chain carboxylic acids.

Soft water Water which contains hardly any dissolved calcium or magnesium salts.

Solubility The number of grams of solute needed to form a saturated solution per 100 grams of solvent used.

Solubility curve A graph showing the mass of solute dissolved to form a saturated solution per 100 grams of solvent at different temperatures.

Solute A substance that is dissolved in a solvent.

Solution A uniform mixture of two or more substances.

Solvent A substance that dissolves a solute.

Sonorous Rings when hit with a hard object.

Spectator ions Ions which do not take part in a reaction.

Standard concentration A concentration of 1 mol of substance in 1 dm^3 of solution under standard conditions.

Standard solution A solution which has a known accurate concentration at a specified temperature and pressure.

State symbols Letters put after a chemical formula showing whether it is a solid, liquid, gas or aqueous solution.

s.t.p. Standard temperature and pressure (0 °C and 1 atmosphere pressure).

Strong acid An acid that ionises completely in solution.

Strong base A base that ionises completely in solution.

Strong electrolytes Electrolytes having a high concentration of ions in the electrolyte.

Structural formula Shows the way the atoms are arranged in a molecule with or without showing the bonds.

Structural isomers Compounds with the same molecular formula but different structural formulae.

Sublimation The direct change of a solid to a gas, or of a gas to a solid, without the liquid state being formed.

Substitution reaction A reaction in which one atom or group of atoms replaces another.

Suspension A mixture of small particles dispersed in another substance, and in which the small particles settle on standing.

Sustainable chemistry See *Green chemistry*.

Synthesis A series of chemical reactions which make a specific product.

Temporary hardness Hardness in water which can be removed by boiling.

Thermal cracking Cracking using high pressure and temperatures above 700 °C.

Thermal decomposition The breakdown of a compound when heated.

Thermometric titration A titration in which the temperature of a reaction mixture is recorded as one solution is added to another.

Titration A method used to determine the amount of substance present in a given volume of solution of acid or alkali.

Titre The final burette reading minus the initial burette reading in a titration.

Triple bond Three covalent bonds between the same two atoms.

 U

Unbranched chain hydrocarbons Hydrocarbons with carbon atoms linked in a chain without alkyl side groups.

Unsaturated compounds Organic compounds containing double or triple bonds (in addition to single bonds).

Upward displacement The movement of a gas upwards due to the pressure of another gas.

 V

Volatile Easily evaporated at room temperature.

Vulcanisation Process used in the manufacture of tyres where sulfur is used to make the rubber harder.

 W

Weak acid An acid which only partially ionises in solution.

Weak base A base which only partially ionises in solution.

Weak electrolytes Electrolytes having a low concentration of ions in the electrolyte.

The Periodic Table of the Elements

Key

relative atomic mass
atomic symbol
name
atomic (proton) number

1.0
H
hydrogen
1

(1)	(2)											(13)	(14)	(15)	(16)	(17)	0
I	II											III	IV	V	VI	VII	(18)
																	4.0 **He** helium 2
6.9 **Li** lithium 3	9.0 **Be** beryllium 4											10.8 **B** boron 5	12.0 **C** carbon 6	14.0 **N** nitrogen 7	16.0 **O** oxygen 8	19.0 **F** fluorine 9	20.2 **Ne** neon 10
23.0 **Na** sodium 11	24.3 **Mg** magnesium 12	(3)	(4)	(5)	(6)	(7)	(8)	(9)	(10)	(11)	(12)	27.0 **Al** aluminium 13	28.1 **Si** silicon 14	31.0 **P** phosphorus 15	32.1 **S** sulfur 16	35.5 **Cl** chlorine 17	39.9 **Ar** argon 18
39.1 **K** potassium 19	40.1 **Ca** calcium 20	45.0 **Sc** scandium 21	47.9 **Ti** titanium 22	50.9 **V** vanadium 23	52.0 **Cr** chromium 24	54.9 **Mn** manganese 25	55.8 **Fe** iron 26	58.9 **Co** cobalt 27	58.7 **Ni** nickel 28	63.5 **Cu** copper 29	65.4 **Zn** zinc 30	69.7 **Ga** gallium 31	72.6 **Ge** germanium 32	74.9 **As** arsenic 33	79.0 **Se** selenium 34	79.9 **Br** bromine 35	83.8 **Kr** krypton 36
85.5 **Rb** rubidium 37	87.6 **Sr** strontium 38	88.9 **Y** yttrium 39	91.2 **Zr** zirconium 40	92.9 **Nb** niobium 41	95.9 **Mo** molybdenum 42	[98] **Tc** technetium 43	101.1 **Ru** ruthenium 44	102.9 **Rh** rhodium 45	106.4 **Pd** palladium 46	107.9 **Ag** silver 47	112.4 **Cd** cadmium 48	114.8 **In** indium 49	118.7 **Sn** tin 50	121.8 **Sb** antimony 51	127.6 **Te** tellurium 52	126.9 **I** iodine 53	131.3 **Xe** xenon 54
132.9 **Cs** caesium 55	137.3 **Ba** barium 56	138.9 **La*** lanthanum 57	178.5 **Hf** hafnium 72	180.9 **Ta** tantalum 73	183.8 **W** tungsten 74	186.2 **Re** rhenium 75	190.2 **Os** osmium 76	192.2 **Ir** iridium 77	195.1 **Pt** platinum 78	197.0 **Au** gold 79	200.6 **Hg** mercury 80	204.4 **Tl** thallium 81	207.2 **Pb** lead 82	209.0 **Bi** bismuth 83	[209] **Po** polonium 84	[210] **At** astatine 85	[222] **Rn** radon 86
[223] **Fr** francium 87	[226] **Ra** radium 88	[227] **Ac†** actinium 89	[261] **Rf** rutherfordium 104	[262] **Db** dubnium 105	[266] **Sg** seaborgium 106	[264] **Bh** bohrium 107	[277] **Hs** hassium 108	[268] **Mt** meitnerium 109	[271] **Ds** darmstadtium 110	[272] **Rg** roentgenium 111							

Elements with atomic numbers 112-116 have been reported but not fully authenticated

* 58 – 71 Lanthanides

140.1 **Ce** cerium 58	140.9 **Pr** praseodymium 59	144.2 **Nd** neodymium 60	144.9 **Pm** promethium 61	150.4 **Sm** samarium 62	152.0 **Eu** europium 63	157.3 **Gd** gadolinium 64	158.9 **Tb** terbium 65	162.5 **Dy** dysprosium 66	164.9 **Ho** holmium 67	167.3 **Er** erbium 68	168.9 **Tm** thulium 69	173.0 **Yb** ytterbium 70	175.0 **Lu** lutetium 71

† 90 – 103 Actinides

232.0 **Th** thorium 90	231.0 **Pa** protactinium 91	238.0 **U** uranium 92	237.0 **Np** neptunium 93	239.1 **Pu** plutonium 94	243.1 **Am** americium 95	247.1 **Cm** curium 96	247.1 **Bk** berkelium 97	252.1 **Cf** californium 98	[252] **Es** einsteinium 99	[257] **Fm** fermium 100	[258] **Md** mendelevium 101	[259] **No** nobelium 102	[260] **Lr** lawrencium 103

Index

Index

Index

Index

Acknowledgements

The authors and publishers would like to thank the following for permission to reproduce photographs:

2.2.4 Howard Davies/Alamy; **2.3.3** Roger Norris; **2.6.1** iStockphoto; **4.1.1** Emilio Segre Visual Archives/American Institute Of Physics/ Science Photo Library; **4.2.1** Sciencephotos/Alamy; **4.3.1** Andrew Lambert Photography/Science Photo Library; **5.4.2** Arnold Fisher/ Science Photo Library; **5.5.3** Ria Novosti/Science Photo Library; **6.1.1** Science Photo Library; **6.2.1** Martyn F. Chillmaid/Science Photo Library; **6.4.1** Mauro Fermariello/Science Photo Library; **7.1.1** Editorial Image, Llc/Alamy; **7.4.1** Roger Norris; **7.4.2** Lenscap/Alamy; **7.4.3** foodcollection.com/Alamy; **7.4.4** Shutterstock; **7.5.2** Martyn F. Chillmaid/Science Photo Library; **7.7.2** Roger Norris; **7.8.2** Andrew Lambert Photography/Science Photo Library; **8.1.1** Shutterstock; **8.2.1** David R. Frazier Photolibrary, Inc./Alamy; **8.3.1** Shutterstock; **9.1.1** iStockphoto; **9.3.2** Andrew Lambert Photography/Science Photo Library; **13.1.3** Eye Ubiquitous/Alamy; **13.4.2** Danita Delimont/Alamy; **13.5.2** Shutterstock; **13.6.3** Steve Bly/Alamy; **14.2.4** Dk/Alamy; **15.1.1** Martyn F. Chillmaid/Science Photo Library; **15.4.2** Howard Davies/Alamy; **16.1.1** Andrew Lambert Photography/Science Photo Library; **16.3.1** 67photo/Alamy; **17.1.3** iStockphoto; **17.2.1** Roger Norris; **18.2.2** David McCarthy/Science Photo Library; **19.1.1** Andrew Lambert Photography/Science Photo Library; **19.2.2** Andrew Lambert Photography/Science Photo Library.

Every effort has been made to trace the copyright holders but if any have been inadvertently overlooked the publisher will be pleased to make the necessary arrangements at the first opportunity.